Further Praise for "Witches" and Wily Women

A singer-songwriter as well as a sociolinguist, Begoña Echeverria deftly studies a set of gendered pronominal particles in popular story and song in Euskera to tell a highly nuanced (and often witty) story of Basque cultural values over the past 500 years. Along the way she makes an impassioned plea for the preservation, and certainly a heightened awareness, of such traces in all endangered language varieties and argues that they may lead to a more equitable and inclusive future.

—*John Dagenais, Department of Spanish and Portuguese, UCLA*

"Intellectual breadth and depth as well as soul shines through this book. Echeverria critically researches the ideologies surrounding the loss of the pronoun *noka*, examining its use in a range of genres—biblical texts, folktales, and folksong. In her analysis of folktales she takes us inside the world of Basque culture so that we hear the voices of women as wives, sisters, friends, daughters, and tricksters. Her journey into understanding gender and culture in Basque society comes fully alive in the analysis of folk songs, treating us to some of her own original compositions. The book is unique in bridging sociolinguistics, language ideology, gender studies, and the lived personal history and experience of being Basque."

—*Marjorie Harness Goodwin, Distinguished Research Professor of Anthropology, UCLA*

In this intriguing and deeply personal book, Begoña Echeverria offers new perspectives on language and gender through a detailed sociohistorical analysis of *noka* (a special set of verbal forms used in Basque to address a woman or girl), building on her own experience and perspective as a sociologist of language and singer-songwriter who grew up speaking Basque in California.

—*José Ignacio Hualde,*
Professor of Spanish and Linguistics, University of Illinois at Urbana-Champaign

This highly readable volume shows the impact that gender bias has on language. Using fascinating historical texts, Echeverria documents the slipping away—or stomping out—of *noka* and asks whether it is too late to reclaim and revitalize it. Even readers who know nothing about Basque language (Euskera) will come away hoping that noka can be saved.

—*Margaret Nash, Professor Emeritus, UC Riverside Graduate School of Education*

Unrelated to any other known language, Basque has long intrigued experts and a wider public. Here Begoña Echeverria draws on her multiple perspectives as a first language speaker of Basque, ethnographer of language, and Basque-medium musical artist to analyze the cultural and linguistic consequences of a seemingly arcane gendered pronoun pattern in Basque (*noka*), which she makes into a window on larger sociocultural concerns. . . . More than a nostalgic preservationist project, this is a call and example for an expanded recognition of a broader and more equitable array of linguistic possibilities for women in Basque culture.

—*Kathryn Woolard, Professor Emerita of Anthropology, UCSD*

"WITCHES" AND WILY WOMEN

Saving *Noka* through Basque Folklore and Song

Begoña Echeverria

CENTER FOR BASQUE STUDIES
UNIVERSITY OF NEVADA, RENO
2020

This book was published with generous financial support from the Basque Government.

Center for Basque Studies
University of Nevada, Reno
1664 North Virginia St,
Reno, Nevada 89557 usa
http://basque.unr.edu

ISBN-13: 978-1-949805-35-2

Cover Design by Ponderosa Pine Design

Library of Congress Cataloguing in Publication Data Forthcoming

Printed in the United States of America

Nere Amaren eta Aitaren izenean
Alejandro eta Pilarcho Echeverria
Goian beude

CONTENTS

1

What Is *Noka* and Why Should We Care?

In a story, there's often one thing that does not make sense. But once you figure that out, you got the whole thing.

—Advice from Professor John L'Heureux, Stanford University Creative Writing Department

This book was born because another one was lost. While working on an academic article 15 years ago, I went to the library for a source that looked promising. It irritated me to find the book missing from the shelf. To make the drive to the library worth my while, I put "Basque" in the search engine and waited for the results, not expecting to find anything new. Surprisingly, I saw a reference I'd never heard of before: an Old Testament fragment written around 1700[1] (which, ironically, had been lost in a private library in Oxford, England, for two hundred years). I giddily made my way to the stacks, flipped through the pages and gasped aloud at what I saw:

The pronouns in this Old Testament were all "wrong"!

In the Basque I had grown up with, speakers used the formal pronoun "*zu*" ("you," pronounced "sue") when addressing a person; I rarely heard "*hi*" ("thee," pronounced like the letter "e" or "he")—and never in dialogues addressing God, as in prayer. But this Old

Testament used the familiar pronoun *hi* all the time. Not only did God use *hi* to rebuke Eve in the Garden of Eden—as might a parent to a disobedient child—but she answered him in the familiar as well. When God used *hi* with Moses on Mount Sinai, he used it right back. I gasped aloud on page after page as I turned them, saying to myself: "No way!" (Fortunately, no other library patrons were around to be disturbed as I did so). "Thee," "thy," "thou," and "thine" covered every page, used for every utterance directed to an individual throughout this text: between Moses and Aaron, Abraham and Sarah, Joseph and Rebecca, even God with the slave Hagar.

I did not know why these uses of pronouns differed so much from what I was used to, but I knew I was on to something. My previous research and experience as a native Basque speaker in the diaspora had taught me a thing or two about the Basque language ("*Euskera*"):[2] pronouns are powerful. Not only do they indicate social status between participants in a conversation as they do in other languages, they also play crucial roles when it comes to gender and identity in Basque society. In my ethnographic work, I had found that despite the definition of a "Basque person" ("*Euskalduna*") as "one who has the Basque language," dominant discourses and images promoted men as the prototypical Basque person. Literature, curricular materials, images, and the public square celebrated male efforts to promote Basque language and culture, although women have played key roles in transmitting *Euskera*, often under politically difficult circumstances. Further, speakers and nonspeakers alike held strong opinions about the familiar singular pronoun *hi*. The only place in *Euskera* that indicates gender, *hi* marks the addressee as female with a form called "*noka*;" that the addressee is male, with "*toka*." But *toka*'s sociolinguistic position surpasses that of *noka*: used in many valued domains, it also has positive connotations of solidarity and masculinity, as will be detailed below. In contrast, speakers rarely use *noka* and attribute it with primarily negative meanings.[3] This intrigued me, for I knew that *noka* and its complicated grammatical constructions were one of the most unique features not only of *Euskera*—an endangered language—but of the world's 6,500 languages more generally. But when I asked why *noka* was held in such low regard or was not used very much, no one could provide me with a convincing explanation.

To paraphrase my college professor John L'Heureux, *noka* was the one thing that didn't make sense to me (or many other Basque speakers) in the story that is Basque sociolinguistic history. John L'Heureux (1934–2019) was a creative writing professor at Stanford University and noted novel and short story writer. I shared with him my struggles to understand some short stories, though I loved them. His advice to me is the epigraph to this chapter. I have found it useful in solving puzzles that emerge from my research as well. Once I figured the puzzle out, I got the whole thing. Or, at least the archival journey on which I have embarked in making sense of *noka* has brought to light—in one place—unheralded stories about gender and language in Basque society that I wish I had known before now.

I hope you enjoy taking this journey with me. To facilitate our travels through Basque pronominal territory, the next section reviews key facts about *Euskera*'s history in general, before detailing important aspects of Basque pronouns in particular.

Goazen aintzinat—Let's go!

"Basque-ing" in *Euskera*: A Primer

Euskera is an isolate, a language unrelated to any other. Without question, *Euskera* is "the sole surviving pre-Indo-European language of western Europe."[4] Traces of Basque can be found on archaeological remains as far back as the Neolithic era (10,000 BCE).[5] The sole-surviving descendant of the Aquitanian language,[6] *Euskera* spread south and west from Gaul.[7] Evidence from place names indicates "Basque was once spoken on both sides of the Pyrenees, as far east as the valley of Aran, in territory which has been Occitan-speaking in historical times."[8]

The region where *Euskera* is now spoken—"*Euskalerria*" or "*Euskal Herria*"—is located in northern Spain and southwest France. About 3,000,000 people currently live in this region, but only 750,000 individuals[9] speak *Euskera* along a narrow swath of the territory comprising about one hundred miles from east to west (starting from outside Bilbao, Bizkaia), and thirty miles north to south (starting from outside Baiona, Lapurdi).[10] Most speakers live in the southern region ("*Hegoalde*") on the Spanish side of the international border (Nafarroa, Gipuzkoa, Bizkaia, and Araba);[11] in fact, two-thirds live just in the provinces of Gipuzkoa and Bizkaia.[12] Only eighty thousand Basque speakers live in the northern, French, provinces ("*Iparralde*": Lapurdi, Baxe Nafarroa, Zuberoa). Tens of thousands also speak *Euskera* elsewhere in France and Spain, as well as in diasporas in Great Britain, Belgium, Latin America, Australia, and the United States (especially Idaho, Nevada, and California).[13]

In addition to the standard variety (*Batua)*[14] used in schools and other official domains today, *Euskera* "is described as having between six and nine dialects"[15]—though Roncalese became extinct[16] with the death of its last speaker, Fidela Bernat. She died in 1991. According to Trask, "the dialects are overwhelmingly congruent in their fundamentals and differ chiefly in vocabulary and in a few rather low-level phonological rules,"[17] that is, pronunciation. Even so, speakers of different varieties can have difficulty understanding each other if they speak in their vernaculars rather than the standard.[18] Contemporary linguistics owes a debt to Luis Lucien Bonaparte when it comes to Basque dialectology. Born to Napolean's brother in exile in England, L.L. Bonaparte was an amateur linguist who turned his attentions to *Euskera* after falling in love with Clemence Richard, a native Basque speaker. In addition to publishing grammatical works and commissioning a translation of the Bible into Basque (discussed in chapter 2), L.L. Bonaparte contributed to Basque linguistics by being the first person to divide *Euskera* "into dialects (and subdialects) with specified boundaries . . . [T]he famous map which he published in 1869 is still today the basis of our classification of Basque dialects."[19]

In fact, it is difficult to ascertain the boundaries of *Euskera* before the mid-nineteenth century when L.L. Bonaparte undertook these efforts. He estimated that 800,000 people spoke Basque, 140,000 of whom lived in *Iparralde*.[20] Ladislao de Velasco gave a much lower estimate in 1879: only 471,000 Basque speakers total, with 80,000 residing in the northern provinces.[21] But *Euskera* had already disappeared in Araba and Nafarroa by the mid-1800s; the number in the rest of *Hegoalde* dropped after the Carlist Wars ended (1879) and mandatory schooling (in Castilian) was introduced.[22] By 1930, only a third of the inhabitants of *Euskalerria* spoke *Euskera*: the number of speakers hovered at 400,000 but the population of the region as a whole had increased to 1,200,000.[23]

The percentage of *Euskera* speakers dropped even further to 20 percent by the end of the Franco dictatorship (1939–1975),[24] during which time it was forbidden to speak regional languages like Basque, Catalan, and Gallego.[25] But in *Hegoalde* (in Spain) not all of this loss can be attributed solely to Franco's repression. Rather, Franco's policies exacerbated the social and economic upheavals in play before the Spanish Civil War (1936–1939) which had already contributed to Basque language loss. Heavy industrialization—and the resulting urbanization—between 1880 and the early 1900s brought tens of thousands of workers from other parts of Spain to the Basque region, especially to Bizkaia and Gipuzkoa.[26] These internal migrants had little incentive to learn *Euskera*, as the language of social mobility, commerce, and prestige was Castilian.[27] Basque elites had adopted Castilian as their main (or only) language of communication, which put pressure on upwardly mobile individuals to do the same. Similarly, Araba's population increased 25-30 percent when it industrialized in the 1950s and 1960s.[28] Nafarroa's population also grew about 17 percent when it began industrializing in 1960.[29] These increases in non-Basque speakers, combined with Franco's repressive policies against regional languages such as *Euskera*, give us a fuller understanding of why the Basque language experienced such a decline by 1975.

As indicated above, the number of Basque speakers in *Iparralde* (in France) has trailed that in *Hegoalde* (in Spain) for the last two hundred years. However, the first books produced in Basque utilized the *Euskera* from *Iparralde*: the Catholic priest Beñaut Etxepare published *Linguae Vasconum Primitiae* in 1545; the Calvinist minister Joanes Leizarraga and his collaborators published the first (Protestant) New Testament in 1571. A hundred years later, the lawyer and historian Arnaud Oihenart followed suit with collections of proverbs and poetry in the Zuberoan dialect. However, the French state's attempts to eliminate Basque began in earnest after the French Revolution; its victors considered *Euskera* and other regional languages (i.e., Breton, Occitan) "obstacles to the spread of civic culture, liberty, and democracy itself."[30] Laws prohibited the use of all languages other than French; Lapurdi, Zuberoa, and Baxe Nafarroa were "merged with non-Basque Béarn into a single new political unit."[31] From this time forward, "the literary [center] of gravity of the language began shifting rapidly from north to south,"[32] a trend that has continued to this day. Further, the *Code Napoleon* (1804) forbade the transfer of a household intact to a single heir, as had been the Basque practice,[33] and thereby upended the cradle of *Euskera*'s intergenerational transmission that was the home.

From Endangered Language to Imperiled Pronoun

Indeed, this weakened intergenerational transmission in the home is one reason why *Euskera* is considered an endangered language. Very few monolingual Basque speakers remain;[34] most now learn it at school and use other language(s) as their daily language for most interactional purposes.[35] Language revitalization efforts have had some success in increasing the knowledge of Basque, especially in the Basque Autonomous Community or BAC (Gipuzkoa, Bizkaia, Araba) of *Hegoalde: Euskera* has enjoyed co-official status with Castilian since the 1982 Statute of Autonomy; standard Basque is used for schooling, for government functions, and by mainstream media. However, the presence of *Euskera* in these domains still pales in comparison to that of dominant languages like Castilian and French; even in the

BAC, jobs in private industry still have no Basque proficiency requirements.[36] *Euskera* enjoys some protections in Nafarroa, but none in *Iparralde*.[37] The most troubling indication that Basque is still not "safe" from extinction is that the use of *Euskera* continues to trail knowledge of it. A street survey conducted in 2016 showed that public use of Basque had fallen in the last five years, to an average of 12.6 percent across all seven provinces.[38] Even Gipuzkoa, the stronghold of Basque language support, averaged only 31.3 percent.[39] In *Iparralde,* this percentage dropped to 6.7 percent, the lowest public use of *Euskera* recorded since the survey was administered there in 1993.[40]

Given all this, one might argue that scholars have enough work to do to strengthen the Basque language as a whole than for me to bother focusing so intently on such a specific (and perhaps, relatively speaking, insignificant) aspect of *Euskera* such as pronouns. We shall see below, however, that pronouns in *Euskera* play outsized roles in the social life of Basque speakers. Specifically, they are fundamental to the social construction of an androcentric Basque identity: one that favors male speakers and centers on male-centered cultural activities. Those of us interested in expanding the universe of Basque speakers in gender-equitable ways, then, would do well to heed their lessons carefully.

Pronouns for (All?) the People

Euskera is not only unique because it is unrelated to the other 6,500 to 7,000 languages spoken today. It is also distinctive in that it has no grammatical gender. Basque does not refer to inanimate objects as if they were female or male, unlike languages like Spanish and French which render some objects "female" ("*la mesa*" or "*la table*" for "the table"), and others "male" ("*el lápiz*" and "*le crayon*" for "the pen"). Like English, Basque refers to "the table," "the pen," and all other inanimate objects in gender-neutral ways ("*mahaia*" and "*arkatza*" with the marker "-a," the equivalent of the article "the" or "a").[41] But unlike English (as well as Castilian and French), *Euskera* does not have natural gender, either. That is, Basque does not use "she/her/hers" or "he/him/his" in referencing the biological gender of a person or animal.[42] Rather, *Euskera* uses gender-neutral pronouns to refer to all third persons—whether "it" be a thing or "s/he," a living being.

However, Basque does find a way to mark gender despite its lack of natural and grammatical gender; the grammatically complex ways it does so also makes *Euskera* unique. Specifically, the use of the familiar second person singular pronoun, "*hi*," sometimes marks the gender of the addressee. This is not the case when the addressee is the subject of an intransitive verb. Thus, "Thou art" would be rendered "*Hi haiz*" whether the addressee is female or male. However, when "thou" takes an object (transitive case), then the auxiliary (helping) verbs take one form (called "*noka*") when the addressee is female, and another form (called "*toka*") when the addressee is male. To take one example, *Euskera* has two "gendered" ways of rendering the English sentence, "You have done work." When addressing a female listener in the familiar, one would say "lan egin du***n***"—with the '***n***' marking that the person addressed is female. For a male addressee in the familiar, one would say "lan egin du<u>k</u>"—the '<u>k</u>' indicating that the addressee is male.[43] The gender of the "person" speaking does not matter; these forms only mark the gender of the addressee. Similarly, *hika*[44] forms mark the gender when the addressee is the indirect object. Thus, "it happened to you," would be "Gertatu zai***n***" in *noka* for a female addressee; "gertatu zai<u>k</u>" marks a male addressee (*toka*).

A more complicated aspect of how *hi* marks the addressee's gender is called "allocutivity," a term coined by L.L. Bonaparte in 1862.[45] This means that the auxiliary verb specifies (or "allocates") the gender of the addressee, even when the addressee does not appear in the sentence as an argument. "A friend sees me," for instance, does not contain the pronoun "you" (or "thou," the familiar equivalent). Yet in speaking to one girl or one woman, the corresponding Basque sentence would be "Lagunak ikusten nai***n***," with the '***n***' specifying that the addressee is female. The same sentence would be "lagunak ikusten nai**<u>k</u>**" when addressing a male, as indicated by the "**k**."[46] Once again, the gender of the speaker does not matter to the conjugation of the helping verbs.[47]

One might be tempted to think that "*hi*" merely represents a grammatically complex version of the familiar pronouns discussed in Brown and Gilman's classic 1960 work.[48] But, alas, the Basque case does not fit neatly in their pronominal box. Brown and Gilman argue that the two second-person pronouns most common in European languages can be traced to Latin: *T* forms addressed a single addressee, while *V* was used to address "you all." However, in the fourth century, speakers used *V* in addressing the Emperor[49]—perhaps because two emperors reigned, so that addressing one implied both. Between the twelfth and fourteenth centuries, a "non-reciprocal power semantic" developed:[50] within a dyad, the more powerful person would use *T* with his or her addressee, but "receive" *V*. Most European languages today are characterized by the "reciprocal solidarity semantic."[51] When two people converse, they address each other with the *T* form ("*tu*" in Spanish and French) rather than the *V* forms ("*usted*" and "*vous*"). Brown and Gilman attribute this shift to a reciprocal "solidarity" pronominal pattern to the development in the nineteenth century of more open, egalitarian societies, which "created a distaste for the face-to-face expression of differential power."[52] Certainly, the ostensible equality between speakers could have been expressed through reciprocal *V*, but the association of this pronoun with the upper classes created an "animus against the pronoun."[53] In England, however, pronoun use shifted away from *T* ("thou") and toward *V* ("you") as a "popular reaction against the radicalism of the Quakers,"[54] whose speech used thou exclusively, eliding status differentials some individuals wished to preserve.[55] (This surprised me when I first learned of it. I had only heard or used "thy" and "thee" in the Lord's Prayer, so these pronouns sounded formal and archaic to me).

Euskera differs from the patterns Brown and Gilman discuss in several ways. First, Basque has four second-person singular pronouns rather than just two. Originally, *hi* was the only second-person singular pronoun ("you"), while *zu* was the second-person plural ("you all").[56] Over time, *zu* evolved into a formal second-person singular pronoun, with *hi* becoming the second person singular familiar.[57] The date when this shift occurred cannot be pinpointed with any certainty. Even in the "earliest documents *zu* appears exclusively with the value of a second person singular of respect, side by side with the familiar *hi*."[58] Thus, as no documents use *hi* exclusively as a singular pronoun alongside *zu* as the plural, we cannot see *zu* "emerge" from the plural singular to the singular formal pronoun. Interestingly, the linguist Resurrección Azkue found that some speakers in Bizkaia continued to use "*zu*" as a plural pronoun into the late nineteenth century.[59]

Historically, *Euskera* has had two other second-person pronouns. "*Berori*," the pronoun of greatest deference, may originate from the "*vuestra merced*" (Your Grace) in Castilian. Used only in *Hegoalde* for august personages such as the parish priest, *berori* has largely disappeared from speech. Further, the eastern dialects in *Iparralde* also have the pronoun "*xu*," considered more formal than *hi*, but not quite as formal as *zu*.[60] Speakers rarely use *xu*, however, and it does not appear in the texts discussed here. As such, this book focuses only on *zu* and *hi*.

Second, unlike surrounding languages, Basque is not shifting to solidarity or reciprocity. While scholars have produced grammatical works on *Euskera* since the seventeenth century, they have written relatively little about pronouns per se, the sources used here notwithstanding. The scant research on these pronouns suggests that *zu* has long been considered the "normal, pragmatically unmarked, form of address."[61] That is, the majority of speakers use *zu* most of the time.

Like other *V* forms, *zu* does connote "prestige" vis-à-vis *hi*: speakers use *zu* with addressees one knows of higher social rank, such as a priest or an elder such as a parent, as well as with strangers, even with those of lower rank than oneself, to show respect.[62] Thus, teachers "should" use *zu* with students, as "should" employers with employees.[63] Unlike speakers of other European languages who use *T* for prayers, Basque speakers use *zu* with

God and other figures pertaining to the supernatural world, such as spirits or the soul. Alberdi, citing a text from 1820, attributes the use of *zu* in Basque prayer to the supposed unsuitability of *hi* "as the language of the Pulpit," as such language required a level of "delicacy" and "cultured style" that *hi* ostensibily lacked.[64] However, my research has shown more variability in this regard, as we shall see in chapters 2 and 3.

Generalizations about *hika* are more difficult to make. Speakers do use *hi* for interactional purposes akin to other *T* forms: to make jokes, insult, curse, and gossip.[65] But the kind of "solidarity" *hi* connotes differs from other *T* forms. Rather than emotional intimacy or friendship, *hika* primarily signifies "a kind of solidarity that . . . consists, above all, in being subject to similar living conditions."[66] This might explain why, in my own research and experience, speakers characterized *hi* as the pronoun of "*konfiantza*" (trust) vis-à-vis *zu*. Speakers use *hi* in addressing persons of similar social rank (siblings and friends of similar age and persons of lower social rank).[67] Trask claims that *hika* with a significantly younger person is possible, so long as "that usage was established when the younger person was a child."[68] My research suggests that pronominal choices are not set in stone. Some immigrants reported that, when they visited the Basque Country after moving to America, their childhood friends addressed them in *zu*, when they had previously used *hi*.

It is within families that we see pronominal asymmetry prevail. Recall that *zu* is the most common pronoun used by Basque speakers; as will be discussed further below, most speakers today do not even know *hi*. The bastion of *hi* use remains the family. In families that use *hi*, asymmetrical *zu/hi* is the norm rather than the exception. Parents use *hi* with their children, but "receive" *zu*. However, there is more nuance here still. De Rijk claims that adults never use *hika* with small children; this extends to parents with their own children, as affection might obtain in these relationships, "but little solidarity."[69] However, de Rilk also reports that sometimes parents begin using *hi* with their children when they get older, though the age can range from as young as six to as old as fifteen.[70]

Further, spouses do not use *hika* with each other, even if they did so before marriage; "the vastly different role patterns assumed in marriage are felt to preclude solidarity [even] between husband and wife."[71] Alberdi's research (see table 1.1), however, demonstrated that such is not always the case. I also have known married couples who use *hika* with each other. One couple told me that they were riding the bus in their hometown one day, speaking to each other in *hika,* as usual. A member of the Basque Language Academy, also from that town, happened to be on the same bus. When he heard the couple speaking *hi* with each other, he approached them: "Aren't you two married? How is it that you speak to each other in *hi*?" Another couple immigrated from *Iparralde* (French Basque provinces) to the United States decades ago. They speak *hi* with each other (still). Years ago, I called the woman when I had a question about a particular *hika* form for a lyric I was writing. She called me back and left a message: the informal Basque she and her husband used was not "good Basque" and I probably shouldn't use it in a song.[72]

Third, speakers use *hika* in contexts not necessarily paralleled by other *T* forms. According to Alberdi, *hika* can be used to address inanimate objects, one's own body, or oneself. Interestingly, some women use the male *hi* forms (*toka*) even when talking to themselves, a pattern I have personally observed. According to Alberdi, *hi* can also be used to address animals;[73] Trask argues that this is only the case when the animal is being berated.[74] However, one of my interviewees told me that *hika* is used to address "unimportant" animals, such as pets, but *zuka* for "important" animals. For example, bees are addressed in *zu* because they produce the wax for the candles used for important rituals such as funerals.

Fourth, use of *hi* is more more restricted than other *T* forms. Since at least the nineteenth century, the farmhouse (*baserri*) has been the mainstay of vernacular Basque,[75] of which *hika* plays a crucial part. Indeed, *hika* forms are difficult to master by anyone who has not "heard it from the cradle."[76] The complicated system of marking gender in *hika*, discussed above, has undoubtedly contributed to its loss over time. *Zu* is the pronoun used in the standard Basque (*Batua*) used in schools, government documents, and mainstream media. Thus, *hika* is rarely learned by those with little access to the rural domains where *hika* can be "picked up" informally, that is second language learners and urban dwellers, who comprise the majority of Basque speakers today. Indeed, until the revitalization efforts on *hika*'s behalf in the 1990s discussed below, even native Basque speakers familiar with *hika* forms only used them within the family and with closest friends.[77]

Finally, and most relevant to the issue at hand in this book, *hi* differs from other *T* forms in that use of the male form (*toka*) far exceeds the female (*noka*) when it comes to actual use. Alberdi illustrates this in his 1996 opus, which (among other things) asked 210 respondents from across the Basque Country to report on the pronouns they used with various family members. Table 1.1 shows the percentage of *hika* used with various family members.[78]

Table 1.1: *Hi* Usage in the Family

Toka		**Noka**	
Wife to husband	21.4%	Husband to wife	12.5%
Girlfriend to boyfriend	33.5%	Boyfriend to girlfriend	21.1%
Brother to brother	90.3%	Sister to sister	49.4%
Sister to brother	72.3%	Brother to sister	50.2%
Male cousin to male cousin	84.2%	Female cousin to female cousin	31.4%
Female to male cousin	51.4%	Male to female cousin	27.7%
Father to son	69.8%	Father to daughter	30.3%
Mother to son	63.0%	Mother to daughter	28.0%
Grandfather to grandson	64.9%	Grandfather to granddaughter	24.6%
Grandmother to grandson	51.0%	Grandmother to granddaughter	26.4%
Uncle to nephew	70.3%	Uncle to niece	20.9%
Aunt to nephew	54.5%	Aunt to niece	23.9%
Father-in-law to son-in-law	43.9%	Father-in-law to daughter-in-law	7.3%
Mother-in-law to son-in-law	26.0%	Mother-in-law to daughter-in-law	7.2%

These data show that *hi* is "coded male." In most cases, respondents reported using *toka* more frequently than *noka* in addressing kin of equivalent relationship. For example, 69.8

percent of respondents reported that fathers used *toka* with their sons, but only 30.3 percent said that fathers used *noka* with their daughters. Similarly, 63 percent reported that mothers used *toka* with their sons, but only 28 percent that mothers used *noka* with their daughters. Only two cases differ from this pattern: wives reportedly use *hika* more often to husbands (21.4 percent) than the reverse (12.5 percent), as do sister(s) to a brother (72.3 percent) than vice versa (50.2 percent). This seeming deviation actually proves my point about the male domain that this *T* form has become: speakers report using *hika* more often—often much more often—with male than female addressees.

In fact, respondents reported the highest rates of *toka* use when *both* the speaker and the addressee were male: brother(s) to brother (90.3 percent); male cousin(s) to male cousin (84.2 percent); and father to son (69.8 percent). Indeed, uncles reportedly use *toka* more often with their nephews (70.3 percent) than mothers did with their own sons (63.0 percent). Only one gender-mixed pairing competes with these numbers: 72.3 percent of respondents said sister(s) used *toka* with their brother, compared to only 50.2 percent of brother(s) to a sister. The latter number compares favorably to its use between sisters: 49.4 percent of respondents reported *noka* use from sister(s) to sister. However, *noka* use drops precipitiously after that: from 31.4 percent female cousin(s) to female cousin to a low of only 7.2 percent for mothers-in-law to daughters-in-law. In contrast, *toka* use in families never drops below 50 percent, if we exclude marital relationships (i.e., husbands and sons-in-law).

My research in the Basque Country and a lifetime in the diaspora corroborate these patterns. In my 1997 research in Donostia, I found that *hika* was used primarily by male speakers to male addressees. In classrooms, I observed teachers using *hika* perhaps a dozen times, to chastise students or get them back on task. In only one case was the teacher a woman; only once was the student a girl. Students exhibited similarly gendered *hika* use. I observed several boys—but no girls—using *hika* in the class, during a field trip, in informal conversations. I also heard students use *hika* in completing group assignments—but never by girls. On one occasion, a boy used *hika* to redirect a girl's attention to the task at hand, but he used *toka* forms in doing so, suggesting that he did not know the "correct" *noka* forms.

Like their children, most parents agreed that men and boys spoke *hika* more often than girls and women. The women who did speak *hika* reported doing so in fewer contexts than men, and expressed greater reservations in doing so. One student's mother, from a town neighboring Donostia, reported being put off when she visited a dentist. Not only did the dentist presume to use *hika* with her, even though they had never met before, "he addressed me with [*toka*], as if I were a man!" Another student's father said that he sometimes used *hika* with his brothers but not with his sisters; his wife interjected he did not even know the *noka* forms.

I found similar patterns in the interviews I conducted among Basque immigrants (from northern Nafarroa) to southern California. Both women and men said that, growing up, males spoke more *hika* than females. Their brothers and male friends were especially prone to use *hika* with each other when playing and joking around. One man said that he didn't speak *noka* with anyone but his sisters growing up. One woman said when people spoke *hika*, they were seen as "wild" ("*basa*"), uneducated ("*ez du eskolik*"), or as a "*menditarra*"—a "mountain-dweller," meant as an epithet. These associations were more acceptable for males than females. Using *noka* (to a female addressee) was seen as particularly disrespectful. In fact, one woman told me that her husband switched from using *zu* to *noka* with his older sisters when they left their husbands for younger men—precisely to show that he had lost respect for them.

Similar gendered patterns hold in the workplace. In Alberdi's survey, 87.8 percent of respondents reported using *hika* with male classmates or workmates; only 27.2 percent reported doing so with female workmates or classmates.[79] In the same way, the male immigrants I interviewed reported speaking *hika* with their male coworkers both in the Basque Country and their fellow countrymen in America. None of the female immigrants did so. Overall, Alberdi reports that 65.7 percent of his respondents only used the *toka* forms—never the *noka* forms. The reverse was never true: no *hika* speakers reported using it exclusively with female addressees. My own observations across California support these claims. *Hika* is commonplace among male immigrants and almost nonexistent among female immigrants. On several occasions in the diaspora, I observed male immigrants using *toka* forms to female addressees, but never immigrants (of any gender) using *noka* to address a man.

These findings show that *noka* is disappearing from contemporary speech at a faster rate than *toka*. Why should this be the case? Since *hi* once served as the only second-person singular pronoun, speakers would have to have used *noka* as a matter of course whenever speaking to one girl or one woman, just as they would have to have used *toka* when addressing one boy or one man.

I have argued that this is, in part, due to the language ideologies ascribed *hi*.[80] I follow Woolard and Shieffelin in defining "language ideology" as "the cultural system of ideas about social and linguistic relationships, together with their loading of moral and political interests."[81] Specifically, I have demonstrated that *hi* "sounds" more appropriate for use by and to male speakers because of its associations with certain "social meanings (e.g., stances, social acts, social activities) that in turn help to constitute gender meanings."[82] That is, while *noka* and *toka* are "lingusticially equal," *hika* "sounds" masculine because of how it is used in valued cultural domains.

One such domain is traditional Basque cultural life. As noted above, much research shows that *hika* is a key marker of solidarity. My research substantiates those claims. The high schoolers I interviewed described *hika* as the pronoun used in close relationships, with best friends, or "*ttikitako lagunak*" ("friends from when you were little"). Even those who did not actually know *hika* themselves talked about *hika* in these terms; in that sense, the association between *hika* and solidarity was "pragmatically salient."[83] Interviewees also repeatedly associated *hika* with "authentic" Basque identity, spoken by "*euskaldun euskaldunak*"—"really, really Basque" people: *Euskaldun Zaharrak* ("Old Basques," or native speakers), those who lived in villages, especially on farms.

Indeed, the media and public square celebrate the cultural forms that originate in Basque rural life. But most of these are male-dominated. Among the most prestigious cultural forms is *bertsolaritza* (ritual verbal dueling). *Bertsos* comprise a significant portion of Basque oral tradition as well as the literature taught in schools. The names of *bertsolariak* from the past grace the names of streets, bookshops, and music stores across the Basque Country; current *bertsolariak* are recognized by name. They perform at major public events and Basque television and radio stations broadcast the annual *bertsolaritza* competition. The participants in these competitions often use *hika* in composing their verses, as do the (male) commentators. While women now participate in *bertsolaritza*—and one such competitor, Maialen Lujanbio, won in 2009 and 2017—this remains a male-dominated domain.

Other prestigious cultural domains include sports such as *pilota* (handball), *harrijasoketa* (rock lifting), and *aizkorajoko* (wood chopping). Female athletes like the rock-lifting champion Idoia Etxeberria notwithstanding, these "traditional" rural sports also remain male dominated. These athletes, too, often use *hika* (*toka* in particular) while playing their sports. Indeed, my sister, Candida Echeverria, plays *pala* (like *pilota* but using a wooden paddle) with men in the diaspora, and sometimes with men in the Basque Country; her male teammates and competitors will use *toka* forms, even with her. As a rule, however, mostly men participate in these activities; as such, *hi* becomes a marker of Basque identity most closely associated with male speakers.

Another domain associated with *hi* is Basque nationalist militancy. The leftist publication *Sabotaia* ("Sabotage") published an interview with an avowed militant Basque nationalist in 1995. While the interview was conducted in *zu*, the interviewee switched to *hi* in demanding that no photographs be taken of him. Similarly, Joseba Zulaika[84] recounts that, right before killing a fellow villager whom they perceived to be a traitor, members of the militant Basque nationalist group ETA (*Euskadi 'ta Askatasuna*) said to him, in *hika*: "You are a dog!" ("*Hi txakur bat haiz*!"). Finally, Aretxaga points out that *bertsolariak* routinely sing verses at the funerals of militants;[85] these, too, are frequently in *hika*. However, as most Basque militants were men, the verses employ *toka* forms in particular.

A related androcentric domain associated with *hika* is what Urla calls "Radical Basque youth culture," one manifestation of which is "free radio."[86] Founded by urban youth disenchanted by party politics, "free radio" stations used vernacular forms in imaginative ways to broadcast local news of particular concern to youth. Programmers used *hika* forms, in particular, to create "a communicative sphere as an imagined community of 'horizontal comradeship' that is in keeping with free radio's vision of radical democracy."[87] Most of the programmers comfortable using these forms were male.[88] When a script called for a woman programmer to use *hika*, she said that while she understood the forms, they did not "come out" as easily for her as they did her male colleagues.[89] Even so, unlike in actual contemporary speech, the scripts called for *hika* by both women as well as men";[90] that is, both *noka* and *toka* forms were used in prerecorded sequences.

While "free radio" stations no longer rule the airwaves as they did in the 1990s,[91] debates continue about the role of the vernacular—and, in particular, *hika* forms—in constructing a voice in *Euskera* that is a "language for living" and a "language for life" (*biziaren hitzuntza*).[92] Indeed, the website www.zuzeu.eus takes up this call explicitly. Consonant with the findings discussed above, the website shows how *toka* has become the "androcentric generic"[93] *hika* form used in public spaces: the male form is taken up as inclusive of both (or all) genders, while the female form remains restricted to the female. A billboard proclaims, "Careful! Basque people are here!" using only the *toka* form ("*Kontuz! Hemen Euskaldunak gaituk*!"); while the -k marker ostensibly marks the addressee as male. In reality it addresses any person who sees the billboard, whether female or male (or anywhere in between). *Toka* also dominates on posters, advertisements, comic strips, and product labels. Bands use *toka* in naming themselves and their records and use *toka* in their lyrics.[94] Yet few musical groups do the same with *noka*, though the website lists my musical trio "NOKA" (www.ilovenoka.com)—composed of Andréa Bidart, Catherine Petrissans, and myself—as one of the few that explicitly does so (see chapter 5).

In these ways, *toka* is presented as a generic form that addresses all audiences, regardless of gender. *Noka*, in contrast, is marked as targeting female audiences or concerns. During my research in 1997, I learned that a member of the Basque Language Academy (*Euskaltzaindia*), while teaching a class to Basque teachers, stated as much: *toka* is unmarked and can be used with both genders, but *noka* is marked, only for female addressees. Indeed, both in the Basque Country and the diaspora, speakers routinely use the terms "*hika*" and "*toka*" interchangeably, but "*noka*" means "*noka*," that is, just the forms for a female addressee. The website www.zuzeu.eus echoes the critique made by many (especially younger) Basque speakers today: The use of *toka* as the generic marginalizes female speakers and listeners—and, presumably—speakers of all genders who wish for a more gender-equitable world. Some younger speakers have attempted to counter this androcentric bias by creating a gender-neutral *hika* form, "diNK,"[95] which incorporates the *-n* and *-k* markers of *noka* and *toka*, respectively.

Only time will tell if such efforts will equip speakers to feel as comfortable using *noka* for as wide a range of interactional purposes for which they use the other varieties in their "verbal repertoire":[96] not only *toka*, but standard Basque, as well as other languages they may know: Castilian, French, or—increasingly—English, which many Basque students study in school. Speakers cannot use their words willy nilly: as Bahktin pointed out, "not all words submit equally to appropriation . . . many words stubbornly resist, others remain alien [or] sound foreign."[97] Ochs adds that gender impacts the extent to which one can "own" one's words, as "gender may generate its own set of voices."[98] The purpose of this book is to uncover the social histories of *noka* in the archives, to demonstrate the myriad ways *noka* was "owned" in the past, in the hopes that these histories may provide (potential) Basque speakers "expressive resources"[99] with which to use *noka* for a "new linguistic future."[100]

However, there is no guarantee that such semantic recovery efforts would be enough to save *noka* from extinction. As noted, only about a third of the residents of the Basque Country even speak *Euskera*, only a minority of those know the informal *hika* forms, and fewer still know *noka* in particular. Further, my ethnographic work shows that there is a sense in which *hika* forms—much less *noka*—are simply inappropriate for female speakers. The high schoolers I interviewed repeatedly said that *hika* "just came out" in spontaneous moments such as anger or joking. Only boys actually used *hika* (usually *toka*) for such interactional purposes; girls switched from Basque to Castilian to joke, express anger—or flirt. One parent told me that *hika* was no concern for girls precisely because *hika* is used for swearing or expressing anger—as if these emotions were simply not ladylike. Several parents described *hika* as "*brutoa*" and "*indartsua*"—brutish and forceful. These adjectives clearly relate to the "masculine" displays of "*indarra*"[101] (strength) of the "Man of Plaza"[102] as exhibited in sports such as handball, *pala*, *jai alai*, rock-lifting, and wood-chopping. One boy said that he used *hika* when arguing with his brother as a way "to score points." Another told me that when deciding whether or not to use *hika* with another boy upon first meeting him, he would look him over to see if he thought the boy could "handle *hika*."

These findings—my own as well as those of other researchers—paint a bleak picture for the future of *noka*. When *hika* was the only singular pronoun, both its forms—*noka* as well as *toka*—had to have been available for use by all speakers for all interactional purposes to every single addressee. But once *zuka* came on the scene, *hika* became linked to male speakers and masculinity, through its use in the positively valued, male-dominated cultural domains I have discussed here. In Gal and Irvine's[103] terms, there is an "iconic" relationship between *hika* and masculinity. Kuipers refers to this process as "essentialization": as *hika* comes to be seen as "essentially or naturally" linked to male speakers and masculinity, use of *hika* by women is "pushed to the periphery where [its] meanings become more ambiguous or uncertain."[104]

Such is particularly the case when it comes to the use of *noka*—especially by women. For my research among high schoolers, I examined several hundred pages of textbooks used for elementary and secondary students. Textbooks described *hika* in terms similar to what I have discussed here: that is, that its use is restricted (compared to *zuka*) and varies from town to town, is more likely to be used by older than younger speakers, and more often in rural areas than the city. *Hika* is described as the pronoun used in families and between close friends. However, the implicit lessons are that *hika* use is "coded male": most exemplars of *hika* use involved interaction between male characters or used the *toka* forms, implying a male addressee. Sometimes *toka* was used in discussing a gender-neutral topic when *noka* forms could have been used just as well. I have found similar patterns in a Basque-English Dictionary designed for American audiences.[105]

In contrast, I found only two texts which employed *noka* forms. In neither case was the speaker male and the context differed sharply from those when male figures used *toka*. Men were shown using *toka* when telling jokes, or hanging out at a bar; one story involved two college-aged men using *hika* when trying to pick up women. While women were rarely shown in such playful moments—they rarely showed up in textbooks at all—they were shown using *zuka* in these situations. I only found two images of women using *noka* with each other. The first was the song "*Lau Andren Besta*" written by Jean Baptiste Elizanburu in 1897 (see chapter 4 for more discussion). The song portrays four women playing a Basque card game, *mus*, which involves bluffing and passing signs (like winking to one's partner). The women use *noka* all the while: One player chastises her partner for being too drunk to pass or read signs correctly. The women on the team opposing them, too, joke and chide one another for not playing the game right. While this might seem like a portrayal of women's joking and having fun akin to those which features men, this situation turns out to be quite different. In the last verse, we learn these female card players and users of *noka* are witches—who have transformed themselves into human women. The second, a stereotypical image of witches (pointed noses, sitting on brooms), that uses *noka* is entitled "*Sorgin-Solasa*" (Witches' Talk) and consists of a nonsense phrase with words formed with the "-n" marker. It is written, in other words, as if the witches were speaking in *noka*.

Certainly, some students might find these images of witches appealing, which could increase their interest in using *noka*. But history has not been kind to women accused of being witches, to say the least. Barring a wider representation of *noka* users in the public imagination, or in their own experience, many speakers may not feel free to use the *noka* forms that they see "voiced"[106] by "witches": especially as Basque "witches" were burned at the stake in 1610 (see chapter 3). Indeed, unlike the wide range of *toka* use and users evident in contemporary Basque life and in the historical record, *noka* is much more restricted not only in use but in social meaning: it is "badly looked upon" (*gaizki ikusia*) or rude. While linguistically equal to *toka*, *noka* has accrued more negative connotations that have contributed to its greater loss over time.[107] There is no female-dominated, unambiguously positive cultural domain associated with *noka* to counter the "semantic derogation"[108] and attrition that *noka* has suffered.

This book attempts to provide such counternarratives. Why should girls and women speak a language that, in many contexts, literally does not speak to them? Does not consider them a listener worth accommodating linguistically? Why should members of the Basque-speaking community settle for a more impoverished set of linguistic resources when speaking to females versus males? I argue that such need not be the case: if one digs deeply enough into the archives, one finds a "new resource in the communicative economy"[109]—alongside *toka*, *zuka*, and even the Castilian and French that surround *Euskera*—that speakers could use to carry out conversations and to construct myriad identities.

Methods and Sources

To understand the "semantic derogation"[110] of *noka*, this book investigates the three main literary genres that have historically been written in *Euskera*: biblical materials (from the sixteenth to nineteenth centuries); folktales (from 1875 to the present day); and songs (from the fifteenth to twenty-first century). In examining these materials, I take a historical sociolinguistic approach that considers "the reconstruction of the history of a given language in its socio-cultural contexts."[111] Specifically, I conducted "[a]n intra-textual investigation examin[ing] the frequency and range of variants in one text or a corpus of texts."[112] Put another way, I systematically examined the entirety of the materials mentioned above and documented every use of *noka*, with a view toward bringing to light the language ideologies underlining such usages.

Outline of Chapters

In chapter 2, I show that the negative cast put on *noka* stems in large part from its use in Roman Catholic texts. While some Catholic prayer books and religious manuals appear as early as the seventeenth century, Protestants published the first Bibles in Basque: a New Testament in 1571 and the aforementioned fragment of the Old Testament, circa 1700. No Roman Catholic translation of the Bible appeared until L.L. Bonaparte commissioned one in the mid-nineteenth century.[113] In line with Protestant theology that attempts to create direct links between believer and God, the 1571 New Testament and 1700 Old Testament fragment used the familiar pronoun throughout, regardless of the gender or status of the participants in the conversation. The Catholic text did the opposite, using the formal *zu* as the default pronoun for the single addressee and reserving the familiar *hi* (almost exclusively *toka*) for negative interactional purposes. It used particularly violent and/or sexualized imagery for the few times it used *noka*, which cast the pronoun with negative connotations. As Catholicism eventually defeated Protestantism in the battle for Basque souls, its pronominal preferences prevailed, contributing to *noka*'s loss over time.

Chapter 3 examines the use of *noka* in Basque folklore. In sharp contrast to the restricted and negative uses of *noka* in Catholic texts, these tales and legends use *noka* frequently for many interactional purposes between and among sirens ("*laminak*"), witches ("*sorginak*"), and the goddess Mari as well as human females with whom they come into contact. As such, these tales model vigorous uses of the *noka* form itself—not restricted for negative purposes such as insulting a female addressee, *noka* can be used between the "divine" and the human, but also for ordinary dialogue directed to wives, sisters, friends, and daughters. These folktales also provide a window into the cultural values and customs of "traditional" Basque culture otherwise lost to the world. Further, the images of the supernatural woman portrayed in these stories differ markedly from accounts of the Basque witch persecutions that occurred in the Basque Country in the early seventeenth century. Rather than Satan-worshipping evil-doers, Basque *sorginak* appear in folktales primarily as relatively harmless tricksters; the devil rarely makes an appearance.

In chapter 4, I conclude *noka*'s social history by examining its use in song. Some songs echo the negative uses of *noka* exemplified by the Catholic texts. But we also "hear" women and girls use *noka* for their own interactional purposes: to express their wishes, assert their opinions, make demands, or take a stand. Sisters and friends use *noka* symmetrically both for solidary and antagonistic purposes; parents use *noka* with daughters asymmetrically when trying to impose their will on them—but they do not always get their way, even when daughters return the pronoun of "respect," *zu*. Heroines and antiheroines alike use *noka*, for ordinary as well as extraordinary interactional purposes. Songs use *noka* to console the grieving and mourn the dead as well as to pine for a lover or the motherland. Thus, even though songs using *noka* comprise but a fraction of the total corpus of Basque song, they provide examples of female agency and female identity that we would not otherwise have. While not all of these portrayals are positive, they provide a more complete portrait of Basque female identity than usually offered by contemporary Basque culture.

Chapter 5 provides additional counternarratives about female identity and possibility by (re)introducing new or overlooked texts that use *noka*. That is, chapters 2 through 4 demonstrated that *noka*'s stigmatization and disappearance have been constituted by sociohistorical circumstances rather than "naturally" flowing from linguistic structures. This chapter attempts to claim a more positive semantic space for *noka* by (re)circulating new texts that use the pronoun, in each genre discussed in this book. As a counter to the negative semantic loading of *noka* in canonical Roman Catholic texts, I discuss the Song of Solomon, which uses *noka* (and *toka*) to construct a surprisingly egalitarian relationship between young lovers. I build on the varied voices inhabiting the supernatural world represented by Basque folklore by analyzing the use of *noka* in Basque fairy tales "starring" characters other than Mari, witches, and sirens. Finally, I contribute lyrics I have written in *noka* to show how it can be used to sing about a wide array of contemporary issues.

Chapter 6 draws out the implications of *noka*'s social history for other languages, in particular those like *Euskera* in danger of extinction. *Noka* is among the most imperiled features of this endangered language; because *Euskera* is also a language isolate, *noka* has no linguistic relatives that can carry on its sociolinguistic inheritance. Thus, the impending death of *noka* represents the closing of the "unique window"[114] it offers to the world—how such a seemingly small part of this endangered language can carry such nuanced information not only about those who use *noka*, but also express the complexity of the worlds in which they move. Given the small number of Basque speakers who use or even know about *noka*, I have no delusions that it can still be saved—those of us who advocate on *noka*'s behalf joined this effort too late. At the very least, then, this book aspires to be a worthy obituary to the rich life *noka* has led.

Notes

1 D'Urte, *The Earliest Translation of the Old Testament into the Basque Language.*
2 I grew up saying "*Eskuara*;" other versions of the language's name are "*Euskara*," "*Uskara*," and "*Heuskara*" (Trask, *The History of Basque*, 320).
3. Echeverria, "(En)gendering the Basque Nation."
4 Trask, *The History of Basque*, 5
5 Urla, *Reclaiming Basque*, 1–2.
6 Trask, *The History of Basque*, 20.
7 Ibid., 39.
8 Ibid.
9 Ibid., 1–2; Urla, *Reclaiming Basque*, 133.
10 Trask, *The History of Basque*, 2–3.
11 I use Basque names for the provinces throughout.
12 Urla, *Reclaiming Basque*, 79.
13 Trask, *The History of Basque*, 1.
14 From the Basque word "bat" for "one."
15 Urla. *Reclaiming Basque.*
16 Trask, *The History of Basque.*
17 Ibid., 5.
18 Ibid.
19 Ibid., 55.
20 Heiberg, *The Making of the Basque Nation*, 247.
21 Ibid.
22 Ibid.
23 Payne, *Basque Nationalism*, 104.
24 Clark, "Euzkadi," 85.
25 Urla, *Reclaiming Basque*, 3.
26 Hooper, *The Spaniards*, 220.
27 In contrast, Catalan prevailed as the language of economic and cultural elites through the Franco era. See Woolard, *Double Talk*, 1989.
28 Nuñez, "Classes Sociales," 47–78; Hernandez & Mercadé, *Estructuras Sociales*, 161.
29 Ibid.
30 Urla, *Reclaiming Basque*, 3.
31 Trask, *The History of Basque*, 21.
32 Ibid., 49.
33 Ibid., 22.
34 Ibid., 5.

35 UNESCO *Red Book of Endangered Languages: Europe.*
36 Urla, *Reclaiming Basque,* 222.
37 Trask, *The History of Basque,* 4–5; Urla, *Reclaiming Basque,* 3.
38 Soziolinguistika Klusterra, "Measurement of the Street Use of Languages," 5.
39 Ibid., 6.
40 Ibid., 6–7.
41 See Oyharçabal, "Verb Agreement with Non-arguments."
42 As these gender-differentiating pronouns are as ancient as Basque itself, they might be forgiven for conceptualizing gender in binary terms.
43 Examples adapted from Oyharçabal, "Verb Agreement with Non-arguments," 90.
44 "*Hika*" is the noun, while "*hi*" is the pronoun. The same is true for "*zuka*" and "*zu*."
45 Antonov, "Verbal Allocutivity in a Crosslinguistic Perspective," 2.
46 Examples adapted from Oyharcabal, "Verb agreement with Non-arguments," 91.
47 Other languages have allocutivity, but they do not mark gender. See Antonov, "Verbal Allocutivity in a Crosslinguisitc Perspective."
48 Brown and Gilman, "The Pronouns of Power and Solidarity."
49 Ibid., 255.
50 Ibid., 256.
51 Ibid., 267.
52 Ibid.
53 Ibid., 265.
54 Ibid., 266.
55 See Silverstein, "Language and the Culture of Gender."
56 Trask, *The History of Basque,* 196.
57 Alberdi, "The Development of the Basque System of Form of Address."
58 Ibid., 280.
59 Trask, *The History of Basque,* 196.
60 Ibid.
61 De Rijk, "Familiarity or Solidarity," 378.
62 Alberdi, "The Development of the Basque System of Terms of Address," 280.
63 Alberdi, "Euskarazko Tratamenduen Ikuspegia,"176.
64 Alberdi, "The Development of the Basque System of Forms of Address," 280.
65 Alberdi, "Euskarazko Tratamenduen Ikuspegia," 175.
66 De Rijk, "Familiarity or Solidarity," 112.
67 Alberdi, "Euskarazko Tratamenduen Ikuspegia," 175.
68 Trask, *The History of Basque,* 96.
69 De Rijk, "Familarity or Solidarity," 112.
70 Ibid.
71 Ibid., 377
72 Interestingly, the lyric was for a lullaby. According to de Rijk (112), "the baby in the cradle is invariably addressed as *zu.*"
73 Ibid.
74 Trask, *The History of Basque,* 196.
75 Urla, *Reclaiming Basque,* 183.
76 Alberdi, "Euskarazko Tratamenduen Ikuspegia," 171.

77 Urla, *Reclaiming Basque*, 181.
78 Alberdi, *Euskararen Tratamenduak: Erabilera*, 371.
79 Alberdi, *Euskararen Tratamenduak: Erabilera*, 390.
80 Echeverria, "Language Ideologies and Practices in (En)gendering the Basque Nation."
81 Woolard and Schiffelin, "Language Ideology," 52.
82 Ochs, "Indexing Gender," 339.
83 Errington, "On the Nature of the Sociolingusitic Sign," 29.
84 Zulaika, "The Tragedy of Carlos," 309.
85 Arretxaga, *Los Funerales en el Nacionalismo Radical Vasco.*
86 Urla, *Reclaiming Basque*, 169–201.
87 Urla, "Outlaw Language," 255.
88 Urla, *Reclaiming Basque*, 181.
89 Ibid.
90 Urla, "Outlaw Language," 255.
91 Urla, *Reclaiming Basque*, 174.
92 Ibid., 147.
93 Romaine, "English: A Man-Made Language?" 132.
94 Urla, "'We Are All Malcolm X!'"
95 Personal communication with Unai Nafarrate-Errasti, native of Arrasate (Bizkaia) and lecturer of Basque Studies and Spanish at UCLA's Department of Spanish and Portuguese.
96 Gumperz, "Linguistic and Social Interaction in Two Communities,"137.
97 Bahktin, "Discourse in the Novel," 294.
98 Ochs, "Indexing Gender," 338.
99 Urla, *Reclaiming Basque*, 138.
100 Ibid., 78.
101 Ott, "Indarra."
102 Fernandez, "Mujer, Ritual y Fiesta," 83.
103 Gal & Irvine, "The Boundaries of Languages and Disciplines."
104 Kuipers, *Language, Identity and Marginality in Indonesia*, 20.
105 Aulestia, *Basque-English Dictionary*, 1989. See Echeverria "Language Lessons, Gender Lessons."
106 Bahktin, "Discourse in the Novel," 294.
107 Echeverria, "Language Ideologies in (En)gendering the Basque Nation," 2003; Echeverria, "Harlots and Whores but Not Lovers."
108 Schulz, "The Semantic Derogation of Woman," 64.
109 Urla, *Reclaiming Basque*, 96.
110 Schulz, "The Semantic Derogation of Woman."
111 Conde-Silvestre and Hernández-Campoy, "Introduction," 1.
112 Auer and Voeste, "Grammatical Variables,"259.
113 Duvoisin, *Bible Saindua*, 1972 [1865].
114 Nettle and Romaine, *Vanishing Voices*, 14.

2

The Devil Made Me Say It: *Noka* in Religious Texts

The Basques are more Catholic than the Pope.

—Common Basque refrain

In the previous chapter, I demonstrated the "linguistic equivalence" of *noka* and *toka:* They occupy the same place in the Basque language, as they are both familiar second person singular pronouns. However, I have also shown that *noka* and *toka* are unequal in sociolinguistic terms. *Noka* has almost disappeared from contemporary speech and is ascribed primarily negative language ideologies. *Toka*, in contrast, is used more widely in daily speech and continues to thrive in positively valued cultural domains such as rural sports, songs, and literature; it indexes solidarity, hegemonic masculinity, and "authentic" Basque identity.[1]

In this chapter, I argue that the negative language ideologies ascribed *noka* stem, in large part, to the ascendency of Roman Catholicism over Protestantism in the Basque Country by the end of the eighteenth century. Consonant with Calvinism's emphasis on the equality of believers under God, and the importance of personal relationships between believer and God, Protestant texts use *hi* with all single addressees, regardless of the status of those involved in the interaction. Pronominal use in Catholic texts, in contrast, use the formal second personal pronoun *zu* to emphasize hierarchy and the importance of intermediaries between God and the believer. On the rare occasions that Catholic texts use *hi*, they do so asymmetrically to index the speaker's "power over" the addressee. While Protestant texts use *hi* for all interactional purposes, Catholic texts use it solely for negative interactional purposes—to condemn, to mock, to curse. But Catholic texts cast particularly harsh social meanings on *noka*, using it to "apostrophize" cities—metaphorically treating these inanimate objects as if biologically female—for disobedience to God, wielding sexualized or violent imagery. Thus, when Catholicism triumphed over Protestantism, so too did the negative language ideologies it cast on *noka*, contributing to its loss over time.

Sources

The sources I draw on include the first two biblical texts in *Euskera*, which were produced centuries apart. As with other languages, Protestants produced the first biblical texts in Basque, even though Roman Catholicism has been the hegemonic religion on both sides of the Basque Country since the tenth century.[2] In 1564, a Calvinist synod held in Pau decided to introduce Protestantism to the "Basque land" by translating the New Testament into Basque. Queen Jeanne d'Albret of Nafarroa commissioned the Calvinist minister Joannes Leizarraga—a former Capuchin priest—for this task and provided him with several assistants.[3] In 1884, a fragment of a Basque Old Testament was discovered in the library of Shirburn Castle in Oxfordshire, England.[4] It had been bequeathed to the Second Earl of Macclesfield, President of the Royal Society,[5] who may have procured it in the mistaken belief that Basque was related to Welsh in which he had a particular interest. Written by Pierre d'Urte in about 1700, the manuscript renders all of Genesis through Exodus 22:11 into the same Lapurdian dialect of Basque as had Leizarraga the New Testament. D'Urte, a native of St. Jean de Luz (Donibane Lohitzune), had fled to England to escape the persecution Protestants faced after the 1685 revocation of the Edict of Nantes,[6] which had extended considerable religious and political rights to French Calvinists, also known as Huguenots.[7] The author based his translation on a Bible published in Geneva in 1588,[8] but whether he produced the manuscript while still in the Basque Country or after he fled to England remains unclear.[9] Either way, d'Urte labored despite straitened circumstances; he applied for aid from London's Huguenot Refugee Society on two occasions.[10]

To my knowledge, these are the only two Prostestant biblical texts extant in *Euskera*. Catholics have produced a variety of religious documents in Basque, such as prayer books and catechisms, since the seventeenth century. Chief among these is Pedro Axular's *Gero*, published in 1643; though a native of Urdazubi in Nafarroa, Axular wrote this text in "an elegant and carefully cultivated version of the French Basque of Lapurdi,"[11] as he was a priest in the village of Sara most of his life. Indeed, the Catholic texts I have come across from the seventeenth century were all published in *Iparralde*: Haramburu's *Debocino Escuarra* (1635); Harizmendi's *L'Office de la Vierge Marie, en Basque Laburdin* (1658); Etcheberri's *Manuel Devotionezcoa* (1669); and Tartas' *Onsa Hilceco Bidia* (1666). All of these were preceded by the *Dotrina Christiana* written by Esteve Materre, a Frenchman who learned Basque as a second language.[12]

However, no Catholic translation of the entire Bible appeared until the mid-nineteenth century, when L.L. Bonaparte commissioned the translation of Catholic scripture into Basque. This will be the focus of the analysis in this chapter, as it is the earliest Catholic document containing all the New and Old Testament texts corresponding to the Leizarraga and d'Urte passages.[13] Though a devout Catholic, L.L. Bonaparte intended not to gain converts with his translations, but to obtain materials for research and deeper knowledge of the Basque language.[14] *Euskera* likely came to him as an object of study because of his long relationship with Clemence Richard, a Basque woman with whom he had a child. He focused on capturing the "living Basque of his own day, in all its local diversity."[15] Toward those ends, he commissioned biblical verses and individual books—usually, the Book of Ruth, the Gospel of John, and the Song of Solomon[16] to be translated into the various Basque dialects. He had the whole Bible rendered into the Lapurdian and Gipuzkoan varieties. I focus on the former, as it is available in its entirety.[17] Bonaparte hired Jean Duvoisin to do the Lapurdian translation. A native of Ainhoa who had already written three books in Basque, Duvoisin quit his job as a customs official, holed up with Bibles in Latin and modern languages and "a manifold collection of commentaries on the Holy Scriptures"[18]—for six years.

Methods

The analysis in this chapter is based on a systematic examination of the pronominal use in the Leizarraga, d'Urte, and Duvoisin texts mentioned above. Given the ostensible inappropriateness of the familiar pronoun (*hi*) for religious purposes, discussed in chapter 1, the section below focuses specifically on whether it was used in interactions involving deity figures, as detailed below.

Findings

We begin our analysis with the New Testament, as it was the first part of the Bible to be translated into Basque. In this section, I examine how pronouns are used in direct speech to a single individual when one of the participants in the interaction is God the Father or Jesus. Specifically, I focus on the Four Gospels (Matthew, Mark, Luke, and John) in which God the Father and/or Jesus converse directly with each other or human beings. I exclude quoted and reported speech, such as that used in parables and prophesies. In table 2.1 below, "use by Jesus" includes chapters in which Jesus speaks to, but is not addressed by, a single addressee. "Use to Jesus" refers to chapters when Jesus is addressed by others as a single addressee but does not reciprocate in kind. In some cases, Jesus makes no response; in others, Jesus responds to more than one person, for which he would use "*zuek*" (you all). "Mutual" interactions refer to chapters in which Jesus and his interlocutor address one another with the same pronoun.

To facilitate analysis of pronoun use, I have categorized the participants in these interactions in the following way:

1. God the Father.
2. The Sick & Possessed: lepers, paralytics, the blind, etc.
3. Apostles: Jesus's twelve apostles.
4. Religious & Secular Authorities: Pharisees, Scribes, "the 70," Jewish leaders, Pontius Pilate, soldiers, centurions.
5. Individuals and Groups: All those not captured in the previous categories: John the Baptist, the Virgin Mary, as well as those simply called "one of the multitude" or "some."

Table 2.1: New Testament Pronominal Uses

Interlocutor	**Protestant (Leizarraga, 1571)**	**Catholic (Duvoisin, 1865)**
God the Father	*Hi* by Jesus (12)	*Zu* by Jesus (12)
	Hi to Jesus (2)	*Zu* to Jesus (2)
Devils, Demons,	*Hi* by Jesus (1)	*Hi* by Jesus (1)
Unclean Spirits	*Hi* to Jesus (3)	*Zu* to Jesus (3)
	Hi & *Zu* (5)	*Hi* & *Zu* (5)
Sick & Possessed	*Hi* by Jesus (17)	*Zu* by Jesus (17)
	Hi to Jesus (3)	*Zu* to Jesus (3)
	Mutual *Hi* (9)	Mutual *Zu* (9)
Apostles	*Hi* by Jesus (10)	*Zu* by Jesus (9)
	Hi to Jesus (36)	*Zu* to Jesus (36)
	Mutual *Hi* (16)	Mutual *Zu* (16)
		Hi & *Zu* (1)
Religious	*Hi* by Jesus (3)	*Hi* to Jesus (1)
& Secular	*Hi* to Jesus (21)	*Zu* by Jesus (2)
Authorities	Mutual *Hi* (14)	*Zu* to Jesus (19)
		Mutual *Zu* (15)
		Hi & *Zu* (1)
Individuals	*Hi* by Jesus (8)	*Hi* by Jesus (5)
& Groups	*Hi* to Jesus (39)	*Hi* to Jesus (8)
	Mutual *Hi* (22)	*Zu* to Jesus (33)
		Mutual *Zu* (22)
	N = 221	**N = 220**

We see that pronominal usage varies greatly between the Protestant and Catholic texts. The Protestant (Leizarraga) text uses exclusive *hi* 100 percent of the time. In contrast, the Catholic (Duvoisin) text uses exclusive *zu* 94 percent of the time (N =

206), exclusive *hi* 3 percent of the time (N = 7), and both *zu* and *hi* 3 percent of the time (N = 7). Below we see these patterns repeated in the Old Testament texts as well.

The Old Testament

As indicated above, d'Urte only translated part of the Old Testament (Genesis 1:1 through Exodus 22:11) into *Euskera*. This section, then, examines only these portions with their counterparts in the Duvoisin text. Specifically, I focus on pronouns used in direct speech to a single individual, when one of the participants in the interaction is God the Father.

Table 2.2: Old Testament Pronominal Usage

Interlocutor	Protestant (d'Urte)	Catholic (Duvoisin)
Adam	Mutual *Hi* (1); *Hi* by God (1)	Mutual *Zu* (1), *Zu* by God (1)
Eve	*Hi* to God	Mutual *Zu* with God
Serpent	*Hi* from God	*Zu* from God
Cain	*Hi* from God	Mutual *Zu* with God
Abel	------	*Zu* from God
Noah	*Hi* by God (3)	*Zu* by God (3)
Abraham	*Hi* by God (5); mutual *Hi* (1)	*Hi* & *Zu* (1); *Zu* by God (2) Mutual *Zu* (2)
Sarah	Mutual *Hi* with God	Mutual *Zu* with God
Hagar	Mutual *Hi* with God	Mutual *Zu* with God
Servant	Zu & *Hi* with God	*Zu* to God
Isaac	*Hi* by God	*Zu* by God
Rebecca	*Hi* & *Zu* by God	*Zu* by God
Moses	*Hi* by God (10); *Zu* to God (1) Mutual *Hi* (4)	*Zu* by God (10); *Zu* to God (1) Mutual *Zu* (5)
Aaron	*Hi* & *Zu* by God	*Zu* by God
	N = 36	**N = 36**

Thus, we see that the Protestant Old Testament (d'Urte) also chooses *hi* as its default form of address to a single interlocutor, while its Catholic counterpart (Duvoisin) uses *zu* most of the time.

Certainly, there could have been important changes in pronominal usage in the intervening centuries between the Leizarraga or d'Urte and Duvoisin texts. But the preference for *zu* in the Catholic texts was established by at latest the early seventeenth century. As noted above, many Catholic texts were published during that time; their pronominal usage parallels that of the Duvoisin text. The Lord's Prayer, for example, consistently used *zu* (Materre, *Dotrina Christiana* [1623]; Etcheberri, *Manuel Devotionezcoa* [1669]; Haramburu, *Debocino Ezcuarra* [1635]; Bonaparte, *Formulaire de Prone,* [1855 (1651)]; Harizmendi, *L'Office de la Vierge Marie* [1901 (1658)]; Tartas, *Onsa Hilceco Bidia,* [1975 (1666)]; in Chamberlayne's edited volume *Oratio Dominica* [1715]; and Nicolás Zubia's *Doctrina Christiana* [1691]).[19]

Further, according to Trask, "[t]he earliest known connected Basque text longer than a couple of words is a prayer, or perhaps rather a magical charm, recorded in a manuscript in the cathedral of Pamplona [Iruñea]" dating to the fourteenth century. Whether prayer or charm, it uses *zu* in making its plea: "Agnus Dei qui . . . guaradela çure [zure] guomendatu gura jruretan d' (Lamb of God . . . that we may be commended of you, that one three times d . . . to save the soul)."[20] These texts demonstrate that *zu* was established as the pronoun of choice in prayer in Basque Catholic texts many centuries before Bonaparte commissioned his Bible translations—which makes the departure to *hi* in the Protestants texts all the more remarkable.

Some Examples

What accounts for the differences in pronoun use between the Protestant and Catholic texts? Why do the Protestant New Testament (Leizarraga) and Old Testament fragment (d'Urte) prefer the *hi* forms (*noka* and *toka*), while the Catholic Bible (Duvoisin) uses primarily *zu*? One way to answer these questions is to examine the pronouns individuals of varying social statuses use to address one another. After all, social status is among the primary social categories pronouns are meant to index.[21]

As a first step toward that goal, texts 2.1 and 2.2 compare how Leizarraga's Protestant text (on the left) and Duvoisin's Catholic text (on the right) use pronouns in the same New Testament passage. (The gender-neutral formal second person singular pronoun ZUKA is in all capitals; <u>gender-neutral familiar forms used</u>

with a male addressee are underlined; **toka forms with transitive verbs, a male indirect object, or allocutive conjugation are both underlined and bolded**):

Text 2.1: God the Father to Jesus

Leizarraga (Protestant)	**Duvoisin (Catholic)**
Eta vozbat cerutic eguin baitzedin, cioela:	Eta mintzo bat egin zen zerutik:
And there was a voice from heaven, saying:	*And a voice from heaven said:*
Hi aiz ene Seme maitea	ZU ZARE ene Seme maitea
Thou art my beloved Son	*You are my beloved Son*
Hitan hartzen **diat** neure atseguin ona	ZURE baithan baitadukat nik gozoa
In thee I take my delight	*In you I have my pleasure*

(Luke 3:22)

Text 2.2: Jesus to God the Father

Leizarraga (Protestant)	**Duvoisin (Catholic)**
Aita, ethorri **duc** orena,	Aita, ethorri da ordua:
Father, the hour has come	*Father, the hour has come*
Glorifica **eçac** eure[22] Semea	GORESTSAZU ZURE Semea
Glorify thy son	Glorify your son
Father, the hour has come, glorify thy son	*Father, the hour has come, glorify your son*
Eure Semeac-ere hi glorifica eçaçat	Gorets ZAITZAN ZURE Semeak ere
So that thy Son will glorify thee	*So that the Son will glorify you, too*

(John 17:1)

Taken together, we see that God the Father and Jesus use the same pronoun with each other. But while the Protestant (Leizarraga) text uses the familiar *hi* (*toka*) reciprocally, the Catholic (Duvoisin) text uses mutual *zu*, the formal pronoun. As Christian theology considers both interactants to be divine, God the Father's and Jesus's symmetrical pronoun use might be seen as mutual acknowledgment of their equal (divine) social status.

However, in text 2.3 below, we see that symmetrical pronoun use is not reserved only for interactions between two deities. It also obtains in an interaction between Jesus and Pontius Pilate, a secular figure with high status. The Protestant text, however, uses the familiar *hi* (*toka*) symmetrically, while the Catholic text uses the formal, *zu:*

Text 2.3: Jesus and Pontius Pilate

Leizarraga (Protestant)	**Duvoisin (Catholic)**
Orduan interroga ceçan:	Pilatok galdatu zioen:
Then Pilate interrogated him:	*Pilate asked him:*
Hura Pilatec, Hi aiz Juduen Reguea?	Juduen errege ZARE ZU?
Art thou the King of the Jews?	*Are you the King of the Jews?*
Eta harc ihardesten çuela erran cieçón: **Hic dioc**	Eta ihardestean, Jesusek erran zioen: DIOZU:
And he answered him, saying: Thou sayest it	*And in answer, Jesus said: You say it*
(Mark 15: 2)	

Perhaps symmetrical pronominal usage characterizes the interactions above because the individuals involved all have high social status, whether in the terrestrial or divine domains. In that case, we should expect nonreciprocal pronoun use when interactants of varying social status converse: the person with higher status uses *T* (*hi*) with the person of lower social status, but the latter returns the pronoun of respect (*zu*). Text 2.4 provides an example of such an interaction; here, Jesus converses with a blind man, with a decidedly lower social status than himself:

Text 2.4: Jesus and a Blind Man

Leizarraga (Protestant)	**Duvoisin (Catholic)**
35. Sinhesten **duc hic** Jaincoaren Semea baithan?	Sinhesten DUZU Jainkoaren Semearen baithan?
Dost thou believe in the Son of God?	*Do you believe in the Son of God?*
36. Ihardets ceçan harc eta erran ceçan:	Ihardetsi eta erran zuen:
He answered and he said:	*He answered and said:*
Eta nor da, Jauna, sinhets deçadan hura baithan?	Zein da hura, Jauna, sinhets dezadan haren baithan?
And who is that, Lord, that I should believe?	*Which is that one, Lord, that I should believe?*
37. Eta erran cieçón Jesusec: Eta ikussi **duc** hura	Eta Jesusek erran zioen: Ikhusi DUZU bada
And Jesus said, The one thou hast seen	*And Jesus said, The one you see, then,*
Eta hirequin minço dena **duc** hura	Eta ZUREKIN mintzo dena hura bera da
The one who is speaking to thee	*The one who is speaking to you, the same*
38. Eta harc dio, Sinhesten **diat**, Jauna	Orduan gizonak erran zuen: Sinhesten DUT Jauna
And he said, I believe, Lord.	*Then the man said: I believe, Lord.*
(John 9: 35-38)	

The evidence thus far suggests that the pronouns *zu* and *hi* index very different social meanings in the Protestant versus Catholic texts. Protestant texts use reciprocal *hi* almost exclusively, while Catholic texts use primarily mutual *zu*. The use of *T* forms *(hi)* in the Leizarraga and d'Urte texts parallels its use in Protestant texts in other languages, so it does not seem too far-fetched to suggest that its use in the Basque intends to promote a solidary relationship between God and human beings, one which would give the believer direct access to God's word. Indeed, we see that even people of low status dare to use *hi* to God in the Protestant texts, but not in the Catholic text. The use of reciprocal *zu* in the Duvoisin texts, however, constructs a more distant relationship typical of Catholicism in which intermediaries such as priests and saints act as go-betweens between God and believer.

The Catholic *Hi* of Disdain: The Devil Is in this Detail

While the Duvoisin Bible overwhelmingly prefers *zu* as the pronoun for the single addressee, it does use *hi* occasionally. Such deviations from the norm, according to Brown and Gilman[23] reflect a "transient attitude" of some kind. Usually, a superior switches from *V* to *T* to express anger or contempt for a subordinate, though the reverse also can occur. The evidence from Duvoisin bears this out in the Basque case as well. Jesus uses *hi* primarily to rebuke the devil or his ilk, as indicated in text 2.5:

Text 2.5: Jesus and the Devil

Duvoisin (Catholic)	**Leizarraga (Protestant)**
9. Jainkoaren Semea BALIMBAZARE	Baldin Jaincoaren Semea bahaiz
If you are the Son of God	*If thou art the Son of God*
Jauz ZAITE hemendik beheiti	**Egotzac** eure burua hemendic beherera
Come down from here	*Take thyself down from here*
10. Izkribatua da ezen, ZUTAZ manatu dituela bere Aingeruak	Ecen scribatua **duc**, bere Aingueruey
Since it is written, his angels	*Since it is written, to his angels*
ZU ZAITZAZTEN begira	Cargu emanen drauela hiçaz, hire beguiratzeco:
Will watch over you	*To take charge of thee, watch over thee*
11. Eta beren eskuez idukiko ZAITUZTELA	Eta escuetan eramanen autela
And they will hold you in their own hands	*And they will hold thee in their hands*
Beldurrez-eta oinaz behaztopa zadien harridan	Eure oinaz harrian behaztopa ezadinçat
Lest you strike your foot against a stone	*Lest thou strike thy foot against a stone*
12. Orduan Jesusek ihardestean erran zioen:	Baina ihardesten duela Jesusec diotsa:
Then Jesus answered, saying:	*But Jesus answered, saying:*

Errana **duk**: *Hire* Jainko Jauna ez **duk** tentaturen	Errana **duc**, **Eztuc** tentaturen *eure* Jainco Jauna.
It is written: Thou shalt not tempt the Lord thy God[PA]	*It is said, Thou shalt not tempt thy Lord God*
(Luke 4: 9-12)	

Thus, in the Duvoisin text, both speakers use *zu* with each other for most of the interaction (and the devil does so throughout). But, in quoting the scripture that finally bests the devil, Jesus uses *hi*. This use of *hi* is also found in Jesus's other interactions with the devil and other demons—all of which are included in the "both" category in table 2.1 (see Matthew 3:3–10; Mark 1:24–25; Luke 8:28–30; Mark 9:24). In all of these interactions, including the exchange shown in text 2.6, the Leizarraga text also uses *hi* (specifically, *toka*).

Similarly, in the Duvoisin text below, Jesus uses *hi* when exorcising a demon possessing a man, even though he uses *zu* to directly address the man himself. In the corresponding passage in Leizarraga, in contrast, Jesus uses mutual *hi* with his addressee—whether that be the man or the demon possessing him:

Text 2.6: Jesus and a Demon

Duvoisin (Catholic)	**Leizarraga (Protestant)**
34. Zer da ZURE eta gure arteko?	Ciola, Ah, cer da hire eta gure artean
What are you to us?	*Saying, Ah, what is between us and thee?*
Jesus Nazaretharra? Gure galtzera ethorria	Jesus Nazarenoa? Gure deseguitera ethorri aiz
Jesus of Nazareth? Have you come to	*Jesus of Nazareth? Thou hast come to undo us.*
Othe ZARE? Badakit nor ZAREN;	**Baceaquiat** nor aicen:
Be rid of us? I know who you are:	*I know who thou art*
Jainkoaren Saindua ZARE ZU:	Hi aiz Jaincoaren saindua
You are the Blessed Lord.	*Thou art the Blessed Lord*
35. Eta Jesusek larderiatuz erran zioen:	Eta mehatcha ceçan hura Jesusec, cioela:
And Jesus, in rebuke, said:	*And Jesus, threatening him, said:*
Ago ichilik, eta hoa gizon harren ganik	Ichil adi, eta ilki adi, horrenganic
Hold thy peace and leave this man	*Be quiet, and leave from there*
(Luke 4:34-35)	

In the same way, in the Duvoisin New Testament, Christ uses *hi* in Mark 9:24 when addressing a demon to exhort him to leave the body of a boy he possesses: "Izpiritu gor eta mutua, nik **dayat** manatzan, haur hortarik ilkhi *hadi*, eta gehiago ez sar horren baithan" ("Stubborn mute spirit, I command thee to leave that child, and never enter him again").[25] Yet in the same passage, Jesus uses *zu* to address the boy himself. The Leizarraga text, in contrast, uses *hi* (*toka*) throughout the interaction, whether it is between Jesus and the boy himself, or between Jesus and the evil spirit.

Jesus uses *hi* in an interaction with his disciple Peter. In the Duvoisin text, Jesus normally uses *zu* with his disciples when addressing them individually. In text 2.7, Jesus resorts to *hi* when he gets particularly angry with Peter, equating his disciple with Satan (see Matthew 16: 16–19, 22–23 for another version of this interaction in which Jesus uses *zu)*:

Text 2.7: Jesus to Peter/Satan

Duvoisin (Catholic)	**Leizarraga (Protestant)**
Jesusek, itzulirik, eta dizipuluei begiratuz	Eta harc itzuliric, eta bere discipuluetarat
Jesus, turning around, and looking at his disciples:	*Turning around, looking at his disciples:*
Larderiatu zuen Piarres erranez:	Behaturic reprotcha ceçan Pierres, cioela:
Rebuked Peter, saying:	*He reproached Peter, saying:*
Gibelerat **egik**, Satan	Guibelerat adi eneganic Satan
Get thee behind me, Satan	*Get thee behind me, Satan*
Zeren Jainkoaren gauzez ez haizen zale	Ecen **eztituc** aditzen Jaincoaren diraden gauçac
For thou dost not love the things of God	*For thou dost not hear the things of God*
Bainan bai gizonenez	Baina guiçonen diradenac.
But those of man	*But those of men*

(Mark 8: 33)

The corresponding Leizarraga passage also uses *hi*, but as we have seen, this is par for the Protestant pronominal course. The use of *hi* in the Duvoisin text, however, deviates from the Catholic norm: It appears the Catholic *hi* is used primarily to rebuke the kind of behavior that only the devil—or his minions—would dare engage in.

This is true in the Old Testament as well. Below is an interaction in which God rebukes the serpent (the devil's) in the Garden of Eden:

Text 2.8: God to Serpent

Duvoisin (Catholic)	**d'Urte (Protestant)**
Eta Jainko Jaunak erraten dio sugeari:	Orduan Jainco eternalac erran çioen sugueari
And the Lord God says to the serpent:	*And so Eternal God[26] said to the serpent:*

Hori egin **dukalakotz**	Çeren hori eguin **duan**
Because thou hast done that	*Because thou didst that*
Madarikatua haiz	Içango aiz madaricatua
Thou are cursed	*Thou shalt be cursed*
Lurreko azienda eta basabere guzien artean:	Eta Larreco bestia gucien gagnetic
Among the tamed and wild beasts	*Among all the earth's beasts*
Herrestatuko haiz hire sabelaren gainean	Hire sabelaren gagnean aiz goango eta
Thou wilt drag on thy belly	*Thou wilt drag on thy belly and*
Eta lurra janen **duk** hire biziko egun oroz	Herrautssa jango **duc** hire biçiegun guçiez
And thou wilt eat of the dirt thy entire life	*Eat dust thy entire life*
(Genesis 3: 14)	

Interestingly, when God curses Eve (Genesis 3:16) and Adam (3:17) for eating of the forbidden fruit, the Duvoisin text uses *zu* for these utterances. The d'Urte text uses *hi* for these passages as well.

Thus far, the evidence from the Duvoisin Bible suggests that *hi* is to be reserved for only the harshest of interactional purposes: to condemn, to castigate, to curse.[27] Other uses of *hi* in the Duvoisin New Testament confirm its status as a pronoun of rebuke. When one of the two "criminals" mocks Jesus on the cross (Luke 23:39), he does so in *hi*: "Hi bahaiz Kristo, salba **zak** hire burua, eta gu ere-bai" ("If thou art Christ, save thyself, and us as well"). This accusatory use of *hi* extends to interactions with humans in addition to the divine: When Judas expresses regret to the high priests for having betrayed Jesus, they dismiss him in *hi*: "Guri zer **dihoakigu**? *Hire* ikhustekoa **duk**?" (What is that to us? See thou to that" (Matthew 27: 4-5). Right after this, Judas kills himself.

The discerning reader of the evidence thus far may have already noticed another significant difference between the Protestant and Catholic New Testaments: the Duvoisin never uses *hi* to address a female person. Indeed, it does not use *noka* even in dialogues analogous to those with male conversants. For example, in text 2.9, a young woman approaches Peter soon after Jesus's arrest (*Gender-neutral familiar forms used with a female addressee are italicized*; ***noka forms with transitive verbs, a female indirect object, or allocative conjugation are italicized and bolded***).

Text 2.9: Woman to Peter

Duvoisin (Catholic)	**Leizarraga (Protestant)**
69. Bada, Piarres kampoko aldean zagoen	Eta Pierres jarriric cegoen lekorean salan:
Then, when Peter was outside	*Then, when Peter was sitting outside*
Ezkarazean jarria; eta neskatcha bat hurbildu	Eta ethor cequion nescatobat,
Sitting in the vestibule, a girl came near to him	*A girl came to him*
Zitzayoen, zerralarik:	Cioela
And said:	*And said:*
Jesus Galilearrekin hintzen hi ere.	Hi-ere Jesus Galileanoarequin incen.
Thou too wast with Jesus the Galilean.	*Thou too wast with Jesus the Galilean*
70.Bainan harek ukhatu zuen	Baina harc uka ceça
But he denied this	*But he denied it*
Guzien aitzinean, zioelarik:	Gucien aitzinean, cioela:
In front of everyone, saying	*In front of everyone, saying*
"Ez dakit DERRATZUN"	"***Etzeaquinat*** cer ***dionan***"
"I do not know what you are saying."	"I know not what thou art saying"
(Matthew 26: 69-70)	

In the Duvoisin text, the woman uses *hi* when confronting Peter about being Jesus's disciple, but Peter uses *zu* in denying her charge. This contrasts sharply from texts 2.5 through 2.7 above, in which Jesus switches from *zu* to *hi* (in particular, *toka*) when asserting himself verbally. It also contrasts with the Leizarraga rendering of this interaction, in which Peter uses *noka* with the young woman. Indeed, as we will see in the next section, the Protestant New Testament avails itself of every opportunity to use *noka* with a female conversational partner for a variety of interactional purposes.

The Protestant *Noka* of Familiarity: Evidence from Leizarraga

While the Catholic (Duvoisin) text hesitates to use *noka*, the Leizarraga text that preceded it by three hundred years embraces it enthusiastically. In table 2.3 below, we see that the Leizarraga text uses *noka* in dialogue directed to female addressees ranging widely in status, from the Virgin Mary and Samaritan woman to "the sinful woman."

Table 2.3: *Noka* Usage in Leizarraga's New Testament

Addressee	Verses	*Noka*
Virgin Mary	Luke 1:27-38, 42-45; Luke 2:34-35	40
	John 2:3-4; John 19:26-27	2
"Sinful woman"	Luke 7:48, 50	2

Woman with hemorrhage	Luke 8:48	4
Resurrected girl	Luke 8:54	1
Martha	Luke 10:41-42	4
Samaritan Woman	John 4:7-42	33
Mary Magdalen	John 20:13; 15-17	8
		94

I discuss these examples below.

The Virgin Mary

The Leizarraga New Testament[28] first uses *noka* in Luke 1:27, when the Angel Gabriel surprises the Virgin Mary with an announcement:

Text 2.10: Angel Gabriel to the Virgin Mary (The Annunciation)[29]

27. David-en etchetico Josef deitzen cen guiçon batequin fedatua cen virjina batgana: eta virjinaren içena cen Maria

To a virgin espoused to a man whose name was Joseph, of the house of David: and the virgin's name was Mary

28. Eta Aingueruac hura baithara sarthurik, erran ceçan, Salutatzen *aut* gratia eguin ***çainana***: Jauna ***dun*** *hirequin*, benedicatua *hi* emazten artean

And the angel came in unto her, and said, Hail, thou that art highly favoured, the Lord is with thee: blessed art thou among women

29. Eta hura, Aingueruа ikussirik trubla cedin haren erranaren gainean, eta pensatzen çuen ceric licen salutatione hura

And when she saw him, she was troubled at his saying, and cast in her mind what manner of salutation this should be

30. Orduan diotsa Aingueruac, Maria, ***eztunala*** beldurric, ecen eriden ***dun*** gratia Jaincoa baithan.

And the angel said unto her, Fear not, Mary: for thou hast found favour with God

31. Eta horra, concebituren ***dun*** *eure* sabelea, eta erdiren *aiz* seme batez eta deithuren ***dun*** haren icena Jesus

And, behold, thou shalt conceive in thy womb, and bring forth a son, and shalt call his name Jesus

32. Hura içanen ***dun*** handi, eta eritziren ***ciayon*** Subiranoaren Seme: eta emanen diraucan Jainco Jaunac bere aita David-en thronoa

He shall be great, and shall be called the Son of the Highest: and the Lord God shall give unto him the throne of his father David:

33. Eta regnaturen ***din*** Jacob-en etchearen gainean eternalqui, eta haren resumaren finic ***eztun*** içanen

And he shall reign over the house of Jacob forever; and of his kingdom there shall be no end

34. Erran cieçón orduan Mariac Aingueruari, Nola içanen da hori, guiçonic ezagutzen eztudanaz gueroz

Then said Mary unto the angel, How shall this be, seeing I know not a man?

35. Eta ihardesten çuela Ainguerauac erran cieçón, Spiritu saindua *hire* gainera ethorriren ***dun*** eta Subiranoaren verthuteac itzal eguinen ***draun*** eta halakotz *hitaric* sorthuren ***den*** saindua, Jaincoaren Seme deithuren ***dun***

And the angel answered and said unto her, The Holy Ghost shall come upon thee, and the power of the Highest shall overshadow thee: therefore also that holy thing which shall be born of thee shall be called the Son of God

36. Eta hara, Elisabeth *hire* lehen gussua, harc ere concebitu ***din*** semebat bere çahartzean, eta hil haur ***din*** seigarrena steril deitzen cenac

And, behold, thy cousin Elisabeth, she hath also conceived a son in her old age: and this is the sixth month with her, who was called barren

37. Ecen ***eztun*** deus inpossibleric içanen Jaincoa baithan

For with God nothing shall be impossible

38. Eta erran ceçan Mariac, Huna Jaunaren nescatoa: eguin bequit *hire* hitcaren araura. Eta parti cedin harenganic Ainguerua

And Mary said, Behold the handmaid of the Lord; be it unto me according to thy word. And the angel departed from her

39. Eta jaiquiric Maria egun hetan joan cedin mendietara lehiatuqui Judako hiri batetara

And Mary arose in those days, and went into the hill country with haste, into a city of Judah;

40. Eta sar cedin Zachariasen etchera, eta saluta ceçan Elisabeth

And entered into the house of Zacharias, and saluted Elisabeth

41. Eta guertha cedin, ençun ceçanean Elisabethec Mariaren salutationea, jauz baitzedin haourra haren sabelean, eta bethe cedin Spiritu sainduaz Elisabeth:

And it came to pass, that, when Elisabeth heard the salutation of Mary, the babe leaped in her womb; and Elisabeth was filled with the Holy Ghost:

42. Eta oihuz jar cedin voz handiz, eta erran ceçan, Benedicatua *hi* emazten artean, ecen benedicatua ***dun*** *hire* sabeleco fructua

And she spake out with a loud voice, and said, Blessed art thou among women, and blessed is the fruit of thy womb

43. Eta nondic haur niri, ethor dadin ene Jaunaren ama enegana?

And whence is this to me, that the mother of my Lord should come to me?

44. Ecen huna, *hire* salutationeare voza ene beharrietara heldu içan den beçain sarri, jauci içan ***dun*** bozcarioz haourra ene sabelean

For, lo, as soon as the voice of thy salutation sounded in mine ears, the babe leaped in my womb for joy

45. Eta dohatsu *aiz* sinhetsi ***baitun***, ceren conplituren baitirade Jaunaz erran ***çaizquinan*** gauçác

And blessed is she that believed: for there shall be a performance of those things which were told her from the Lord

(Luke 1:27–45)

The above usage resembles *T* usage in other languages in which individuals use *T* with one another as a matter of course, regardless of their status: the angel Gabriel to the Virgin Mary as well as between the Virgin Mary and her (significantly older) aunt Elizabeth.

The next use of *noka* to the Virgin Mary occurs during the presentation of Jesus to the temple, when Simeon, "a pious man longing for 'the consolation of Israel' (the messianic age)"[30] gives the Virgin Mary this message:

Text 2.11: Simeon to Virgin Mary

34. Eta benedica citzan Simeonec, eta erran cieçón haren ama

Mariari, Huna, eçarri içan ***dun*** haur anhitzen destructioneta, eta anhitzen resurrectionetan Israelen, eta signotan ceini nehor contrastaturen baitzayo:

And Simeon blessed them, and said unto Mary his mother, Behold, this child is set for the fall and rising again of many in Israel; and for a sign which shall be spoken against:

35. Are *eurorren* arima ere iraganen ***din*** ezpata batec, aguer ditecençat anhitz bihotzetaco pensamenduac

Yea, a sword shall pierce through thy own soul also, that the thoughts of many hearts may be revealed

(Luke 2:34-35)

With these words, Simeon wishes to convey to Mary that her newborn son will eventually "bring truth to light and will effect decision and judgment. However, in so doing he will face opposition and death."[31] That time is not yet nigh, as Jesus makes clear to his mother many years later at the wedding at Canaan:

Text 2.12: Jesus to Virgin Mary at the Wedding in Canaan

3. Eta faltatu cenean mahatsarnoa, bere amac diotsa, Jesusi, Mahatsarnoric eztie

And when they wanted wine, the mother of Jesus saith unto him, They have no wine

4. Diotsa Jesusec, Zer dut nik *hirequin* emaztea? oraino ***eztun*** ethorri ene orena.

Jesus saith unto her, Woman, what have I to do with thee? Mine hour is not yet come.

5. Dioste haren amac cerbitzariey, Cer ere erran baitieçaçue, egiçue

His mother saith unto the servants, Whatsoever he saith unto you, do it.

(John 2:3-5)

By the time Jesus addresses his mother in *noka* again, he faces the death that Simeon (and others, not discussed here) had prophesied:

Text 2.13 Jesus to Virgin Mary at His Crucifixion

25. Eta ceuden Jesusen crutzearen aldean, haren ama eta haren amaren ahizpa, Maria Cleopasena eta Maria Magdalena

Now there stood by the cross of Jesus his mother, and his mother's sister, Mary the wife of Cleophas, and Mary Magdalen

26. Ikus citzanean bada Jesusec bere ama, eta maite çuen discipulua han cegoela, diotsa bere amari, Emaztea, horra *hire* semea.

When Jesus therefore saw his mother, and the disciple standing by, whom he loved, he saith unto his mother, Woman, behold thy son!

27. Guero diotsa discipuluari, Horra *hire* ama. Eta orduandanic recebi ceçan hura discipuluac beregana.

Then saith he to the disciple, Behold thy mother! And from that hour that disciple took her unto his own home.

(John 19:25-27)

In sum, in just a few short passages, the Leizarraga text uses *noka* to the "most blessed of women" for a variety of positive interactional purposes: to announce she has been chosen to bear the Son of God (text 2.10); to declare that her newborn son will be the salvation of all the world (text 2.11); and to commission her to love one of Jesus's disciples as her own son when Jesus dies on the cross (text 2.13). Only one of these uses—Jesus's deflection of his mother's comment about the lack of wine at the wedding in text 2.12—can be read as negative. However, the Virgin Mary nonetheless instructs the servants to carry out Jesus's instruction, which ultimately leads to Jesus's miraculous turning of water into wine. In so doing, "Jesus has performed the first of his signs, whose purpose, to indicate who he is (to manifest his glory), is now fulfilled in the disciples' response of faith."[32]

We shall see below that Jesus uses *noka* for similar salvific purposes with other women as well.

Mary and Martha

Mary and Martha, along with their brother Lazarus whom Jesus raises from the dead, are among Jesus's closest disciples. In

Luke 10:38-42, Martha "invites Jesus into her home, apparently as head of household."[33] While she busies herself welcoming her guest, her sister Mary sits at his feet listening to his teachings. Martha complains to Jesus of this and asks him to tell Mary to assist her:

Text 2.14: Jesus to Martha

41\. Eta ihardesten çuela erran cieçón Jesusec, Martha, Martha: Arrangura ***dun***, eta tormentatzen *aiz* anhitz gauçaren ondoan:

And Jesus answered and said unto her, Martha, Martha, thou art careful and troubled about many things:

42\. Ordea gauçabat ***dun*** necessario. Baina Mariac parte ona hautatu ***din***, cein ezpaitzayo edequiren

But one thing is needful: and Mary hath chosen that good part, which shall not be taken away from her

(Luke 10:41-42)

Like text 2.13, one could take Jesus's words only at face value, as chastisement. However, this passage as a whole can also be read as an "affirm[ation] of the primacy of prayer and contemplation. Both women were disciples who offered hospitality to Jesus—Martha provided food and other courtesies, but Mary, who chose the 'better part' of hospitality, 'sat at the Lord's feet and listened to what he was saying.' The story is remarkable as a revelation of women as disciples and as an affirmation of listening to Jesus."[34] Jesus shows his particular esteem for Martha in other ways as well: "Martha is named first, before Mary and Lazarus, as loved by Jesus (11:5) . . . she receives teachings concerning the resurrection, acknowledges him as Lord, and confesses faith in him as 'the Christ, the Son of God'"(11:20-27).[35]

Jesus next uses the familiar pronoun to "save" three women, in different ways. The first woman—unnamed except for her designation as "sinful"—washes his feet with oil as Jesus dines in the home of Simon, a Pharisee. Knowing the woman repulses Simon because of her sinfulness, Jesus nonetheless allows her to anoint his feet, then forgives her sins: "Barkatu ***çaizquin*** *eure* bekatuak . . . *Eure* fedeac salbatu *au: oha* bakerequin" (Thy sins are forgiven . . . Thy faith has saved thee: go in peace). (Luke 7:48, 50). In Luke 8, Jesus performs two miracles. In verse 48, he heals a woman seeking relief from a hemorrhage she's had for seven years: "Alaba aun bihotz on *eure* fedeac sendatu *au: oha* bakerequin" (Daughter, thy faith hath made thee whole; go in peace." In verse 54, Jesus resurrects a young girl from the dead: "Eta harc, guciac canpora iraitziric, eta haren escua harturic, oihu egin ceçan, cioela, Neskatcha, iaqui *adi*" ("And he put them all out, and took her by the hand, and called, saying, Maid, arise").

The Gospel of John contains perhaps the most famous female characters in the New Testament: the Samaritan Woman and Mary Magdalen. In John 4, Jesus goes to a well and asks a woman from Samaria—an ancient enemy of the Jews[36]—to fetch him some water. The request surprises her.

Text 2.15: Jesus and the Samaritan Woman

10. Ihardets ceçan Jesusec eta erra cieçón, Baldin *bahaqui* Jaincoaren dohaina, eta nor ***den*** *hiri* erraiten ***draunana***, ***indan*** edatera, *hi* escatu inçayqueon hari, eta eman ***baitzerauquenan*** ur vizirik.

Jesus answered and said unto her, If thou knewest the gift of God, and who it is that saith to thee, Give me to drink; thou wouldest have asked of him, and he would have given thee living water.

11. Diotsa emazteac, Jauna, **eztuc** cerçaz idoci deçan, eta putzua **duc** barna: nondic **duc** beraz ur vizi hori?

The woman saith unto him, Sir, thou hast nothing to draw with, and the well is deep: from whence then hast thou that living water?

12. Ala gure aita Jacob baino handiago *aiz hi*, ceinec eman baitraucu putzu haur, eta berac hunetaric edan baitu, eta haren haourrec, eta haren abrek?

Art thou greater than our father Jacob, which gave us the well, and drank thereof himself, and his children, and his cattle?

13. Ihardets ceçan Jesusec eta erran cieçón, ur hunetaric edaten duen gucia egarrituren ***dun*** berriz:

Jesus answered and said unto her, Whosoever drinketh of this water shall thirst again:

14. Baina norc ere edanen baitu nic emanen ***draucadan*** uretic, ***eztun*** egarriture seculan: baina nic emanen ***draucadan*** ura, eguinen ***dun*** hura baithan ur jauzten denezco ithurri, vizitze eternalecotzat.

But whosoever drinketh of the water that I shall give him shall never thirst; but the water that I shall give him shall be in him a well of water springing up into everlasting life.

15. Diotsa emazteac, Jauna, **indac** ur horretaric, egarri eznadin, eta ethor eznadin huna idoquitera

The woman saith unto him, Sir, give me this water, that I thirst not, neither come hither to draw.

16. Diotsa Jesusec, *Habil* dei ***eçan*** *eure* senharra, eta *athor* huna

Jesus saith unto her, Go, call thy husband, and come hither

17. Ihardets ceçan emazteac eta erran cieçón, **Eztiat** senharric. Diotsa Jesusec, Ungi erran ***dun***, **Eztiat** senharric.

The woman answered and said, I have no husband. Jesus said unto her, Thou hast well said, I have no husband:

18. Ecen borz senhar ucan ***ditun***, eta orain ***dunana***, ***eztun*** *hire* senhar: hori eguiaz erran ***dun***.

For thou hast had five husbands; and he whom thou now hast is not thy husband: in that saidst thou truly

19. Diotsa emazteac, Jauna, **badiacussat** ecen Propheta aizela hi.

The woman saith unto him, Sir, I perceive that thou art a prophet.

20. Gure aitec mendi hunetan adoratu ucan die: eta çuec dioçue ecen Jerusalemen dela lekua non adoratu behar baita.

Our fathers worshipped on this mountain; and ye say, that in Jerusalem is the place where men ought to worship

21. Diotsa Jesusec, Emaztea, sinhets neçan ni, ecen ethorten dela orena noiz ezpaituçue mendi hunetan ez Jerusalemen adoraturen Aita.

Jesus saith unto her, Woman, believe me, the hour cometh, when ye shall neither on this mountain, nor yet at Jerusalem, worship the Father

22. Zueç adoratzen duçue eztaquiçuena, guc adoratzen ***dinagu*** daquiguna: ecen salbamendua Juduetaric ***dun***.

Ye worship ye know not what: we know what we worship: for salvation is of the Jews.

23. Baina ethorten ***dun*** orena, eta orain ***dun***, noiz adoraçale eguiazcoec adoraturen baitute Aita spirituz eta eguiaz: ecen Aita ere halaco adoraçalen galdez ***diagon***.

But the hour cometh, and now is, when the true worshippers shall worship the Father in spirit and in truth: for the Father seeketh such to worship him.

24. Jaincoa ***dun*** Spiritu: eta hura adoratzen dutenec, Spirituz eta eguiaz adoratu behar ***dine***.

God is a Spirit: and they that worship him must worship him in spirit and in truth.

25. Diotsa emazteac, **Bazeaquiat** ezen Messiasa ethorteco dela, Christ deitze dena, harc dathorrenean declarature **dirauzquiguc** gauça guciak.

The woman saith unto him, I know that the Messias cometh, which is called Christ: when he is come, he will tell us all things.

26. Diotsa Jesusec, Ni ***naun*** hura, *hirequin* minzo naicena.

Jesus saith unto her, I that speak unto thee am he

(John 4:10-26)

Taken aback at how much Jesus knew of her life and at his prophesies, the Samaritan Woman goes to the city and proclaims him the Christ. The men she speaks to concur with her opinion: "***Eztinagu*** goitiric *hire* erranagatic sinhesten: ecen geurok ençun ***dinagu***, eta ***baceaquinagu*** ecen haur dela eguiazqui Christ munduaren Salbadorea" ("Now we believe, not because of thy saying: for we have heard him ourselves, and know that this is indeed the Christ, the Savior of the world").

Finally, John 20 relates the story of Mary Magdalen at Christ's Tomb. Mary Magdalen is "mentioned first in every listing of Jesus's female disciples . . . She therefore seems to have been the leader of a group of women who 'followed' and 'served Jesus constantly from the outset of his ministry in Galilee to his death and beyond."[37] Having witnessed Jesus at his crucifixion (see text 2.13 above), she goes to attend to his dead body at the tomb only to find it empty:

Text 2.16: Mary Magdalen at the Tomb

12. Eta ikus citza bi Aingueru churiz veztituac, jarriric ceudela, bata burura eta bercea oinetara, Jesusen gorputza etzan içan cen lekuan.

And she seeth two angels in white sitting, the one at the head, and the other at the feet, where the body of Jesus had lain.

13. Eta hec erran ***cieçoten,*** Emaztea, cergatic nigarrez *ago*? Dioste, Ceren kendu baitute ene Jauna, eta ezpaitaquit non ezarri duten.

And they say unto her, Woman, why weepest thou? She saith unto them, Because they have taken away my Lord, and I know not where they have laid him.

14. Eta haur erran çuenean itzul cedin guibelerat, eta ikus ceçan Jesus han cegoela, eta etzaquian Jesus cela.

And when she had thus said, she turned herself back, and saw Jesus standing, and knew not that it was Jesus.

15. Diotsa Jesusec, Emaztea, cergatic nigarrez *ago*? noren bilha *abila*? Harc ustez ecen baratzeçaina cela, diotsa, Jauna, baldin **hic** eraman **baduc** hura, **erradac** non ecarri **duan**: eta nic kenduren **diat**.

Jesus saith unto her, Woman, why weepest thou? whom seekest thou? She, supposing him to be the gardener, saith unto him, Sir, if thou have borne him hence, tell me where thou hast laid him, and I will take him away.

16. Diotsa Jesusec, Maria: Itzuliric harc diotsa, Rabboni, erran nahi baita, Majistrua.

Jesus saith unto her: Mary. She turned herself, and saith unto him, Rabboni; which is to say, Master.

17. Diotsa Jesusec, ***Ezneçanala*** hunqui: ecen oraino ***eznaun*** igan neure Aitagana: baina *habil* ene anayetara, eta erran ***iecen***, Igaiten naiz neure Aitagana, eta çuen Aitagana, eta neure Jaincoagana eta çuen Jaincoagana.

Jesus saith unto her, Touch me not; for I am not yet ascended to my Father: but go to my brethren, and say unto them, I ascend unto my Father, and your Father; and to my God, and your God.

(John 20:12-17)

Immediately thereafter, Mary goes to Jesus's disciples to tell them he has risen from the dead, the origin for her appellation as "The Apostle to the Apostles."[38] As such, Mary Magdalen joins the Virgin Mary, Elisabeth (mother of John the Baptist) and Martha as respected individuals with whom the Leizarraga New Testament uses *noka*. The other females with whom Jesus uses *noka* played key roles in his salvific mission as either beneficiaries of his miracles (the "sinful woman," woman with the hemorrhage, or resurrected girl) or bear important witness to his prophesies (the Samaritan Woman). These passages use *noka* for positive interactional purposes: to bless, to send forth, to proclaim, to heal, to save. Thus, Duvoisin had many models for *noka* usage when he translated his New Testament three hundred years later. But he did not follow Leizarraga's lead; Duvoisin uses no *noka* in his New Testament. The next section, then, examines *noka* usage in the Old Testament, beginning with the oldest such text, d'Urte's fragment of 1700.

Findings: The Protestant Old Testament

Pierre d'Urte's fragment encompasses all of Genesis but ends abruptly after Exodus 22:11, suggesting d'Urte may have died before he completed his work. Only Genesis contains any *noka*, as this book features many female characters. The Exodus excerpt ends with the Israelites' encampment in Sinai,[39] which features primarily male figures such as Moses, Aaron, and the Pharoah, with whom *noka* would not have been used.

Table 2.4: *Noka* in d'Urte's Old Testament Fragment

Addressee	Verses	*Noka*
Eve	Gen 12, 3:13, 16	9
Sarah	Gen 12:11-12; 16:6; 18:15; 20:13-16	17
Hagar	Gen 16:8-12; 21:17-18	20
Rebecca	Gen 24:58-60; 27:11-13	10
Midwife	Gen 35:17	3
Rachel	Gen 37:17	3
Potiphar's wife	Gen 39:9	4
		66

As with Leizarraga's text, d'Urte uses *noka* with a wide range of females, for disparate interactional purposes. The section below discusses these in more detail.

The Protestant *Noka* of Familiarity: Evidence from d'Urte

Many female characters appear in this short Old Testament fragment. The first use of *noka* occurs in the Garden of Eden, during the "Divine Judgment"[40] when God—called the "The Eternal One" by d'Urte, which "had the mint-mark of Protestant acceptance and could not be omitted"[41]—banishes Adam and Eve from Paradise for eating of the forbidden Tree of Knowledge:

Text 2.17: God and Eve

13: Eta Jainco Eternalac erran çioen Emazteari, çergatic eguin ***dun*** hori? . . . eta emazteac ihardetssi çuen, sugueac enganatu **<u>niauc</u>**, eta jan **<u>diat</u>** handic.

And the Eternal One said unto the woman, What is this that thou hast done? And the woman said, The serpent beguiled me, and I did eat.

16: eta erran çioen Emazteari, hagutic berretuco ***dignat*** *hire* içorra nequea: nequerequign erdico *aiz* haurrrez, eta *hire* gutiçiac *hire* senharrarengana goanen ***tun*** eta horrec erreguignatuco ***dign*** *hire* gagnean

Unto the woman he said, I will greatly multiply thy sorrow and thy conception; in sorrow thou shalt bring forth children; and thy desire shall be to thy husband, and he shall rule over thee.

(Genesis 3:13,16).

The punishment of Eve illustrates a pattern in Genesis 4–11 characterized by "[b]rokenness, disharmony, the sundering of relationships between God and humanity, between man and woman, and between the human and the nonhuman world."[42] The d'Urte text, not surprisingly, uses *noka* for some negative interactional purposes in such passages. We see this also in Genesis 12:11. God has promised Abraham many descendants who would then possess Canaan.[43] Nonetheless, Abraham leaves Canaan when famine descends upon it and goes to Egypt. Fearing that Egyptian men will covet Sarah and kill him to take her for themselves, Abraham directs Sarah to tell a lie that endangers her role as ancestress and thereby the fulfillment of God's promises:[44] "***Erran*** daquidantçat eta *hi aiçela* moyen ene biçia salba dadintçat" (Say, I pray thee, thou art my sister: that it may be well with me for thy sake; and my soul shall live because of thee).

We next see *noka* in a scene in which Sarah is endangered in another way. Barren, she "gives" her maid Hagar to Abraham in the hopes that she can bear him a child—that will legally belong to Sarah; "[s]uch substitute childbearing . . . was apparently an accepted social institution in the ancient Near East."[45] Yet when Sarah overhears the news that Hagar expects Abraham's child, she laughs in disbelief. God confronts her:

Text 2.18: God to Sarah

15: Sarac ukhatu çuen çiotssala, **eztiat** hirri eguign: eçen beldurtu çen. Eta erran çuen, ***eztun*** horrela: eçen hirri eguin ***dun***

Then Sarah denied it, saying, I laughed not; for she was afraid. And he said, Nay; but thou didst laugh.

(Genesis 18:15)

This is the third use of *noka* thus far for negative interactional purposes, which would seem to contradict the argument I am making in this chapter as a whole. But text 2.18 deviates in a significant way from the patterns outlined by Brown and Gilman. Rather than a superior shifting from *V* to *T* to berate a subordinate, Sarah reciprocates God's use of *noka* with her by using *toka* with him.

The final use of *noka* to Sarah occurs in Genesis 20: 13-16.

Presented as Abraham's half-sister rather than his wife, Sarah converses with Abimelech, King of Gerar (in current-day Israel).

Text 2.19: Sarah and Abimelech

13. Eta guerthatu içan da, Jaincoac eraman nauen orduan harat hunat, ene aitaren etçhetic campora, erran içan diodala, hemen ***dun*** gracia *hik* niri . . . eguignen ***darotanana***: ethorrico garen lekhu gucietan, erran nitaz, ene Anaia da

And it came to pass, when God caused me to wander from my father's house, that I said unto her, This is thy kindness which thou shalt shew unto me; at every place whither we shall come, say of me, He is my brother

14. Orduan Abimelec hartu çituen ardiac, idiac, muthillac eta nescatoac, eta eman çiotçan Abrahani, eta errendatu çioen Sara bere emaztea

And Abimelech took sheep, and oxen, and menservants, and women servants, and gave them unto Abraham, and restored him Sarah his wife

15. Eta erran çuen, horra, ene herria hire . . . manuco: egon adi non ere . . . placer içanen **baituc** eta han

And Abimelech said, Behold, my land is before thee: dwell where it pleaseth thee

16. Eta erran cioen Sarari, horra, eman ***çiotçanat*** *hire* anairi milla çillhar pheça: horra, begui estalquibat çaign *hiri hirequin* diren guçien aldera: horrela içatu cen erreprehenditua

And unto Sarah he said, Behold, I have given thy brother a thousand pieces of silver: behold, he is to thee a covering of the eyes, unto all that are with thee, and with all other: thus she was reproved

(Genesis 20: 13-16)

Here, then, a king uses *noka* to bless, rather than to curse, Sarah—and she returns the pronominal favor by using the familiar (*toka*) with him.

The flexibility of *noka* for positive and negative purposes is affirmed in its use with the servant, Hagar. When Hagar becomes pregnant with Abraham's child, she looks upon Sarah with disdain;

Sarah complains of this to Abraham. He answers: "Horra *hire* nescatoa *heure* escuan ***dun***, eguin dio . . . nahi ***dunan*** becala. Saric bada aflijtu çuen hagna eta ihessi goan cen haren aitcignetican." (But Abraham said unto Sarah, Behold, thy maid is in thy hand; do to her as it pleaseth thee. And when Sarah dealt hardly with her, she fled from her face). Hagar flees from Sarah's abuse, but then an angel coaxes her back with the announcement in text 2.20.

Text 2.20: The Eternal One and Hagar

7. Bagnan Eternalaren aurkhitu içan çuen hagna ithurri ur baten aldean, dessertuan, sçurreco bidean den ithurriaren ondoan

And the angel of the Eternal One found her by a fountain of water in the wilderness, by the fountain in the way to Shur

8. hala erran cioen, Agar Sarairen nescatoa, nondic heldu *aiz*? Eta norat *oha*? Eta ihardetssi çuen, ihessi **nihoac** Sarai ene etcheco andrearen aitcignetic

And he said, Hagar, Sarah's maid, whence camest thou? and whither wilt thou go? And she said, I flee from the face of my mistress Sarah.

9. eta Eternalaren Ainguеruac erran çioen, bihur *adi hire* etçheco andreagana, eta humilia *adi* haren azpian

And the angel of the LORD said unto her, Return to thy mistress, and submit thyself under her hands.

10. guehiago Eternalaren Aingueruac erran çioen, berretuco **diat** hagutic hire ondorea: halaco maneraz non eçin condatudo baita hagn haundia içanen **duc**

And the angel of the LORD said unto her, I will multiply thy seed exceedingly, that it shall not be numbered for multitude

11. Eternalaren Aingueruac erran çioen oragno . . . horra, contcebitu ***dun***, eta erdico *aiz* semebatez çegnaren içena deithuco ***baitun*** Ismael: eçen Eternalac entçun ***dign*** *hire* aflicсionea

And the angel of the LORD said unto her, Behold, thou art with child, and shalt bear a son, and shalt call his name Ishmael; because the LORD hath heard thy affliction

12. eta hagna içanen ***dun*** . . . guiçona bassa astoa: horren escua

içanen ***dun*** batbederaren contra, eta batbederaren escuac horren contra: bere anaia guçien escugnean egongo da

And he will be a wild man; his hand will be against every man, and every man's hand against him; and he shall dwell in the presence of all his brethren.

(Genesis 16:8-12)

However, the rivalry between Sarah and Hagar continues even after Sarah herself has borne Abraham a son. Fearing that Hagar's son, Ishmael, threatens her son Isaac's position as heir, Sarah coaxes Abraham to banish Hagar and Ishmael.[46] God comes to Hagar's aid once again:

Text 2.21: The Eternal One and Hagar

17: Eta Jaincoac aditu çuen haurreren boca, Jaincoaren aingueruac deithu çuen çeruetari Agar: eta erran çioen çer ***dun***, Agar? ***Eztunala*** beldurric, ecen Jaincoac aditu ***dign*** haurraren boça, den lekhutic

And God heard the voice of the lad; and the angel of God called Hagar out of heaven, and said unto her, What aileth thee, Hagar? Fear not; for God hath heard the voice of the lad where he is

18: Jaiqui *adi*, altçha ***çan*** haurra eta ***hartçan*** *hire* escuarequiagn: ecen egui-naraçico ***dignat*** naçione haundibat

Arise, lift up the lad, and hold him in thine hand; for I will make him a great nation

(Genesis 21:17-18)

Thus, by the twenty-first book in Genesis, the Protestant reader would have seen *noka* used by speakers as disparate in status as God the Father to Hagar the slave, and for conversational purposes ranging from the negative (punishing, cursing, casting out) to positive (blessing and announcing the pregnancy of an heir). We see the flexibility of *noka* usage continue in interactions involving Rebecca, who marries Abraham's son, Isaac, in text 2.22.

Text 2.22: The Wooing of Rebecca

58. Deithua içan çuten bada Rebecca, eta erran çioten, nahi ***dun*** goan guicon hunequin? Cegnac ihardetsi baitcuen, goango naiz.

And they called Rebecca, and said unto her, Wilt thou go with this man? And she said, I will go

59. Hala bidaldu içan çuten Rebecca bere Arreba eta haren unhidea, elkharrequign Abrahanen muthilla eta haren jendeac

And they sent away Rebecca their sister, and her nurse, and Abraham's servant, and his men.

60. eta bedincatu çuten Rebecca eta erran çioten, gure Arreba *aiz*, içan *adi* fruitutssu milla milliunea, eta *hire* ondoreac possedi beça higuindaco ***dutenan*** athea

And they blessed Rebecca, and said unto her, Thou art our sister, be thou the mother of thousands of millions, and let thy seed possess the gate of those which hate them

(Genesis 24:58-60)

This passage likens Rebecca to Abraham: she, too, "is an essential link in the transmission of the divine promise and is thus called by Yahweh, as Abraham was, to her matriarchal role . . . in agreeing to the marriage with Isaac, [Rebecca] moves toward the blessing and becomes a member of the blessed family."[47] Indeed, that Rebecca is a force to be reckoned with is evidenced by her agency in passages of "The Deception of Isaac." Overhearing that Isaac plans to give his blessing to their son Esau, Rebecca concocts a plan to disguise Jacob—her favorite son—so that Isaac blesses him instead. But Jacob himself fears the consequences that may arise from her plan,[48] as is seen in text 2.23.

Text 2.23: Rebecca and Jacob

11. Eta Jacobec ihardetssi çioen Rebecca[49] . . . bere Amari, horra, Esau ene Anaia . . . guiçon Illetss ***dun*** bagnan ni ***naun*** guicon Ille gabea . . .

And Jacob said to Rebecca his mother, Behold, Esau my brother is a hairy man, and I am a smooth man:

12\. benturaz ene aitac ***niaun*** uquituco . . . eta ***niaun*** iduquico . . . engana-Laribatentçat eta benediçionea era-***dignat*** (-) kharrico . . . ene gagnera madariçionea:

My father peradventure will touch me, and I shall seem to him as a deceiver; and I shall bring a curse upon me, and not a blessing.

13\. eta bere Amac erran çioen, Ene semea, hire madariçionea içan dadillala ene gagnean: solament obedio **dioçoc** ene hitcari eta oha har **dieçadac** erran ***darodana***

And his mother said unto him, Upon me be thy curse, my son: only obey my voice, and go fetch me them.

(Genesis 27:11-13)

Ultimately, the image that emerges of Rebecca is a powerful one: she is "an energetic and resourceful woman who acts on behalf of her son and thus serves the hidden purposes of God."[50]

Two passages using *noka* remain in d'Urte's text. In Genesis 39:9, Joseph fends off the advances of his guard Potiphar's wife as he sits in jail: "***Eztun*** etçhe huntan ni bagno haundiagoric, eta etçiarotan debecatu deussere. *Hi* baiçen, *hi* haren emazte *aiçen* becala: eta nola eguingo nuque gaizqui . . . horren haundi hori eta eguingo nuque bekhatu Jaincoaren contra?" (There is none greater in this house than I; neither hath he kept back any thing from me but thee, because thou art his wife: how then can I do this great wickedness, and sin against God?). In Genesis 35:17, a midwife relays good news to Rachel, Rebecca's niece, as she delivers her baby: "Eta nola baitçen erditçeco mignetan, emaguignac erran içan cioen, ***eztunala*** beldurric: eçen hori ***çaign*** oragno *hiri* hemen semebat" (And it came to pass, when she was in hard labor, that the midwife said unto her, Fear not; thou shalt have this son also).

In sum, d'Urte's Old Testament resembles Leizarraga's New Testament in that it uses *noka* to address women across the social spectrum: from the ancestresses Eve, Sarah, Rebecca, and Rachel to the slave Hagar and the unnamed guard's wife. Each of these women returns the familiar pronoun in kind, whether they address their spouse (Sarah with Abraham), their son (Rachel with Jacob), or The Eternal One (Eve, Sarah and Hagar). Once again, Duvoisin does not follow these pronominal leads, choosing instead to use *noka* for the most restricted and most negative of purposes.

The Duvoisin Old Testament: Semantic Derogation of *Noka*

While the Protestant texts model the ubiquitous use of *noka* to and between a variety of female characters for a wide range of interactional purposes, the Duvoisin text takes up but few of these in rendering the Old Testament into Basque. Table 2.5 provides a summary of my findings.

Table 2.5: *Noka* Usage in Duvoisin's Old Testament

Addressee	**Chapters**	***Noka***
Donkey	Numbers	3
Woman	Kings 3:22	14
Babylon	Psalm 136	3
	Isaiah 1, 47	52
	Jeremiah 50, 51	10
Sidon, Tyre	Isaiah 23	10
Jerusalem	Isaiah 1, 22, 51, 57	55
	Jeremiah 11	3
	Ezekiel 5, 6, 20, 22-23, 25-26	603
Egypt	Jeremiah 46	12
Didon	Jeremiah 48	6
Hesbon/maiden	Jeremiah 49	
Forest of the South	Ezekiel 20	4
Israel/Judah	Micah 6	18
	TOTAL	**783**

In all, Duvoisin's Old Testament uses *noka* in one book each in Numbers, Kings, Psalms, and Micah, with the bulk used in Isaiah, Jeremiah, and Ezekiel. Most of these passages use *noka* as "prosopopeia" (or "apostrophe"), addressing an inanimate object metaphorically as if it were a living (in this case, female) entity. I begin with the context for those usages below.

The Book of Psalms

Duvoisin first uses *noka* metaphorically in Psalm 136, which is both a lamentation and a curse, like a funeral dirge.[51] Verses 1 through 4 "lament[. . .] the impossibility of chanting songs honouring Jerusalem in enemy lands" and verses 5 through 9 use *noka* to describe Babylon burning down Jerusalem:

Text 2.24: *Noka* to Babylon

8. Babilonako alaba zorigaichtokoa, dohatsu *hiri* bihurturen ***dainana hik*** guri egin gaizkiak!

"Wretched daughter of Babylon, to whom will be returned happily the ills thou didst us!"

Dohatsu hartuko dituena *hire* haur cheheak eta harriaren gainean phorroskatuko dituena!

"Happy the one who shall take thy little children and shall dash them on a stone!"

(Psalm 136:8-9)

Harsh words indeed. Below we shall see that this mean-spirited use of *noka* occurs throughout Duvoisin's Old Testament.

The Latter Prophets

Duvoisin uses *noka* primarily in the Latter Prophets, which are part of the fifteen central books of the Hebrew Bible.[52] Specifically, the *noka* passages occur in the Books of Isaiah, Jeremiah, Ezekiel, and Micah, whose settings range from the eighteenth to the fifth centuries BCE.[53] This time period spans the destruction of Jerusalem by the Babylonians to the "Persian-period restoration of Jerusalem and the Temple."[54]

The Book of Isaiah

In the Book of Isaiah, an educated man of high status[55] or an advisor to kings[56] "grapples with the theological problem of evil" in the face of "Assyrian invasion and Babylonian exile."[57] Isaiah sounds "the familiar themes of social justice, the obligation to aid and not oppress the weak, and the obligation to worship only Yahweh."[58] Table 2.6 provides a summary of *noka* usage in Isaiah.

Table 2.6: *Noka* in Isaiah

Addressee	Chapters	*Noka*
"Faithful city"	Isaiah 1	5
Jerusalem	Isaiah 22, 51, 57	50
Sidon, Tyre	Isaiah 23	10
Babylon	Isaiah 47	54
	TOTAL	**119**

Table 2.6 shows that four of the six books of Isaiah address the city of Jerusalem. Isaiah 1:22 tells the "faithful city" (understood to be Jerusalem) that "[t]hy silver has become slag and thy wine has been mixed with water." *Noka* passages castigate Jerusalem's leaders as "faithless" (v 22) and "friends of thieves . . . running after profit" (v 23). Isaiah 22:1 through 3 and 7 address Jerusalem as "the valley of vision"[59] whose leaders "have fled as one;" Jerusalem is told: "thy choice valleys shall be filled with chariots and horsemen will be placed in thy gate" (v 7).

Isaiah 57 uses *noka* to address a "post-exilic Israel . . . addressing the past, present and future people of God, including God-fearing foreigners."[60] Specifically, *noka* passages chastise the addressee for "offer[ing] sacrifices" (v 6), "immolat[ing] victims" (v 7), "receiv[ing] to thyself the obscene man" (v 8), "adorn[ing] thy head with ointment . . . humiliat[ing] thyself all the way to hell . . . [for] with thy deeds thou didst find a living, and didst not say any prayers" (v 10). Verse 11 chides Israel for "forget[ting] me because I did not remain quiet and as if I could not see." Even the "righteousness" (v 12) of the few "will not benefit thee."[61] Yet God proclaims that, in the future, "whoever trusts in me will inherit the earth, and will exalt my sacred mountain" (v 13).

Isaiah also uses *noka* in the "oracles against the nations" 52 times—out of the total 119 tokens. Isaiah 23:12, for example, calls the "daughter of Sidon" a "dishonored maiden" (v 15), and tells her to "[t]ake the guitar, go round the city, whore who has been forgotten about; sing well, repeat the song, so that someone remembers thee" (v 16). By far the greatest vitriol is reserved to "humiliate" Babylon[62] as we see in text 2.25:

Text 2.25: *Noka* to Babylon

1. Jauts *hadi*, jar *hadi* herrautsean, dontzeila, Babilonako alaba; jar *hadi* lurrean; ez ***dun*** tronurik gehiago Kaldearren alabarentzat; ezen ez *haiz* guria eta samurra deithuren gehiago.

"Descend, sit in the dust, damsel daughter of Babylon; sit on the ground; there is no longer a throne for the daughter of the Chaldean; for thou shalt no longer be called soft and tender"

2. Har ***zan*** ihara, eta eho ***zan*** irina; ager ***zan*** *hire* itsukeria, ager sorbalda, ager ichterrak, iragan hibayak

Take the millstone, and grind the flour; show thy ugliness, show thy shoulder, show thy thighs, cross the rivers

3. Agertua izanen ***dun*** *hire* hidoya; ikhusiko ***diten*** *hire* laidoa: harturen dut asperkunde, eta ez da gizonik niri itchikiko darotanik

Thy indecency shall be revealed; they shall see thy dishonor: I will take revenge, and no man shall retain me

5. Jar *hadi* ichil-ichila, ea ilhumbeetan sar *hadi*, Kaldearren alaba; ezen ez *haute* gehiago deithuren erresumetako erregina.

Sit in silence, and enter in darkness, Chaldean's daughter; for they shall call thee no longer queen of realms

9. Agortasuna eta alhaguntasuna, horiek biak terrepentean eta egun batez ethorriren ***zaizkin*** gainera. Oro gainera eroriko ***zaizkin***, *hire* gaizkinkerien elemenia gatik, eta *hire* charma-egileen gogortasun gaitza gatik.

Sterility and widowhood, both will come upon thee suddenly, in one day. Everything will fall upon thee, because of the abundance of thy misdeeds, and because of the great severity of thy spells

10. *Hire* tzarkerietan *bahuen* sinheste; erran ***dun***: ez da nihor ikhusten nauenik. *Hire* zuhurtziak eta jakitateak, horiek *haute* enganatu. Eta *hire* bihotzean erran ***dun***: Ni banaiz, ea nitaz landan ez da bertze bat.

Though trustedst in thy evil deeds; thou saidst: There is no one that sees me. Thy wisdom and knowledge, they deceive thee. And in thy heart thou hast said: I am, and aside from me there is no other

11. Gaitza ethorriren ***zain*** gainera, eta ez ***dun*** jakinen nondik ilkhitzen

den; eta gainera eroriko ***zain*** ezin jabalduko ***dunan*** zorigaitza; terrepentean ethorriko ***zain***, ezagutu ez ***dunan*** erromeseria.

Evil will fall upon thee, and thou shalt not know where it comes from; and on thee will fall a misfortune that thou canst not undo; an unknown misery will suddenly afflict thee

12. Athera *hadi hire* charma-egileekin eta *hire* gaizkinkeria gaztedanik erabili ***ditunan*** guziekin, ikhusteko hean zerbait baliatuko ***zaizkinan***, edo hean hazkarrago egin *haitakeen.*

Come out with thy spells and with all thy sorceries which thou hast employed since thy youth, to see whether they are of any use to thee, or whether thou may be strengthened.

(Isaiah 47:1-12)

This passage from Second Isaiah was composed between 539 and 535 BCE, soon after Persia's King Cyrus captured Babylon. God (through Isaiah) spews invective at Babylon. But the extent to which this invective utilizes sexualized, violent imagery is worthy of note. Babylon is brutally punished for her arrogance, for considering herself "queen of the realms" (v 5), thinking to herself that "there is none but me" (v 8). She will also soon suffer sterility, widowhood, and misfortune (v 8-10). Babylon has relied on "sorceries" and "sky-diviners" but they will not rescue her when her "indecency," "dishonor," and "ugliness" are revealed. The once-mighty Babylon has been humiliated as if she were some lowly, errant young woman—worse, an adulteress whom no one tries to save.[63]

The Book of Jeremiah

The Book of Jeremiah encompasses events beginning with Judah's loss of independence after the death of King Josiah in 609 BCE to Jerusalem's destruction by Babylon and the subsequent exile of its people in 587 BCE.[64] Table 2.7 outlines *noka* usage in Jeremiah.

Table 2.7: *Noka* in Jeremiah

Addressee	Chapters	*Noka*
Judah/Jerusalem	Jeremiah 11	3
Egyptian maid	Jeremiah 46	12

Daughter of Didon	Jeremiah 48	6
Hesbon/maid	Jeremiah 49	15
Babylon	Jeremiah 50, 51	10
	TOTAL	**46**

Table 2.7 shows that only one chapter in Jeremiah uses *noka* in addressing the Jewish people. Chapter 11 uses *noka* three times to condemn Judah for "thou hadst as many gods as cities; and thou, Jerusalem, for each road set up altars of shame, altars for sacrifice to Baal" (v 13). However, the majority of the forty-six uses of *noka* in Jeremiah are directed to enemies of the Jewish people. Jeremiah 48: 18 tells the daughter of Didon to "[d]escend from thy glory and sit in thirst, dwelling of the daughter of Didon; for Mohab's vanquisher is coming up to thee and will rip asunder thy strongholds" (v 18). The forty-ninth chapter uses *noka* to tell Heshbon to be patient in the face of some destruction; it chastises the "sensitive maid" for "whoring off in thy valleys" (v 2–3). Jeremiah 50 uses *noka* to berate Babylon for "provok[ing] the Lord" after God has caught her in a trap he set (v 24). Chapter 51 uses *noka* three more times to threaten Babylon: even though she "dwellest on great waters, smothered with wealth" (v 13), the "Lord of armies has made this vow upon himself: By my word, I will cover thee with men like locusts, and a song of war shall be sung about thee" (v 14).

However, *noka* most often addresses the country of Egypt. One oracle (v 2–12, see text 2.26 below, v 11–12) claims that Egypt's defeat is Yahweh's revenge for Pharoah's killing of King Josiah in 609 BCE.[65] Similarly, a second oracle (v 13–24) interprets Babylon's imminent defeat of Egypt (circa 586 BCE) as punishment from Yahweh:

Text 2.26: *Noka* to Egypt

11. Galaadera igan *hadi* eta har ***zan*** baltsamua, Egiptoar neskatcha gaztea; alferretan erabiliren ***ditun*** asko sendakari; sendatzerik *hiretzat* ez ***dun***

Go up to Galead and take balsam, young Egyptian maiden; in vain wilt thou try many medicines; there is no healing for thee

12. Jendayek entzun ***dine*** *hire* laidoa eta *hire* orrobiek bethe ***dine***

lurra; zeren hazkarrak hazkarrari jazarri baitio eta biek batean jo baitute lurra
The nations have heard of thy dishonor, and thy howls have filled the land; for the strong has assailed the strong and both have fallen together
(Jeremiah 46: 11-12)

The Book of Ezekiel

In 597 BCE, Nebuchadnezzar and King Johoiachin of Judah took Ezekiel, along with other priests and royal family members, with them into exile in Babylonia.[66] This book "describes the departure of God's 'glory' from the temple"[67] as well as the temple's ultimate restoration. Table 2.8 outlines *noka* usage in Ezekiel.

Table 2.8: *Noka* in Ezekiel

Addressee	**Chapters**	***Noka***
Jerusalem	Ezekiel 5, 16, 22, 23	443
Israel	Ezekiel 7	27
Forest of the South	Ezekiel 20	4
Ammon, Moab, Edom, Philistia	Ezekiel 25	13
Tyre	Ezekiel 26	49
	TOTAL	**522**

The Book of Ezekiel uses *noka* primarily to address Jerusalem. But it uses *noka* for the most virulent and graphically sexual imagery we have seen thus far. Ezekiel 5 admonishes Jerusalem for her "abomination" (v 9); "wickedness and evil doings" (v 11); vowing to punish her through cannibalism: "fathers will eat their sons in thy midst, and sons their fathers" (v 10); by "break[ing] thee; and my eyes will not spare thee, and I will not take pity" (v 11); "blight[ing] [Jerusalem] by famine . . . scatter[ing] . . . to all the winds . . . draw[ing] the sword" (v 12); and sending "famine and the fiercest of beasts . . . pestilence and blood" (v 29). These punishments will make Jerusalem serve as a "reproach and a blasphemy, a spectacle and a horror among the nations around thee, when I shall implement my rulings in my fit of indignation, anger and fury" (v 8).

Chapter 7 heaps more invective upon the temple of Jerusalem in Israel. The God of Israel vows to "pour my anger upon thee . . .

judge thee according to thy path, and burden thee with all thy wicked deeds" (v 3). The Lord God promises "not to take pity [but] cause thy bad ways to fall upon thee [so that] thy abominations will remain in thy midst" (v 4). In chapter 20, God calls upon the Son of Man to tell the "forest of the south" (v 46) that he will "light a fire in thy midst . . .burn in thy midst . . . burn all thy trees . . . and all the faces shall be charred in it, from south to north" (v 47).

Thus, in just a few passages, Ezekiel 5 and 7 uses the terms "evil" and "abominations" twice to discuss Jerusalem's behavior, for which he calls for severe punishments by beast, burning, famine, and cannibalism. Chapters 16 and 23 level more egregious charges against Jerusalem still; both chapters use marriage as a metaphor for the relationship between God and the Jewish people. Ezekiel 16 emphasizes Jerusalem's "horrible deeds" (v 1), reminding her that her "Amorite father and Hittite mother" (v 2) "did not purify thee with water for thy salvation, nor salt thee with salt, nor swaddle thee in cloths" (v 4). Rather, Jerusalem was "cast . . . on the ground" (v 5) at birth; God found her "trampled underfoot in thy blood" (v 6) and took pity, "rais[ing] thee like a herb in the fields . . [until] thou camest of age and to a womanly shape" (v 7). God covered Jerusalem's "dishonor" with a cloak (v 8), dressing her in "colorful dress and purple shoes" (v 10), adorning her with jewels (v 11), including a "gold ornament" (v 12), a "beautiful diadem" (v 12), "gold and silver" (v 13), and "raised [her] on wheat flour, honey and oil" (v 14).

Then God excoriates Jerusalem for abusing the beauty and gifts he bestowed on her: "Thy name circulated among the nations on account of the attractiveness of thy face, because thou wert truly beautiful" (v 14)." Yet she grew "conceited about thy beauty, thou didst sully thy name; and thou didst show thy indecency to all the passers-by" (v 15); "sew[ing] obscene coverings" to wear (v 15) . . . [and] profan[ing] thyself as nobody has ever done before or ever will" (v 16). She made "human shapes" (v 17) from the gold and silver God gave her, "plac[ing] . . . before them" (v 18, 19) the perfumes, oil, [and] honey; sacrificed her children to them "to be devoured" (v 20); immolating her children "consecrating them to them" (v 21). Finally, "after all those horrors and defilement, thou didst not remember thy days of youth, when thou wert naked, covered with shame, trampled in thy blood" (v 22).

In addition to exploiting her God-given beauty for her own sake, then, Jerusalem also offers her own children to worship idols other than the God who protected her and bestowed gifts upon her. Yet Jerusalem is guilty of sexual improprieties as well, and Ezekiel 16 uses *noka* in laying out his case of licentiousness against her. By setting up a "house of debauchery" (v 24), "thou [Jerusalem] hast opened thy legs to any passer-by, and thy acts of debauchery have piled up" (v 25); to punish her, God will "leave thee to the mercy of the Palestinian girls who detest thee" (v 27). Yet Jerusalem continues to "commit debauchery" with Assyrian boys (v 20), Canaanites (v 20), begging the question: "How am I to clean thy heart . . . when thou dost perform all the acts of a slutty, shameless woman?" (v 30). Indeed, "in offering and declining with disgust, thou hast now become like a whore who raises her prices" (v 31), akin to a prostitute (v 32–33); "in giving rather than receiving a price, what happens in thy case is unlike anywhere else" (v 34). God will punish Jerusalem for her misdeeds by "reveal[ling] thy dishonor [so that all] shall see how repugnant thou art" (v 37), "cause thy blood to be shed" (v 38), and thrown to her enemies, who will demolish her "place of lewdness" (v 39), strip her of her jewels, clothes (v 39), bring forth a crowd that will stone her (v 40) and set her house afire (v 41). When Jerusalem has endured all these punishments, then God's "rage will cease" (v 42).

In the meantime, Ezekiel 16 resumes the tirade diatribe against Jerusalem and her family. Ezekiel reminds Jerusalem (again) that her mother left her father and abandoned her children (v 45). He mocks her that she will soon exceed the depravity of her infamous sisters, Samaria and Sodom (v 47–49), whom God "wiped . . . out" for their "conceit" and the "horrors [they committed] in my presence" (v 50). Ezekiel 16 concludes by reminding Jerusalem (yet again) of her birth in "disgrace" (v

58), of God's coming to her rescue (v 59-60). He tells Jerusalem: "remember thy wrong steps and shalt be ashamed," (v 61) and he will make another pact with her.

Thus, an unambiguously negative image of Jerusalem emerges from Ezekiel 16. Rather than be grateful to God for rescuing her as an orphan and his generosity, Jerusalem has worshipped graven images, wasted her beauty, and lived a sexually dissolute life. These passages use *noka* throughout, casting aspersions on the pronoun as well.

Ezekiel 23 elaborates upon the long list of atrocities and abominations in Ezekiel 16, which uses *noka* liberally in the dialogue of the "Allegory of the Two Sisters," Ohola and Oholibah; they represent Samaria and Jerusalem, respectively.[68] Verses 1 through 10 detail the "dirty embraces" (v 7) and "scandalous [sexual] behavior" engaged in by the two sisters. Verse 11 claims Oholibah's "shameless offers are greater debaucheries than her sisters" (v 11). Text 2.27 provides an excerpt from this passage:

Text 2.27: *Noka* to Samaria and Jerusalem

21. Eta berritu ***ditun*** *hire* gaztaroko tzarkeriak, *hire* bulharrak Egipton zaphatuak, eta *hire* lorea histua izan zirenekoak

And thou hast repeated the evils of thy youth, thy breasts squashed in Egypt, when thy flower was withered

25. Eta ezarriren ***dinat*** *hire* kontra ene kharra zeinari errabian emanan baitiote *hire* gainean bide; ebakiren ***darozkine*** sudurra eta beharriak; eta *hitarik* gelditzen dena arthikiren ***dine*** ezpataren azpira; harturen ***ditine*** *hire* seme-alabak; eta suaz iretsiak izanen dire *hire* azken ondarrik

And I will set my zeal against thee, whom they shall deal with angrily; they shall cut thy nose and ears off; and what remains of thee, they shall cast under the sword; they shall take away thy children; and thy last residue will be consumed by fire

26. Biluziren *haute hire* soinekoetarik, eta eramanen ***ditine*** *hire* sendagailazko edergailuak.

They shall strip off thy clothes, and they shall carry away thy beautiful jewels

27. Eta *hire* ganik geldiaraziren **ditinat** *hire* tzarkeria, eta Egiptoko lurretikako *hire* lohikeriak; eta ez **ditun** gehiago hekien gainera goitituren *hire* begiak, eta ez *haiz* gehiago Egiptoaz orhoituren

And I will cause your bad behavior to cease from thee, and thy fornication from the land of Egypt; and thou shalt no longer lift up thy eyes upon them, and shalt not remember Egypt any more

29. Eta gaitzireizkorekin lothuko ***zaizkin***, eta eramanen ***ditine*** *hire* onak, eta igorriren *haute* buluzik eta laidoz estalia; eta agertuak izanen ***ditun*** *hire* lohikeria ahalkagarriak, *hire* tzakeria eta *hire* lizunkeriak

And they shall set to work on thee with hatred, and shall take away thy good, and shall send thee off naked and covered with shame; and thy shameful fornications, thy wicked ways and thy disgraceful behavior will be exposed

34. Eta hartarik edanen ***dun***, eta ondakineraino hustuko ***dun***, eta iretsiko ***ditun*** haren puskak, eta aztaparka larrutuko ***ditun*** *hire* bulharrak; ezen ni ***naun*** mintzatu, dio Jainko Jaunak

And thou shalt drink from it, and thou shalt drain it to the dregs, and thou shalt swallow its pieces, and thou shalt claw the skill off thy breasts; for I have spoken, says the Lord God

(Ezekiel 23:21-34)

In its conclusion, Ezekiel 21 rebukes Jerusalem for forgetting God, for her "wrongdoing" and "fornication" (v 35), for "paint[ing] thy eyebrows with antimony" (v 49), and setting "sweet balms and fragrances" before other men (v 41). This Allegory of the Two Sisters intentionally uses graphic language "to shock [the] reader into realizing how drastically they have violated their covenant relationship with God."[69] Oholibah (Jerusalem) should have heeded the poor example of her older sister Samaria whom the Assyrians destroyed.[70] Instead, Jerusalem has also "committed adultery with the Assyrians and compounded that sin by inviting the Babylonians to commit adultery with her, even while she was still seeing her Egyptian lovers;"[71] this alludes to

Judah's history of allying itself with worshippers of other gods in Assyria, Babylon, and Egypt. Oholibah has fled into the arms of her lovers and now subjects herself to their mercy as she faces punishment. But they will show her no mercy; instead, they will "rise against" her (v 22), strip her (v 26), squash her breasts (v 21), attack her with belts and shovels (v 24), cut off her nose and ears, and take away her children (v 25).

Thus, Jerusalem has received her comeuppance by the end of Ezekiel 23: her lovers (and other nations) have set against her with their judgment and weaponry, robbed her of her finery and her children, dismembered her and will burn what little remains. These horrific punishments have been meted out because of her sexual promiscuity, taken as a metaphor for her disloyalty to God.[72] All this hatred is spat upon Jerusalem in *noka*, associating the pronoun with negative connotations.

The Book of Micah

Finally, Duvoisin uses *noka* in the Book of Micah, whose life spanned the reign of three Judean Kings: Jothan (742–735 BCE), Ahaz (735–715 BCE), and Hezekiah (715–687 BCE).[73] As a native of a rural area outside Jerusalem, Micah "represents the feelings and concerns of the rural farmers and villagers who lived to bear the brunt of the Assyrian army's rape and pillaging,"[74] In chapter 6:1 through chapter 7:20, Micah promises God's people deliverance from this abuse and suffering if they would only return to living by his covenant. Yet Micah uses *noka* not to deliver this message about deliverance but in articulating "God's Intention to Punish."[75] Addressed to "my people," God states (through Micah) that "I began to strike thee with destruction on account of thy sins" (verse 13): Jerusalem will eat without being sated, lose what she attempts to save, will fail to harvest what she sows and to drink wine from the grapes she tread (verse 14). Despite Micah's purported messages of hope, then, we see that it, too, uses *noka* to portend punishment.

Conclusion

In this chapter, I have shown that Protestant and Catholic texts use *noka*—and *toka*—very differently. The Protestant New Testament (Leizarraga, 1571) and Old Testament fragment (d'Urte, 1700) use *noka/toka* as a matter of course in speech directed to every single addressee, for all interactional purposes—the pedestrian, profound, and profane. In contrast, Duvoisin's 1865 Catholic texts uses *hika* sparingly and for exclusively negative functions—to curse, condemn, challenge, castigate, or cast out. It uses *noka* in especially disparaging ways. Save for the exception discussed in text 2.29 below, Duvoisin only uses *noka* with inanimate addressees, metaphorically cased as female, using sexual, violent imagery.

One might argue that a simple explanation underlies these differences: perhaps Leizarraga and d'Urte simply projected their own linguistic habits onto their translations. After all, they wrote their texts 150 to 300 years before Duvoisin wrote his Bible. It is certainly possible that pronominal patterns shifted in the intervening years; *noka/toka* usage could have been more widespread in the sixteenth and eighteenth centuries in which Leizarraga and d'Urte wrote than in the mid-nineteenth century of Duvoisin. We might even expect as much, given the whirl of changes in pronominal systems that occurred throughout Europe during this time period (see chapter 1). Or perhaps d'Urte merely modeled the pronoun use in his Old Testament fragment after Leizarraga's New Testament published 130 years before. Indeed, if d'Urte had access to the entirety of Leizarraga's text (which we have no way of knowing), he would have seen that Leizarraga also used *hika*—more accurately, *toka*—for many prayers, psalms, the Ten Commandments, and the rite of baptism.[76]

However, the documentary evidence argues against such a simple explanation; both Protestant authors made different pronominal choices in other texts. For example, Leizarraga prefaces his New Testament with a dedication to Queen Jeanne d'Albret, who commissioned it. He uses *zu* in addressing her,[77] suggesting that he deemed the use of *noka* to an actual female of such high status inappropriate.

In a catechism he published in 1571, Leizarraga employs the asymmetrical pronoun pattern typical of Catholic texts: the priest uses *hi* (specifically, *toka*) in providing a child religious instruction, but the child answers him in *zu*.[78] Similarly, when d'Urte contributed a Basque version of The Lord's Prayer for a collection edited by Chamberlayne in 1715[79] he uses *zu*, although he had used *hi* in his own grammar of 1712.[80] In that grammar, d'Urte also provided dialogues in French and Basque. While the French always used mutual *T* (*tu*), only two of the nine exchanges in Basque use any *T* (in both cases, *toka*).[81] Thus, Leizarraga and d'Urte did not translate the *T* directly from their source materials into Basque *hi*; nor did they simply reflect whatever their own linguistic habits were onto the written page in a transparent way. Even if they did use *hi* liberally in their own speech (which we cannot know one way or another), both Leizarraga and d'Urte seemed hesistant to extend—or model—such usage in nonscriptural texts.

We have seen that the Duvoisin text uses *hi* in a much more restricted way than do Leizarraga's New Testament and d'Urte's Old Testament fragment. I have argued that such is in line with Catholic theology that emphasizes hierarchy, as will be discussed in more detail below. One might quibble with an argument about Catholicism writ largely based on just one document. However, I have focused on the Duvoisin Bible in this chapter only because it is the earliest Catholic text containing all the passages corresponding to the Leizarraga and d'Urte texts. I found pronominal usage paralleling that of Duvoisin in all other Catholic texts I have examined. These include the catechisms, spiritual guides, and prayer books published between Leizarraga's and d'Urte's texts: Materre (1623), Haramburu (1635),[82] Axular (1648),[83] Harizmendi (1658);[84] Etcheberri (1669),[85] Tartas (1666),[86] and Chamberlayne (1715). The same is true of the one Catholic text that preceded Leizarraga's New Testment of 1571: Beñaut Etxepare's *Linguae Vacsconum Primitiae*, published in 1545. While not a religious book per se, it was written by a Catholic priest and contains "The Christian Doctrine." All these texts use *zu* as a matter of course, and *hika* (exclusively *toka*) sparingly for negative interactional purposes. And this book never uses *noka.*

These findings show that *zu* has been the "pragmatically unmarked"[87] pronoun for Basque Catholics for centuries. In line with Catholicism's emphasis on authority and intermediaries between God and believer, Catholic texts have long favored *zu* as the default pronoun of "respect." Catholic texts very infrequently also use *hi*, but asymmetrically—as a way to signal the speaker's "power over" the addressee, and/or to condemn, to mock, to curse. Basque Protestants, I suggest, used *hi* in their sacred texts to "protest" against the hierarchical theology of Catholicism. Put another way, the Leizarraga and d'Urte documents attempt to create a sense of solidarity among the "imagined community"[88] of Protestant believers not only by using Basque instead of Latin, but by using symmetrical *hi* rather than *zu*.

In contrast, not only does the Duvoisin text use *hika* sparingly and for negative purposes—as do all the Catholic texts discussed in the chapter—this is especially true for the *noka* forms employed for a female addressee. Save for the exception discussed in text 2.29 below, Duvoisin uses *noka* only to "apostrophize" cities—metaphorically treating these inanimate objects as if biologically female—for disobedience to God, wielding sexualized or violent imagery. One might argue that Duvoisin was merely following the textual traditions in the source languages he used; Latin and French also used female names for countries and cities. However, I also found one example in which the Duvoisin text casts the city of Bethlehem as male, suggesting that the author did not follow his source languages' leads blindly:

Text 2.28: Chief Priests and Scribes to Herod (quoting prophesy):[89]

Eta <u>hi</u>, Bethlehem, Judako lurra, ez <u>haiz</u> segur chumeena Judako lehembizikoen artean, ezen <u>hire</u> baitharik **<u>duk</u>** ilkhiren Israelgo ene populuari hotsemanen dioena.

And, thou, Bethlehem, the land of the Jews, thou art not the least among the leaders of the Jews, since from thee will come one who will lead my people Israel

(Matthew 2:6)

Thus, for this positive use of *hi*, Duvoisin addresses a city as if it were male, in contrast to the hundreds of *noka* used to "apostrophize" cities for negative purposes. This suggests that Duvoisin made a choice as to which pronoun to use; it was not a decision constrained by his source languages. For whatever reason, Duvoisin chose to use *noka* only to condemn cities, not laud them. And this usage is consistent with his one and only use of *noka* to address human female characters, as in the infamous scene in which two women claim the same boy as their son, risking his dismemberment by King Solomon:[90]

Text 2.29: Solomon and the Two Feuding Mothers

22. Bertze emaztekiak ihardesi zuen: Ez ***dun hik dionan*** bezala, bainan *hire* semea hila ***dun***, eta enea bizi. Bertzeak bertze aldera zioen: Gezurra ***dion***, ***ezan*** ene semea ***dun*** bizi, eta *hirea* hila ***dun***. Eta horreletan hizkatzen ziren erregeren aitzinean

The other woman replied: It is not as thou sayst, but thy son died, and mine lives. The other, for her part, said: That's a lie, it's my son that lives and thine is dead. And so they gabbled on in front of the king

23. Orduan erregek erran zuen: Hunek dio: Ene semea bizi da, eta *hirea* hila ***dun***. Eta horrek ihardesten du: ez, *hire* semea hila ***dun***; enea, berriz, bizi

Then the king said: This one says: My son is alive, and thine is dead. And that one answers: No, thy son is dead; mine lives

24. Erregek erran zuen beraz: Ekhar darotazue marrauza bat. Eta marrauza ekharri zutenean erregeren aitzinera

So the king said: Bring me a knife. And when they had brought a knife to the king,

25. Erran zuen: Haur bizia bi zathi egizue; emozuete batari erdi bat, eta bertzeari bertze erdia.

He said: Divide the living child in two; give one half to one, and the other half to the other.

26. Bainan semea bizia zuen emaztekiak erregeri erran zaroen (ezen barnea laztu zitzayoen bere semearen gainean: Othoi, jauna,

haurra bizirik emozue horri, eta etzazuela hil. Bertzeak zioen aitzitik: Ez bedi izan ez *hiretzat,* ez enetzat, bainan zathi bedi.

But the woman whose son was alive said to the king (for she suffered inside on account of her son): Please, sir, give her the child alive, and don't kill it. The other said: Let it be neither for you nor for me, let it be divided.

(III Kings 3:22-26)

Noting that only the true mother would give up her child to the other woman rather than have him be killed, King Solomon grants the child to her. Even so, the text only goes so far in according this woman respect. Corroborating my argument, the Duvoisin text calls both women "*emazteki lilitcho*" (little flowers)–a common euphemism for "prostitute."[91] *Noka* is used only to address females, whether metaphorical or biological, who inhabit marginalized or disparaged social categories.

While we may not know why Duvoisin made the pronominal choices he did, we can see their interactional effects. *Noka* is never used "simply" as a familiar pronoun addressing a woman or girl; it is not used with actual (animate) girls or women—for neutral or positive purposes. The lack of such uses in the most sacred documents constitute important aspects of *noka*'s "semantic derogation"[92] that other scholars have overlooked. Given the hegemonic role Catholicism has played in Basque culture, the pronominal usage included in, or excluded from, its texts matter. Rather than a familiar mode of address that can be used for a range of interactional purposes, *noka* is read (or heard in Mass) as appropriate only for the most denigrated of women, adulteresses, and harlots—metaphorically, traitors to God and nation. Perhaps it should not surprise us, then, that Basque speakers avoided using the pronoun associated with such accusations, thereby leading to its disuse over time.

In the next chapter, we shall see rampant *noka* use among other female characters inhabiting yet another world trounced by Catholicism: the "witches" and "sirens" of Basque folklore and the female humans in their midst.

Notes

1 Echeverria, "Language Ideologies and Practices in (En)gendering the Basque Nation.".

2 Trask, *The History of Basque*, 13.

3 *Diccionario Enciclopedico Vasco*, 233.

4 D'Urte, *The Earliest Translation*, vii.

5 Ibid., vii.

6 Ibid., viii.

7 Ibid., xiii.

8 Ibid., xvi.

9 Ibid., xx.

10 Ibid., xiii.

11 Trask, *The History of Basque*, 48.

12 Ibid.

13 Jean Hareneder, priest of St. Jean de Luz, published *Jesu-Christo Gure Jaunaren Testament Berria Lehenago* in 1855. While the title claims the volume to be the first translation of the New Testament, it only contains the Four Gospels (Dodgson, "Appendix B. *List of Translations of the Bible or Parts of it into Basque*, 159).

14 Duvoisin, *Bible Saindua*, 2.

15 Ibid., 3.

16 D'Urte, *The Earliest Translation*, xxiv.

17 Acccording to Dodgson, Uriarte "only published the Books of Genesis, Exodus and Leviticus . . . though the title announces the whole Bible" ("Appendix B," 160).

18 Duvoisin, *Bible Saindua*, 4.

19 As cited in Michelena, *Textos Arcaicos Vascos*, 167–168.

20 Trask, *The History of Basque*, 45.

21 Brown and Gilman, "The Pronouns of Power and Solidarity."

22 *Eure*" ('thy' or 'thine') is a variation of "*hire*."

23 Brown and Gilman, "The Pronouns of Power and Solidarity," 274.

24 English translations of the New Testament are taken or adapted from: quod.lib.umich.edu/ k/kjv/browlse.html.

25 My translation.

26 According to Llewelyn Thomas, who edited the d'Urte Old Testament fragment published in 1894, the word *Eternal* "had the mint-mark of the Protestant acceptance and could not be eliminated" (d'Urte, xvii).

27 This usage is consistent with Axular's 1643 text *Gero*. As mentioned above, Axular usually addresses the reader in *zu*. But he switches to *hi* to admonish the lazy or sinful (267): "Hiregatik du dilubio handi hartan, Noeren denborako uholdean, hondatu, eta itho **ginituan**" (Because of thee, we were ruined and drowned in the flood during Noah's time). The sun rebukes a man who has stayed too long in bed (14): "Nik atzo, **hik** baiño bide gehiago iragan **nian**, inguratu bainuen mundu guztia, eta orai ere, hi baiño goizago jaiki **nauk**" (Yesterday, I traveled more than thee, because I circled the entire world. And yet

I have gotten up earlier than thee). A soul leaving a sinful body is condemned in (female) *hika* forms (263): "Amaren sabelatik iltki *intzen* ponturik, pontu hunetaraino, bethiere jarraiki ***natzain***, ***eznatzain*** behin ere apartatu. Anhitz enseiu egin ***dinat***, *hire* horretarik begiratzeko, eta orai darmanena bide gaixtoaren huts eragiteko. Baina alferrik guztiak. Zeren nola baituen libertatea, eta *heure* burua *heure* eskuko, hala egin ***dun*** *heure* plazera eta borondatea: garaitu ***naun***, ***eztun*** nitzaz konturik egin: ez *aiz* nitzaz gobernatu. Galdu ***dinat*** nik neure trabaillua, eta bai ***hik*** ere, sekula fingabekotzat *heure* burua." (From the time I left my mother's womb until now, thou hast always followed me, and thou hast never surpassed me. I have tried many tests, so that thou wouldst learn from them, so that by now thou wouldst have left behind thy evil ways. But all was naught. Because where there was freedom, to make up thy own mind, thou didst whatever thou wished and whatever pleased thee: thou hadst defeated me, thou didst not pay attention to me: thou art not governmed by me. I have lost in my efforts, and thou too, to make thee a disciplined person").

28 Leizarraga, *Jesus Christ Gure Jaunaren Testamentu Berria,* 1990 [1571].

29 I preserve the spelling and grammar of the original Basque throughout this chapter.

30 Craddock, "Luke," 932.

31 Ibid.

32 Smith, "John," 961.

33 Achtemeier, ed., *The HarperCollins Bible Dictionary,* 657.

34 McBrien, *Encyclopedia of Catholicism,* 828.

35 Achtemeier, ed., *The HarperCollins Bible Dictionary,* 657.

36 Smith, "John," 964.

37 Achtemeier, ed., *The HarperCollins Bible Dictionary,* 657–658.

38 See Haskins, *Mary Magdalen*, especially pages 24, 55, 150–155.

39 McCarter Jr., "Exodus," 136.

40 Kselman, "Genesis," 86–87.

41 D'Urte, *The Earliest Translation,* xviii.

42 Achtemeier, ed., *The HarperCollins Bible Dictionary,* 86–87.

43 Ibid., 972.

44 Kselman, "Genesis," 91.

45 Ibid., 93.

46 Achtemeier, ed., *The HarperCollins Bible Dictionary,* 396.

47 Kselman, "Genesis," 97.

48 Ibid., 99–100.

49 Ellipses in original.

50 Ibid.

51 Stuhlmueller, "Psalms," 442. Alan R. King translated the Old Testament passages.

52 Blenkinsopp, "Introduction to the Latter Prophets," 480.

53 "Before the Common Era," previously labeled "BC" ("Before Christ").

54 Sweeney, *Tanak,* 266.

55 Matthews, *The Hebrew Prophets,* 99–100.
56 Sweeney, *Tanak*, 27.
57 Ibid., 274.
58 Mathews, *The Hebrew Prophets,* 101.
59 "A designation for Jerusalem" (Sweeney, *Tanak*, 281).
60 Sheppard, "Isaiah," 527–528. For an exhaustive list of *noka* excerpts in Isaiah 47, see Echeverria, "Harlots and Whore but Not Lovers," appendix 1.
61 Ibid., 531.
62 Sweeney, *Tanak*, 286; Sheppard, "Isaiah," 522.
63 Sheppard, "Isaiah," 522.
64 Sweeney, *Tanak*, 293.
65 Overholt, "Jeremiah," 574.
66 Sweeney, *Tanak,* 319.
67 Matthews, *The Hebrew Prophets*, 160.
68 Wilson, "Ezekiel". For a discussion of the threat posed by sisters, see Kalmanofsky, "The Dangerous Sisters of Jeremiah and Ezekiel." For an exhaustive list of *noka* excerpts in Duvoisin's Ezekiel 23, see Echeverria, "Harlots and Whore but Not Lovers," appendix 2.
69 Wilson, "Ezekiel," 610.
70 Ibid.
71 Ibid., 611.
72 Wilson, "Ezekiel," 611.
73 Sweeney, *Tanak*, 357.
74 Matthews, *The Hebrew Prophets,* 11.
75 March, "Micah," 664.
76 Leizarraga, *Jesus Christ*, 1263–1282; 1398–1424.
77 Ibid., 249–253.
78 Ibid., 1293–1354.
79 Chamberlayne, *Oratio Dominica*, 44.
80 D'Urte, *Grammaire Cantabrique Basque,* 13.
81 Ibid., 503–537.
82 *Debocino Escuarra*, 1635.
83 *Gero*, 1643.
84 *L'Office de la Vierge Marie, en Basque Laburdin,* 1658.
85 *Manuel Devotionezcoa,* 1669.
86 *Onsa Hilceco Bidia,* 1666.
87 Errington, "On the Nature of the Sociolinguistic Sign."
88 Anderson, *Imagined Communities.*
89 These uses of *hika* are not included in table 2.1 as it includes only direct speech, not speech reported on someone else's behalf, such as in prophesies.
90 For the remaining *noka* passages in III Kings, see Echeverria, "Harlots and Whore But Not Lovers," appendix 3.
91 Lhande, *Diccionaire Basque-Français,* 678.
92 Schulz, "The Semantic Derogation of Woman."

3

Who's Afraid of the Big Basque Witch? *Noka* in Basque Folklore

That there are witches, one should not believe. That there are not, one should not say.

—José Miguel Barandiaran, *Euskal Herriaren Mitologia*

The quote above suggests the ambivalence about witchcraft haunting the Basque Country. On the one hand, as we saw in the previous chapter, Roman Catholicism has reigned supreme over other institutionalized religions since it expelled the last Protestants from Basque shores by the end of the eighteenth century. On the other hand, underlying—and some have argued, preceding—Christianity has lingered a decidedly unchristian belief system dominated by female figures such as sirens (*laminak*), witches (*sorginak*), and the chief witch or goddess, Mari. In this chapter, I focus on the sociolinguistic rather than the theological effects of these competing belief systems. That is, rather than attempt to ascertain the extent to which Basques have "believed" in these supernatural figures, I examine the kinds of identities and roles taken up by them, and the social meanings thereby ascribed the *noka* forms they use as they do so.

I will show that, in sharp contrast to the restricted and negative uses of *noka* in Catholic texts, Basque myths and legends use *noka* among individuals of varying social statuses for a range of interactional purposes. Further, these tales model vigorous uses of the *noka* form itself—not restricted for negative purposes or for insulting the female addressee, but the whole range of conversational purposes. It can be used between the "divine" and the human, but also for ordinary dialogue directed to wives, sisters, friends, and daughters. Finally, these tales illustrate robust uses of *noka* by women. Of the thirty-one stories for whom attribution was given, women told twenty; men narrated eleven. Thus, these folktales provide a window into the cultural values and customs of "traditional" Basque culture otherwise lost to us. They also show the important roles women have played in disseminating that culture as protagonists, rather than just as consumers.

These tales also show that the *sorginak* of Basque folklore have nothing in common with the Basque "witches" persecuted and burned at the stake. In fact, the inquisitors' views of witchcraft were "so irrelevant to the functional popular belief in witches that [they] did not become a permanent tradition, but [were] forgotten (or became anecdotal history) in the intervals between the great witchcraft epidemics, and that people therefore had to be instructed through preachers or secular agitators before a new mass persecution could be initiated."[1] Unfortunately, such "agitators" abounded on both sides of the Basque Country in the early seventeenth century.

Basque "Witch" Persecutions in *Hegoalde*: Logroño, 1610

As I wrote about in the fictionalized *The Hammer of Witches,* on November 8, 1610, thirty-one people were tried as witches at the *Auto de Fe* ("Act of Faith") in Logroño, LaRioja. Six were burned at the stake; thirteen had already died in prison awaiting trial. A Catholic priest and monk denied they were witches, under torture, and were punished with temporary exile from Nafarroa and permanent banishment from their dioceses. The remaining ten people made false confessions so they could be spared the pyre and "reconciled" to the Church. All those who walked away from the stake that day had to wear a *sambenito,* a penitential garment with figures indicating the nature of the wearers' crimes and their sentences; their property was also confiscated.[2]

The "crimes" to which the reconciled witches confessed—often under duress—or of which they were accused alarmed the estimated thirty thousand people listening to the public recitation: offering young children to Satan; partaking in Masses with the Devil; renouncing God, the Virgin Mary, the saints, and the sacraments; feasting on dead witches and human children; concocting powders to destroy crops; and "doing evil to men, in the villages and on the roads."[3] Within a few years, it would become clear that "the existence of an organized witch cult [had] no basis in fact whatsoever."[4] Inquisitors would issue more "enlightened" procedures for investigating witchcraft and eventually the persecution of "witches" would come to an end. However, Basques would endure much suffering in the interim.

It was the Inquisition's custom to write official accounts of what it did in its *Autos de Fe* to demonstrate the power and the mercy of the Church, that is, not only that inquisitors had thoroughly investigated accusations of witchcraft (and other heresies), and given the accused ample opportunity to confess and be embraced anew by the Catholic Church—but also that they punished those who remained intransigent. The Inquisition's official account, or "*relación*," outlines what transpired in these public tribunals; it lists the names of the accused, their alleged crimes, whether they confessed and what punishment or penance they received. These *relaciones* were then distributed to the public, to demonstrate that the Inquisition had rooted out the heretics in its midst.[5]

In addition to the official *relación* of the 1610 Logroño trial, spectators churned out their own versions of what had happened—in their own words and even in a written ballad (that is now lost to us). These stories made their way back to the Basque villages, fueling new accusations of witchcraft, and this time the villagers did not wait for the Inquisition to root out the "witches" supposedly (still) in their midst. They meted out vigilante justice. Villagers in Nafarroa made the accused "walk the ladder":

"witches" were placed between the rungs of a ladder, held horizontally by accusers at either end. The ladder would be jerked back and forth, knocking the "witches" down on their faces then their backs as they were paraded around town. Sometimes, villagers took the ladder torture one step further. After parading the alleged witches around the town, they lowered them—still bound to the ladder—from a bridge until they touched the water and let them hang there. Then they slacked the rope so they would sink to the bottom of the river, ducking them over and over again until they were exhausted or drowned.[6] Others accused of witchcraft were bound by rope to benches or trees; then the "ropes [were tightened] so that they suffer hideous pain."[7] At least two women died as a result of this torture.

Alarmed by this violence, for they believed that they had rid these lands of witches, the inquisitors sent its most junior member, canon lawyer Alonso Salazar de Frías, to make a "visitation" to investigate these new allegations. He brought with him the "Edict of Grace" translated into *Euskera*; this edict pardoned anyone of their sins against the Church, including witchcraft, so long as they confessed within a specified period of time (usually, four months). Unlike the previous visitation that had been made, which had culminated in the 1610 Logroño trial, Salazar ensured those who confessed that their property would not be confiscated and that their names would remain confidential.[8]

In the course of his investigation, Salazar learned of the coercion that had procured the initial witchcraft accusations and confessions. A sixteen-year-old boy told him that he had been tied naked to a bed and beaten until he confessed—by his own uncle, an agent of the Inquisition. Two sisters told Salazar their father had held a dagger to their throats until they admitted to being witches and named others. An Inquisition official had told their father that if the girls made such a "voluntary" confession, they would not be punished. Inquisitor Salazar heard such stories over and over again and came to the only logical conclusion: "I have not found a single proof nor even the slightest indication from which to infer that one act of witchcraft has actually taken place."[9] Thus, he issued an Edict of Silence:

> An absolute silence is to be imposed in view of the undesirable consequences of the public discussion of these matters which have divided people into factions and led to each man carrying out private investigations to confirm his own opinion. Let this be made very clear to the commissioners and confessors. It is furthermore to be announced that the matter can only be raised when someone has to make a confession. However, both before and after making his statement the person in question is under the same obligation to preserve secrecy as in other cases dealt with by the Holy Office.[10]

Even though the persecution of witches abated after the edict's publication, witches did not disappear from the public imagination: "witches" (*sorginak*) and their kind abound in Basque legend. But we shall see below that the *sorginak* of Basque folkore, though unruly tricksters, are not the handmaidens of the devil the 1610 Logroño trials falsely accused them of being. To contextualize how the latter view took root, with such devastating consequences in the Basque Country, the following section reviews how early modern Europe understood "witchcraft."

Basque "Witch" Persecutions in the European Context

Gustav Henningsen delineates the larger European context in which the Basque witch persecutions occurred, especially the events culminating in the 1610 *Auto de Fe*:

> The decades around 1600 marked the peak of the European witch persecution. The excitement was whipped up by popular prints with revelations in text and pictures about the abominable sect. . . . Side by side with this propaganda there appeared a succession of learned

> treaties that were almost a sort of manual of witch persecution. . . . In France, there were Jean Bodin's *De la Démonomanie des Sorciers* (1580), Nicholas Rémy's *Demonolatreiae* (1595), and Henri Boguet's *Discourse des Sorciers* (1602); in Germany, Johan Gerog Godelmann's *Disputatio de Magis* (1584), Peter Binself's *Tractatus de Confessionibus Maleficorum* (1589), and Henning Grosius' *Magica* (1587); in Italy, Francesco Maria Guazzo's *Compendium Maleficarum* (1608), just to mention the important titles.[11]

We do not know if Spanish legal and religious authorities knew of these works or, if they did, if they took them seriously. Inquisitor San Vicente did not mention them in his 1630s inquisitor's manual—and he himself had prosecuted the Logroño witches in 1610.[12] Most of the 347 books in his library focused on religion and law; none concerned demonology.[13] Similarly, most of the 1,425 volumes in Inquisitor Salazar's library pertained to the law. Even so, Henningsen cautions that Salazar may have owned editions of the *Malleus Maleficarum*—the classic witch tract first published by German inquisitor Heinrich Kramer in 1486—but they may have been subsequently lost; his probate inventory notates a three-volume collection.[14] Additionally, the edition that Salazar may have owned had a publication date of 1620, ten years after the Logroño trial. We have no way of knowing if Salazar had access to editions before the 1610 trial that may have influenced his deliberations.

Certainly, Basques did not wait for the publication of the *Malleus* to carry out their own witchhunts. Tribunals tried female "witches" south of the Pyreness as early as 1329,[15] many decades before the *Malleus*'s first edition. Further, "the Basque word for witch, *sorguina* [*sorgina*], first appeared in a libel suit from Pamplona in 1415."[16] Witch persecutions occurred in the Basque region in 1507, 1517, and in the 1520s.[17] When they erupted again in 1538, the inquisitor received "enlightened instructions"[18] urging him to "talk to the leading and more enlightened residents, explaining that when the harvest fails or the crops are damaged . . . they should not imagine that only witches do these things. And you should not believe everything in the *Malleus Maleficarum*."[19] These cautions apparently fell on deaf ears in Nafarroa; three more people were burned as witches there in 1575.

Incidents such as these suggest that Basques already believed in, even feared, witches well before the Spanish Inquisition came calling. Further, stories about the supposed goings-on at the witches' Sabbath ("*akelarre*") had circulated long beforehand. The Basque term "*akelarre*" or the "meadow of the goat [signifies] a plain situated in front of the entrance to the cave called '*Akelarren-leza*' 'cave of the Akelarre' in Zugarramurdi"[20] (in Nafarroa) where the witches allegedly gathered. But "the Basque anthropologist Mikel Azurmendi has claimed that *aker* cannot lose its *r*, and therefore suggested that *aquelarre* [*akelarre*] derives from *alklarre*, or 'meadow with *alka* flowers.' *Alka* (*Dactylis hispanica*) is a poisonous plant that can make cows ill when they eat it. Probably there was some translation error during the interrogations."[21]

Regardless of the origin of the term, fifteenth-century Valencian poet Jaume Roig wrote about witches assembling at night in a cave to worship a goat and renounce God, after which they had a feast and flew home. Thus, "the phenomenon of witchcraft was in fact not at all the constant factor we normally regard it to have been, but was a dynamic and flickering element, now present, now absent"[22] ready to be ignited in times of crisis or misfortune. Basque beliefs about witches eventually merged with discourses about witchcraft produced by members of the "learned" classes—such as Pierre de Lancre.

Basque "Witch" Persecutions in *Iparralde*: Pierre de Lancre, 1609

On December 10, 1608, France's King Henry IV appointed Pierre de Lancre to investigate allegations of witchcraft in Lapurdi: "The nobility of the region had apparently complained about impieties (alluding to the recent religious strife between Protestants and

Catholics in the region),[23] as well as crimes of witchcraft, and petitioned the Parliament for help against the witch menace."[24] De Lancre seemed well suited for this task: a lawyer of Basque descent and a member of the Bordeaux Parliament since 1582, he had already written a witch tract two years before this appointment. He spent four months investigating allegations of witchcraft in Lapurdi.

However, de Lancre "embrac[ed] the 'realist' view initiated by Heinrich Kramer (Institoris) in the *Malleus Maleficarum* (1487) and shared by prominent demonologists like Jean Bodin and Martin del Río. That is, they believed that witches existed in reality not just in the imagination. They asserted witches actually flew to the Sabbath to worship Satan—not just dreamed that they did, as skeptics pointed out—to plan the evil deeds (*maleficia*) that they would perpetuate when they return to their homes."[25] As such, the documents written by "experts" such as Pierre de Lancre should be taken with a grain of salt; they conducted their investigations hoping to confirm their belief that witches existed and engaged in heretical activities, not to find counter-evidence that would exonerate the accused. Indeed, de Lancre had the "authority to interrogate under torture and pronounce summary death sentences."[26] And pronounce, he did: over eighty Basques were burned as witches.[27]

On the Inconstancy of Witches, de Lancre's report of his witchcraft investigation in Lapurdi, consists of six books organized into subsections. Book 1 contains a supposed "description of the Sabbath, of the poisons produced there, and some depositions of very experienced witches that clearly prove the reality of witches being transported."[28] Book 2 describes what allegedly occurs "[w]hen the Sabbath takes place and in what forms the devil appears."[29] De Lancre claims that Satan "sits as a billy-goat in his golden throne, he dances on the Sabbath with the girls and women, and with the most beautiful, now leading the dance, now submitting himself to those he favors most; and he mates in this form with them."[30] De Lancre also alleges that the witches, at Satan's command, repudiate the fear of hellfire by jumping through flames and debase the church's sacraments as they feast on the dead, concoct "poisons," and perform other "diabolical functions."[31] After reciting the Mass, Satan supposedly delivers a homily in Basque and—after raising a triangular (rather than round) host—"in a sign of the greatest execration, thr[ows] it down immediately and tr[eads] on it."[32]

De Lancre also describes the diabolical dances that allegedly occurred at the sabbaths. While he does not mention women as being musicians themselves, he comments that "the [female] witches think that they go to some place where . . . [they] hear so many diverse and melodious instruments that they are enraptured, and believe themselves to be in some terrestrial Paradise."[33] Under one of Book 3's subsections, "The witches' dance at the Sabbath," de Lancre states that "a girl never returns from the [Sabbath] ball as pure as she went there,"[34] for the witches participate in circle dances in which "they come so close together that they touch each other and have their backs touch each other, every man touching a woman. And, dancing to a certain beat, they bump each other and wantonly bring their backsides up against each other."[35] De Lancre highlights the role babies and children play at these gatherings. He claims that witches eat some babies at the Sabbath meal and sacrifice others to the Devil; the witches supposedly "[kneel] on the ground and [say] to him submissively: 'Great Lord whom I adore, I bring you this new servant, who wants to be your slave for eternity.'"[36]

These imaginings by de Lancre hewed close to previous constructions of "witches" and their supposedly nefarious ways. For example, the *Malleus Maleficarum* (1487) asserts that "witches raise hailstorms and hurtful tempests and lightnings; cause sterility in men and animals; offer to devils, or otherwise kill, the children whom they do not devour; they can turn the minds of men to inordinate love or hatred."[37] Early modern discourses and iconography seem to have a particularly prurient interest in the carnal relations in which female witches engage with the devil at their sabbaths.[38]

In the same way, the coerced testimony of the Basque "witches" in the 1610 Logroño trial closely resembles de Lancre's account. One "witch" described the devil as "a dark-skinned man with wide, glaring, horrible eyes. . . . He had three horns on his head. His hands were like a cock's feet, with bony fingers and nails like hawk's claws."[39] The accused falsely confessed that they participated in Black Masses in which "the Host resembled the black sole of a shoe and bore the devil's portrait. . . . And the kneeling witches would answer in chorus: *aquerragoiti, aquerrebeiti!* [up with the goat, down with the goat!]."[40] After mass, the "witches" said they "would devote themselves to the customary carnal pleasures."[41] Other *akelarre* activities supposedly included feasting on the corpses of witches or humans (including babies) that the witches had killed and making a concoction with the bones: allegedly, "the poisonous property of that evil liquid is such that anyone touched by it on any part of the body dies very shortly after, there being no known remedy."[42]

The similarities between the investigations by de Lancre and in the Baztan Valley (which led to the 1610 Logroño trial) should not surprise us. The two events occurred around the same time, across the border from each other. Evidence suggests that the woman who made the initial allegations of witchcraft (ultimately found to be false) in Baztan had spent time in Lapurdi during the time de Lancre was conducting his investigation. She, and other Basques from the region, would have been familiar with what Basque "witches" supposedly did.[43] The investigations took place under intimidating circumstances: powerful inquisitors asked leading questions in a language the accused (except for the priest and monk) did not understand. A priest likely aligned with the Inquisition served as translator when needed. Inquisitors informed the accused that (unnamed) witnesses had identified them as witches, rendering denial futile; their property could be confiscated if they did not cooperate. By telling the inquisitors what they wanted to hear, they were spared horrific deaths at the stake.

Inquisitor Salazar's reinvestigation and his Edict of Silence did have its intended chilling effect on the witch craze. Salazar returned to the Basque region in 1617 to assess the state of affairs among the 1800 "witches" supposedly in the area, the 4,000 others suspected of being witches, as well as their dependents and local authorities. He was amazed to find that everyone was "in such a state of peace and understanding . . . that it seems utterly incredible. No one . . . could have imagined that with the imposition of silence on the witch question it would have been possible to combat the craze to such an extent that today it is as if the problem had never existed."[44]

Further, the version of witchcraft in Basque folklore differs considerably from the foregoing examples found in de Lancre's report and the 1610 Logroño trial accounts. To contextualize these tales, the next section provides a brief primer of Basque religion and mythology.

Basque Religion and Mythology

Even though Catholicism has been the religion of Basques since their conversion to Christianity, it did not take real hold for some time:

> It is clear there was a significant Christian presence in the Ebro valley from the fourth century onwards, and a bishopric is attested in Pamplona from 589. On the other hand, the Basque heartland in the mountains is devoid of any trace of Christianity before the tenth century: even the bishopric of Bayonne is not attested earlier than this date . . . Around 630 or 640 the missionary bishop Amanscus made an attempt to convert the Basques, but his mission met nothing but opposition and failure. The famous cemetery of Argineta in Elorrio (Bizkaia), generally dated to 883, shows discoidal tombstones with no trace of a cross, and is thought to represent pre-Christian burial practices. Arab writers not infrequently referred to the Basques as

> magus "wizards, pagans." Consequently, most historians other than Christian apologists have concluded that the Basques of Bizkaia, Gipuzkoa, and the French Basque Country did not accept Christianity before the tenth century and in some cases, later than that.[45]

Thus, we have few details of the Christianization of the Basques; we have fewer still of the indigenous religion that preceded it. "*Ilunberrixus Anderexus*" ("The Woman of the New Moon") appears frequently on inscriptions dating back to Roman times, which might speak to her importance.[46] However, I have not found any references to this figure in Basque folklore. Due to the dearth of information about Basques' pre-Christian beliefs, some scholars have turned to Basque folklore in search of its vestiges, "which may or may not preserve fragments of earlier religious belief. The enigmatic figure of Mari, the lady of the mountains, is thought by some to represent a continuation of an ancient goddess, though one doubtless overlaid by the Christian Virgin."[47] According to Basque priest and anthropologist José Miguel Barandiaran, "[f]olk tales correspond to the natural needs of the human soul, and their structures appear to be shaped by those needs as well, at least in the case of tales of wonder."[48] More specifically, the "origins of both the story and the legend lie within human nature and man's desire to explain phenomena and actions that take place in the world around him."[49] In Basque folklore, female mythological figures play prominent roles in thus explaining the world: the goddess Mari, witches (*sorginak*), and fairies or sirens called *laminak* (variously spelled *lamiñak* or *lamiak*).

Sources

We may never know for certain whether Basque folklore reveals traces of an indigenous religion, just "made up" stories told for amusement akin to fairy stories elsewhere, or something else. I take no stand with regard to this issue; rather, I focus on the pronominal legacy of Basque folktales: which pronouns are used for talk directed to single addressees for which conversational purposes, and what are the identities constructed in doing so? The first collections of folktales published in *Euskera* hailed from the northern Basque Country: Jean François Cerquand's *Legéndes et Recits du Pays Basque* (1875–1876) and Jean Barbier's *Legéndes du Pays Basque d'après la Tradition* (1931).[50] Their mantle was taken up by the scholar-priests José Miguel Barandiaran and Resurreccion Azkue, who collected folktales primarily from the southern Basque Country. In conducting this historical socio-linguistic investigation of pronominal use, I examined each page of every collection of Basque legends published in *Euskera* since 1875. Given my interest on the social history of *noka* and the importance of female characters in Basque folktales, this chapter narrows the focus to those folktales "starring" Mari, witches (*sorginak*), or sirens (*laminak*) that use *noka*.

Table 3.1 provides a summary of *noka* usage by and to female addressees–supernatural and human—in the seventy-seven tales that compose my corpus.

Table 3.1: *Noka* and the Supernatural Woman

Protagonist	No. Stories	*Noka*	Female Narrators
Mari	6	42	1
Witches (*Sorginak*)	39	162	13
Sirens (*Laminak*)	32	152	6
	77	**356**	**20**

Below, I discuss stories about each female protagonist in turn.

Mari and *Noka*

In Basque folklore, Mari is the "mistress of all the witches."[51] Stories about her abound particularly in Gipuzkoa and Bizkaia, which refer to her as "Lady" (*Dama*) or "Mistress" (*Señora*):

> Mari here is not Mary, but Andere, the pre-Christian beginning of all womanhood, most of the universe, and likewise mother of the moon, the sun, human beings,

> animals, and plants, a being who inhabits a harmonious, miraculous and perfect paradise of folk memory. However, we have transformed Mari, Europe's last goddess, into a diabolical being and become fearful of her. But not completely! For even in today's Euskal Herria [Basque Country], one way or another, we worship Mari in her temples of stone. Deep, deep inside we sense that we were born of Mari and one day we will return to her bosom.[52]

Mari has the power to fly from place to place—usually the mountains—"surrounded by fire, and great noises are produced when she hides in one of her holes."[53] She makes skeins of gold using ram horns—sometimes appearing as a vulture. Some stories portray Mari with a spouse named "*Majue*" or "*Maju*"; hail falls when they unite. Mari is also a mother in some stories, with either seven children, or two—one good *(Atarrabi)* and one bad *(Mikelats)*.[54] In other accounts, Mari is a seductress: she "lures the shepherds to her rooms, which are full of gold and precious stones . . . if she gives them any of it, it becomes worthless when they leave. However, there is no shortage of cases in which a piece of coal given by her turns into pure gold."[55] According to anthropologist Julio Caro Baroja, Mari might also be linked to "the half-animal figures in pre-historical engravings and paintings in caves . . . not only present-day traditional ones but also old ones."[56]

Table 3.2 outlines the stories about Mari that use *noka*.[57] ***(Female narrators are italicized and bolded;*** <u>male narrators are underlined</u>):

Table 3.2: *Noka* Stories about Mari (N = 6)

Title	**Provenance**	***Noka***
1. A Mother's Curse	No informant indicated	10
2. The Origin of the Lady of Anboto	<u>Domingo Arroita</u> (B), 1982	9
3. The Lady of Anboto	***Maria Artetxe*** (B*)*, 1987	2
4. The Lady of Olarra in Upo	<u>Roke Abrisketa</u> (B), 1920	7
5. Mari Screaming, Cave to Cave	Bizkaia	12
6. The Witches and Young Girl	<u>Ignazio Ulazia Artano</u> (G), 1991	1
	TOTAL	**41**

Most of these stories about about Mari recount her origin story. Below is one such example, "A Mother's Curse." (*Gender-neutral familiar forms used with a female addressee are italicized*; *noka* forms with transitive verbs, ***a female indirect object or allocative conjugation are italicized and bolded;*** gender-neutral familiar forms used with a male addressee are underlined; **toka forms with transitive verbs, a male indirect object or allocutive conjugation are underlined and bolded**):

Text 3.1: Ama Baten Madarikazioa[58]

Bazen behin Zegaman artzain neska gazte polit bat. Artaldearekin mendian zegoela, ekaitz erauntsi beldurgarri batek jo zuen, eta, ikaraturik, lasterka etxera joan zen, ardiak mendian bakarrik utzita. Ardirik gabe itzuli zela ikusirik, amak, haserre, kargu hartu zion: "Zer *habil*, zuntzuna halakoa! Non ***ditun*** ardiak?"

"Mendian, ama," erantzun zuen erdi negarrez eta izu-izu neskatoak.

"Zer esan ***dun***? Mendian? Hori al ***dun*** gure azienda zaintzeko modua?" egin zion orru amak, esku altxaturik masailekoa emateko prest. "Tuntuna *haiz*, gero! Ez ***dun*** ezertarako balio! Mila debruk eramango ahal *haute*!" Eta hitz horiek esan orduko, amaren esku zafratzaileak alabaren aurpegi ukitu ere baino lehen halako zarata gorgarri batean mila tximistak jo izan balute bezala, lurra dardarka hasi zen, eta hodei beltz batek estalia bezala, ilun-ilun geratu zen dena. Minutu batzuk geroxeago, egoera bere onera itzuli zenean, artzain neska falta zen.

Handik egun batzuetara, Aizkorriko mendian galdutako ahari baten bila zebilen artzain bat Aketegiko haitzuloan barrendu zen. Eta hara non, bila ari zen animalia galdua ez ezik neskato bat animaliaren gainean hankalatraba jarria aurkitu zuen barruan. Desagertutako artzain neska gajoa zen.

Artzainak behin eta berriro igurtzi zituen begiak, ametsetan ez zegoela sinesteko. Eta . . .

"Zer ari *haiz* hemen, holako leku ilun batean bakarrik?" galdetu zion neskatoari.

"Deabruaren gatibu nago, amaren madarikazio batengatik."

"*Hator* nirekin. Amak barkatuko *hau*, seguru!" esan zion artzainak, kemen pixka bat ematearren, eta eskua luzatu zion.

"Ezin naiz hemendik atera amarekin ez bada."

Hori esan eta neskatoa haitzuloaren atze hondoan desagertu, dena bat izan zen. Artzaina harri eta zur geratu zen. Heskatoaren bila ibili zen gero denbora luzean, bainan alferrik, ez zuen aurkitu, eta aharia hartuta haitzulotik atera zen. Handik Zegamara jaitsi lasterka, eta neskatoaren amarengana joan zen, gertatutakoaren berri ematera. Ama orde ez zen sekula alabaren bila mendira igo, herrian ez baitzuten artain neska hura gehiago ikusi.

Urteak joan urteak etorri, neskato hura emakume ederra bilakatu zen: Akertegiko Dama deitzen omen diote inguruetako baserritarrek.

A Mother's Curse

Once upon a time there was a pretty young shepherd girl in Zegama [Gipuzkoa]. One day when she was up in the mountain there was a great, frightening storm. She raced home in fear, abandoning the sheep in the hills. Her mother, on seeing her return home without her flock, shouted at her in anger:

"What do you think you're doing, silly girl? What have you done with the sheep?"

"They are on the mountain, mother," the frightened girl answered. She was close to tears.

"What did you say? On the mountain? Is that how you look after our property?" yelled the mother, raising her hand to slap her daughter's cheek. "You are such a foolish girl! You are useless! May a thousand devils take you!"

No sooner did she say that, without time even for the mother's hand to hit the daughter's face, a deafening noise like thunder was heard. As if a thousand bolts of lightning had hit the front door all at once, the ground began to tremble and it grew very dark, as though a black cloud had covered the sky. Just a few minutes later when everything went back to normal, the shepherd girl was gone. A few days after that, a shepherd searching for a ram lost on Aizkorri mountain found his way into her cave. And to his surprise, inside he found not just the lost animal but a girl sitting astride it. She was the poor shepherd girl who had vanished!

The shepherd rubbed his eyes in case he was dreaming.

"What are you doing alone in such a dark place as this?" he asked her.

"I am the devil's prisoner on account of my mother's curse."

"Come along with me. I am certain your mother will forgive you!" said the shepherd encouragingly, and offered her his hand.

"I cannot leave here unless it is with my mother."

No sooner had the girl spoken these words than she disappeared into the depths of the cave, to the shepherd's astonishment. He searched everywhere for her in vain: she was nowhere to be found, so he took the ram and left the cave. He ran down the mountain to Zegama and went to see the girl's mother to tell her what had happened. But the mother never went up the mountain to find her daughter and the shepherd girl was never seen again in the town. The years passed and the young girl grew into a beautiful woman. The country folk around there call her the Lady of Aketegi.

This story and its variations, such as "Mari Screaming, Cave to Cave" (*Mari Garretan Kobarik Koba)* and "The Witches and the Cursed Young Girl on the White Horse" (*Sorginak, Neska Gaztea Zaldi Zuri Baten Gainean Konjuru Ezak*) reveals the origins of Mari to be quite humble indeed. Rather than spring from the head of Zeus as does Athena in Greek mythology, the foremost female figure in the Basque mythological pantheon had formerly been an easily frightened peasant girl who failed to carry out her duties on the farm. In contrast to most stories (discussed below) which punish laziness or incompetance, the peasant girl from Zegama is rewarded by her transformation into Mari. The shepherd finds her straddling a ram; recall that Mari weaves skeins of gold using rams' horns.[59] On a pronominal note, we already see a contrast to the Catholic texts with regard to *noka* usage: while the mother uses *noka* seven times to berate her daughter, the shepherd also uses *noka* three times with the girl, but in expressing concern for her.

In a pattern typical of origin stories about Mari—even those that do not use *noka*—a curse initiates a peasant girl's transformation into Mari in the story below as well. "Mari" appears as the Lady of Anboto, a mountain in Bizkaia:

Text 3.2: Anbotoko Senorea Sorrera[60]

Anbotoko Señorea, inok be ez dakigu zelan fundatu zen. Nik neuk maldizino batetik fundatu zelazkoa daukat entzunda. Behin baten, ama-alaba bi bizi ei ziren baserriren baten eta ama fina eta behargina zen bitartean, alaba alperretik be pasatua. Beti ei zegoen buruko uleak orraztu eta orraztu eguzkiaren ordu guztietan. Bainan egun baten, amak ezin zuen gehiago eta haserre aldi baten, odolak ur egiteko gutxiren faltan badinotso maldizinoka bere alaba alperrari:

"Ez ***dinat*** ikusi nahi nire begien bistan be eta joan *hadi* betiko Anbotoko koba-zulora!"

Alabak, berbok entzun zituenean, zuzian eta garretan urten zuen egaz letxe eta ez zen gehiago agertu. Zazpi urte pasatu zirenean, amari Anbotora joatea gogoratu zitzaion bere alabari sorots egiteko eta halaxe egin zuen. Iritsi zen Anbotoko koba-zuloaren atakara eta han zegoen bere alaba Anboto Señora eginik. Bizimodu onean, jan-edanen falta barik eta pozik herritarren langutzari esker.

Amak ha egoera ha ikustean ***badinotso*** berriro maldizioka: "*Hi* hemen ondoegi bizi *haiz* eta joan *hadi* hemetik Gorbeko kobazulora beste zazpi urterako."

Su eta garretan joan zen Anbotoko Señora Gorbeiarantz eta Superlegorreko koban hazi zen bizitzen. Egun gutxi barru, inguruko artzainak eta herritarrak zer gura eta haxe eroaten zioten Anbotoko Señorari eta Anboton baino hobeto bizi zen. Superlegorreko koban zegoenako zazpi urteotan koxitza txarrak baino ez zituen hartzen bere amak eta ez zeukan bakerik.

Horregatik, zazpigarren urtean, berrien berriz joatea erabaki zuen alabari maldizioka ekiteko.

Joan zen ba ama hori Gorbeiara eta bere alaba Anboton baino hobeto bizi zela ikustean badinotso: "*Hi* lehen baino hobeto eta ni neu lehen baino txarrago? Ez horixe, joan *hadi* berriro Anbotora eta ez ***dinat*** bakean utziko."

Anbotoko Señora, garretan joan zen berriro Anbotora eta holan ei dabil batetik bestera noiz arte ez dakigula.

The Origin of the Lady of Anboto

Nobody knows for sure how the legend of the Lady of Anboto started. I have heard that it arose from a curse. Once, a mother and daughter lived on a farm; the mother was industrious and hardworking but the daughter was very lazy. They say she just sat combing her hair at all hours of the day.

But one day, her mother could not stand it any more and in a fit of anger, when her blood was about to boil, she swears at her lazy daughter: "I don't want to see you with my eyes again; off with you to the cave of Mount Anboto forever!"

When the girl heard these words, she flew away in a burst of fire and never came back. When seven years had passed, the mother took it into her head to go to Mount Anboto to see what her daughter was up to. And so she did. She reached the mouth of the cave of Mount Anboto and there she found her daughter, who was now the Lady of Anboto. She had a good life, and lacked neither food nor drink but lived happily thanks to the help of the peasants.

When her mother saw her situation, she curses her again, saying: "You are too well off here, off with you to the cave of Mount Gorbeia for another seven years!"

Off went the Lady of Anboto to Mount Gorbeia in a burst of fire and took up residence in the cave called Superlegor. A few days later, the local shepherds and peasants were bringing the Lady of Anboto whatever she fancied, and she lived even more comfortably than on Mount Anboto. For the seven years that she lived in the cave of Superlegor, the mother had nothing but poor harvests and had no peace, so in the seventh year she decided to go and curse her daughter once again.

The mother went to Mount Gorbeia, and when she saw her daughter living even better than on Mount Anboto, says to her: "So, you're living better than ever and I'm worse off than ever? Oh no you don't! Off with you back to Mount Anboto, and I will never let you alone!"

Off went the Lady of Anboto in a burst of fire back to Mount Anboto, and so she goes back back and forth, according to legend, until who knows when.

In this story, then, the reward given the girl exceeds that of text 3.1. Her laziness explicitly contrasts with her mother's industriousness. Yet with each passing year, she lives better and better because peasants bestow offerings upon her—while the mother's fortunes continue to decline. A 101-year-old woman from Artea-Arratia (Bizkaia), Maria Artetxe, related another origin story, "The Lady of Anboto: The Shop Assistant in Flames with Her Distaff."[61] Mari evolves from a "cruel seamstress" who would not forgive a customer's debt even after the customer died. The customer comes back from the dead to earn enough wages to pay the seamstress back: "Here is your money, I have paid my debt!" (Hemen ***dituna*** diruok, kitutu ***dinat*** zor guztia!).[62] Immediately thereafter, the seamstress flies off to Mount Anboto in flames, "where she became the Lady of Anboto. And ever since, they say that she goes about her business traveling back and forth between Anboto and the cave of Zuperlegor on Mount Gorbeia."[63] Once again, we have asymmetrical use of *noka*, but not necessarily from a superior to a subordinate. Who has the upper hand here—the seamstress or the customer? Even if initially in an inferior position, the customer ultimately becomes Mari, quite the prize indeed. As we saw above, her powers included the ability to cause fire or storms. Animals such as bulls, goats, horses, and serpents do her bidding. Often depicted as an elegantly dressed woman, sometimes she also resides in a golden palace where she loves to spend time combing her hair—with a comb made of gold.

(And someone steals it.) Mari wields other powers with her comb as well. When asked why she always combed her hair, the "Lady" answered: 'I'm going to Nafarroa to reap.' And on that day she destroyed the wheatfields of Nafarroa. They say on Fridays, her husband Maiu [Maju] comes to comb her hair, and it is said that when the husband and wife come together there are storms."[64]

However, in a pattern we shall see repeated in stories about female supernatural figures subordinate to her—*sorginak* (witches) and *lamiñak* (sirens)—Mari's powers do have their limits. Roke Abrisketa Añibarro, a seventy-three-year-old man from Ugaokoa (Bizkaia), told this story:

Text 3.3 Olarreko Señorea Upon:[65]

Olarreko Señorea deritzona, Zeberikok Upon egoten ei zelazkoa daukatzu entzunda eta Upotik Txakarrera ibiltez ei zela bere haronakoak egiten. Upon eguzkiak joten zuenean, Upon geratuten zen bere ule gorriak orraztuten eta Upoko eguzkia joaten zenean, Txakarrera etorri eta beste hainbeste egiten zuen. Señora galanten batek izan behar zuen. Ez zeukan fama onik ze, sari ikusten ei zuten erdi biluzik inguruko artzain, mandazain eta bidazkiei on baino kalte gehiago egiten.

Egun baten, Olorreko andre bat joan zen Upora Señora horri kartilla kantatzeko asmoz eta ikustean badinotso: "*Hi* zer egiten ***duna*** erdi biluzik gizonak guztiak proboketan? *Hi* personea barik inpernuko zezena *haiz* eta utz gaitzak bakean!"

"Ja-Ja-Ja! Niri neuri ahoa berotzen *hator*? Joan *hadi* etxera eta ikusiko ***duna*** zer den niri atentzioa deitzea!"

Ha andrea joan zen ba bere etxera eta helduz batera surten egosten utzi zuen esne guztiak ganaz egin ziola konturatu zen eta bainoen berekitan: "Horrek Olarreko Señora horrek maldizioa bota zidak baina ez berearekin urtengo, ez horixe!"

Geroagorako utzi barik, andre hori D. Pedro abadeagana joan zen eta bizitako guztia kontatu. Abadeak, hurrengo egunean, Upoko ermitara joan eta bedeinkatu egin zuen ha paraje guztia eta Olarreko Señoreak Txarkarrera joan behar izan zuen. Txakerre bera be bedeinkatu egin ei zuten eta gero ez daki inok handik norako bideaeri eragon zion, baina gehiago ez zena egertu ondo jakitun gaude. Bakea langoa!

The Lady of Olarra in Upo

I have heard that the so-called Lady of Olarra used to stay at Upo (Zeberio) [Bizkaia] and that she used to go from Upo to Txakarre on her errands. When the sun shone on Upo she would stay at Upo combing her red hair, and when the sun left Upo she would go to Txakarre and do likewise. She must have been a beautiful lady. She did not have a good reputation because she was often seen half-naked and doing more evil than good to the shepherds, the mule herders, and travelers in the vicinity.

One day, an Olarra woman went to Upo to tell the Lady of Upo off. When she saw her she said: "Hey you, what are you up to, going about half naked and teasing all the menfolk? You are not a person, you're a bull from hell; leave us alone!"

"Ha, ha, ha! Are you looking for an argument with me? Go home and you will find out out what comes from telling me off!"

The woman went home and discovered that all the milk she had left boiling on the fire had gone sour, and she said to herself: "That Lady of Olarra has put a curse on me, but she won't get away with it, you'll see!"

The woman went to Father Peter without delay, and told him all that had happened to her. The following day, the priest went to the place, and the Lady of Olarra had to go to Txakarre. They also blessed Txakarre. Nobody knows where she went after that, but we all know that she never came back to that place again. Good riddance!

Thus, with the assistance of her village priest, the woman in this story ultimately bests Mari (in the guise of the Lady of Olarra). The use of pronouns here also suggests the level playing field on which the woman and Mari wage their battle: they use mutual *noka* with each other. As we saw in chapter 2, Catholic texts never deign to put the familiar pronoun in the mouth of a lowly woman in addressing a divine figure (God, Jesus) or one divine-adjacent (the Virgin Mary).

Sorginak and *Noka*

Given the primacy of Mari in Basque mythological hierarchy, I was surprised to find that the number of tales about her pales in comparison to supernatural figures subordinate to her, such as *sorginak*.

Table 3.3: *Noka* Stories about "Witches"[66] (N = 39)

Title	Provenance	*Noka*
1. Burning a Witch's Face	Aranberri Azkue[67] (G), 1991	1
2. Burning the Cat-Witch	***Ramona Otamendi*** (Bedaio, G), 1992	1
3. A Cross Shoos Away the Witch	***Ramona Otamendi*** (Bedaio, G), 1992	3
4. The Egg and the Serpent	No informant indicated	4
5. "In a farmhouse"	No informant indicated	1
6. In Petralanda	No informant indicated	1
7. In Sorginzu and Arrantzu	Juan Irureta (G), 1921	1
8. Journey to the Akelarre A	***"A female informant"*** (Liginaga, Z)	4
9. Journey to the Akelarre B	***"A female informant"*** (Liginaga, Z)	2
10. Journey to the Akelarre C	***"A female informant"*** (Liginaga, Z)	1
11. The King's daughter	***Angela Bilabo*** (Orozko, B), 199268	21
12. The Lady Witch . . .	Joakin Balerdi (Amezketa, G)	3
13. "A Man From Bedaio"	Jose Maria Aguirrezabala (G), 1926	3
14. "The Master of Zaro . . ."	"My informant"	3
15. The Mother-Daughter Witches	***Ramona Jauregi*** (Amezketa, G)	2
16. "A Mule Driver from Sakana . . .	Juan Migel Agirre (G), 1919	6
17. The Muleteer and the Witches	Ataun (G), 1973	17
18. Old Woman . . . Broken Leg	Bizkaia	2
19. "One Day Two Mule Drivers . . ."	***"An old woman"*** (A), 1919	1
20. "Salabarren is a Suburb . . ."	***M. de Madariaga*** (B), 1929	1
21. The Shepherd King	No informant indicated	11
22. "Some Young Girls . . ."	Juan Migel Agirre (G), 1919	2
23. The Story of the Muleteers	Aramaio (A), 1921	15
24. The Story of the Stealing Witch	No informant indicated	5
25. "There Were Two Sisters . . ."	"My informant"	4
26. The Thieving Witch	Ataun (G), 1973	6
27. The Three Waves	No informant indicated	9
28. Two Hunchbacks	No informant indicated	8
29. Two Witches at Edar Spring	***Josefa Antonia Agirrezabala*** (G), 1992	2
30. The Wicked Witch	Ataun (G), 1973	1
31. The Wife-Witch . . . Horse	***Kontxi Altuna*** (Amezketa, G), 1991	3
32. The Witch	No informant indicated	5
33. Witchcraft in Sorgintzu . . .	Zarautz (G), 1973	4
34. The Witches at the Akelarre	No informant indicated	1
35. The Witch from Gorriti	Bizkaia	1
36. The Witch's Misfortune	Liginaga (Z), 1973	5
37. The Witch . . . Unable to Walk	***Josefa Antonia Agirrezabala*** (G), 1992	1
38. A Witch Who Looks Like a Cat . . .	Migel Mutua Mendizabal (Altzo), 1991	1
39. A Witch Who Looks Like a Cat	***Errosario Salzedo*** (B), 1983	1
	TOTAL	**163**

I suggested at the beginning of this chapter that folk stories about Basque *sorginak* have little in common with their representations by de Lancre and the *Malleus Maleficarum*, or the crimes falsely attributed to the "witches" burned at Logroño in 1610. This becomes clear by examining folk tales describing "stereotypical" witch activities: how they traveled to their gatherings and what they did when they got there.

Sorginak at the *Akelarre*

As we have seen, witches' supposed doings at their gatherings preoccupy early modern documents. Consonant with such accounts, Basque "witches" falsely confessed to worshipping the devil at the *akelarre*:

> Before the witches set off, they anointed themselves with a very evil-smelling fluid of a greenish-black color. They rubbed it on their hands, temples, face, breast, genitals, and the soles of their feet, saying these words: I am the devil. From now on I am to be one with the Devil/I shall be a devil/And I shall have nothing to do with God.[69]
>
> With this they depart through the air to the *akelarre*, sometimes in their own form, sometimes in the shapes of dogs and cats, and always accompanied by their "dressed toads." On arrival, they fall on their knees before the Devil, worship him and kiss him under the said parts. Taking with them the remains of the liquid extracted from the toads they pour it into a vast cauldron together with that brought by the rest of the witches and from this brew are concocted poisons and powders.[70]

José Miguel Barandiaran, an ethnologist and priest who collected folktales throughout his 103-year-long life, provides a different version of the witches' Sabbaths. He collected the following account from (an unfortunately unnamed) "female informant":

Text 3.4: Viaje al *Akelarre* B[71]

Neskatila batek eta motiko bateko ezkongei zizien. Motikua eskalampuñeo zen. Eta gai batez juan ziozun neskatilai eskalampu eli baten eamaitia.

Nestatilak erran ziozun: "Nik behar **diat** juan."

"Nuat?"

"Sabatualat. Ni belagile nük."

"Nie nahi ***nun*** *hiekin* jun."

"Bena han **eztukek** behar zeñatu, ez Jinkua aipatâ. Bestela han bagatuen *hiz*."

Juaiteko, eskuak pomada batez fretatu zitizien, eta cheminien gora aidatu, tta jun zütutzun sabatualat. Han dantzatu zututzun. Eta gero orok behar beitzien debriai uzkien pot egin.

Motikuak, pot egin plazan, eskalampu egiteko puntxua üzkiti sartu ziozun: Debriak erran ziozun: "Nor zen hoi?"

"Billankozeko aotza."

"Errozie geoko jin aldiko bizarre egin dezan"

Journey to the *Akelarre* B

A girl and a boy were engaged. The boy was a clog maker. One day he went to take a pair of clogs to his girl.

The girl said to him: "I must go."

"Where to?"

"To the *akelarre*. I am a witch".

"I would like to go with you."

"But once there you must not make the sign of the cross or mention God, or else you will have to remain there."They rubbed their hands with an ointment so that they could go, and they flew up the chimney and went to the *akelarre*. They danced there. Later, they all had to kiss the devil's arse.

The boy, instead of kissing him, stuck the awl for making clogs up his arse.

The devil said: "Who was that?"

"The carpenter from Billankoze."

"Tell him to shave next time."

Thus, despite the ignominious activities in which witches supposedly engage at *akelarres*, the boy quite readily agrees to go there with his witch-girlfriend. As in other Basque stories, the witches anoint themselves with a special ointment that gives them the ability to fly. But only in this story does the devil appear, and the boy undermines rather than confirms his authority by subverting the ritual display of worship the devil apparently expects.

In another version of this story collected by Barandiaran by (perhaps the same) "female informant," the engaged couple already have a child whom the young man finds crying alone at his fiancée's house. His fiancée and her mother eventually come home and "he hears the daughter telling her mother: '"Oh mother, I'm exhausted!'/'Of course, my child: we have just been in Madrid, Spain, and now we are here'" (Aisa, haurra: adesa Madril España'kuan ***güntuña***, eta oai emetxe.)[72] In yet another version told by another female informant, the witches travel even further afield. A coal maker's apprentice misses work one night, claiming two witches diverted the boat he uses for transport. He reports on the conversation he overheard between them: "You are pregnant: we are three here" (*Hi* haur ***espantziozun*** bestiai: hemen ***bagütun*** hiru/"I'm not in any such condition: you are" (E ***nün*** ni hala; *hi* au *hiz* hala).[73] But after the witches curse the boat, it sets out for Bueno Aires, and the apprentice returns on it the next morning.

Human encounters with witches do not always turn out so well. In the story below, a muleteer overhears witches discussing a long illness the king's daughter has suffered, for which only they know the cure:

Text 3.5: Mandazaina eta *Sorginak*[74] (excerpt)

"Bada, aurreko iganden, neska mezetan zela, joan ***zunan*** besteak bezala komunioa hartzera, baina ogi bedeinkatua eman ziotenean lurrera erori ***zitzaionan*** ogi zatixo bat. Ogi zatia aldare azpiko harlauza baten zirrikitutik behera joan ***zunan*** eta harlauza azpian zegoen zapo batek harrapatu ***zinan***, baina kontrako eztarritik joan ***zitzaionan***. Orain zintzurrean ein irentsita ***din*** ogi zaita zapoak. Zapoari ogi zatia kentzen badiote eta halako iturritan garbitu ondoren gaixoari janarazten badiote, berehalaxe sendatuko ***dun***; bestela ez ***dun*** sendatuko sekula.

The Muleteer and the Witches

"Well, last Sunday when the lass was at mass, she went with everyone else to receive communion, but when she was given the sacred host she dropped a small piece of it, which fell through a crack in the stone slab underneath the altar, and a toad that was under the stone swallowed it but it went down the wrong way and now it's stuck in the toad's throat and it can't dislodge it. If someone removes the piece of the host from the toad and after cleaning it in such-and-such a fountain gives it to the princess to eat, she will get better immediately. Otherwise she will never recover."

The muleteer repairs to the palace, tells the king what he has heard, and they extract the toad-with-host from the princess's throat; the king showers the muleteer with riches as a reward. The muleteer's brother, hoping for the same good fortune, goes to the same spot where the muleteer had overheard the witches. But the witches sense his presence, find him, and beat him up: "He never again worked as a muleteer!"[75] "An old woman" from Etxaguen (Araba) told a version of this story to Barandiaran, in which the muleteer is rewarded with enough money to buy a new pack of mules. A version told to Barbier, "The Shepherd King" (*Artzaina Errege*),[76] varies in plot in that a lone shepherd overhears the witches; the witches have no second shepherd to punish for attempting to reap the reward given to the first shepherd.

The *noka* stories about witches echo other Basque stories that do not use *noka*, and songs about witches (see chapter 4). Whereas seventeenth century accounts of the witchcraft investigations would lead us to expect witches engaging in sexual union with the devil, feasting on babies and concocting poisons, none of this occurs in Basque versions of witch antics.

Dueso's account of the "Two Hunchbacks" (*Bi Konkordun*)[77] provides perhaps the worst fate befalling humans at an *akelarre*. In this story, a hunchback meets in secret with his fiancée, a young woman who "shows him true love and took no notice of his physical deformity."[78] But the girl refuses to meet with him on Saturdays; when he confronts her about this, she admits she attends a witches' coven every Saturday. She assuages his concerns, telling him that the *akelarres* are like going to church—but more fun. Indeed, the witch informs him that now that he knows her secret, he must accompany her to the *akelarre*. He immediately agrees, but she tells him that once there he must never utter the word "Sunday" for according to her "head witch" (whom she likens to his "head priest"), that day does not exist. When the allotted day arrives for his first *akelarre*, the hunchback's fiancée anoints his body "with something oily, then she greased him under the arms and between the legs with a hot and cold ointment,"[79] and they both appear in the middle of a big lawn full of people. However, when the head witch calls on the hunchback to name the days of the week as part of his initiation, he inadvertently names Sunday as well. In punishment, the head witch puts on the hunchback's chest a hump that had been previously removed from another hunchback (about which there are several stories, albeit not using *noka*). In other stories, however, escape from the witches proves quite easy to accomplish. Sixty-eight-year-old Ramona Jauregi Amondarin of Bedaio, Gipuzkoa, related the following tale:

Text 3.6: Ama-Alaba *Sorginak*, Morroia eta *Akelarrea*[80]

Etxe batean, ama-alaba sorginak bizi ziren beren morroi gazte batekin. Gauez, bi sorgin hauek mutila bakarrik utzi eta alde egiten zuten eta behin horrela, morroiak zer gertatzen ote zen jakitea pentsatu zuen; horretarako zizailu batean etzan eta lo-itxurak egiten jarri zen.

Hau honela ikusirik, alabak amari esan zion: "Hori lo dago," eta amak erantzun: "Ai, neska, mutilek tranpa asko izaten ***dinate!*** Jostorratz sartu behar ***zionagu***."

Jostorratza sartu zioten bainan mutilak lo itxuran jarraitu zuen.

Bi sorginak, pomada miragarriz gorputza igurtzi ondoren, tximinitik gora atera ziren honela esanez: "Hodoi guztien azpitik eta sasi guztien gainetik."

Mutil saiatu zen gauza bera egitera bainan oker esan zuen: "Hodoi guztien gainetik eta sasi guztien azpitik." Honela arpegi guztia odoletan zuela akelarre batera joan zen. Hemen sorgin bat txakolina ematen hasi zitzaion eta mutilak sorgina ezagutuz honela agurtu zuen: "Jesus, etxekoandrea, zu ere hemen!"

Jesus izena entzutearekin, bapatean sorgin guztiak alde egin eta ezkutatu egin ziren, mutila bakardade osoan gelditurik. Morroi gazte hark urteak igaro zituen herrira itzuli gabe.

The Mother and Daughter Witches, the Servant, and the *Akelarre*

A mother witch and a daughter witch lived in a house with their young servant. By night, the two witches would leave the servant alone in the house and go out. One day the servant thought he would find out what was going on, so he lay down on a bench and pretended to be asleep. When they saw him the daughter said to her mother: "He's fast asleep!" to which the mother replied: "My dear girl, boys are full of tricks! We must prick him with a needle."

They pricked him with a needle but the lad kept on pretending he was asleep. The two witches spread magic ointment all over their bodies and left the house through the chimney, as they chanted: "Under the clouds and over the bushes!"

The boy tried to copy them but got it wrong and said: "Over the clouds and under the bushes!" So he ended up with his face all bleeding in an *akelarre* where a witch gave him some *txakoli* [sparking white wine] to drink. Recognizing her, he exclaimed: "Jesus, mistress! Are you here too?!"

As soon as they heard the word "Jesus," all the witches ran away to hide, leaving the boy all alone. For many years that young servant did not return to the town.

Thus, witches' journeys to and activities at *akelarres* prove quite innocuous compared to seventeenth century accounts of them. While they do need a special ointment to fly to their gatherings, they apparently do not require a broom or a devil to chauffeur them there. Neither do the *sorginak* engage in human sacrifice or cannibalism of infants; in fact, young children do not appear in stories of the *akelarre*. While an unfortunate fate befell the hunchback who unwittingly violated the witches "no mentions of Sunday" code in "The Two Hunchbacks," in other versions of this story—not in *noka*—the hunchback faces no punishment at all for the same infraction.

But in Basque folklore, most stories about witches take place outside the *akelarre* in more mundane contexts. The section below examines such stories: perhaps the witches live up to their notoriety there?

Sorginak Outside the *Akelarre*

As we saw above, de Lancre's account alleged that Basque witches did "evil to men in the villages and on the roads."[81] Many a Basque tale portrays *sorginak* encountering human beings as they go about their daily lives. For the most part, however, they engage in quite benign activities. Sixty-six-year-old Josefa Antonia Agirrezabala of Bedaio (Gipuzkoa) recounts one such story:

Text 3.7: Bi Sorgin Bedaioko Edar Iturrin[82]

Bedaion, *Bedaio Barrena* izeneko baserriko etxekoandreak alabari honela esan zion: "Bihar goizean lixiba jo behar ***dun***."

Iritsi zen goiza eta berez Edar Iturrira joan zen, hobeki esateko, iturri hartara hurbildu zen. Eta hurbildu ahala, lixiba jotzearen soinua entzun zuen. Bertaratzean amona handi bat gona gorria eta purrutxetarekin (buruko paineluarekin) aurkitu zuen, neska gazte bat ondoan zuela begira-begira. Bedaio Barreneko neska, ezezagun haiek ikustean, ikaratu eta etxera itzuli zen. Etxean, amak zer gertatzen zitzaion galdetzean, alabak hala erantzun zion: "Gure Edar Iturrin bi lagun arrotz lixiba-joatzen ari dira." Hau entzun orduko, amak esan zion hori ezin zitekeela, baina hala eta guztiz ere bertara joan eta bidali egin behar zituztela.

Ama-alabak aipaturiko iturrira joan ziren, baina han ez zuten inor aurkitu, ez zen ageri sorginen arrastorik. Gero, Bedaio Barreniko neskak lixiba jo zuen eta etxerantz abiatzen, sorginek oihu egin zioten atzetik, hau esanez: "Hurrengoan ere gu hemen izango ***gaitun***!"

Two Witches at Edar Springs in Bedaio

In Bedaio, the farmwife at Bedaio Barrena farm said to her daughter: "Tomorrow morning you have to go and do the washing."

Morning came and she went to the spring they had there, called Edar Spring, or rather she started heading toward it. As she came closer, she could hear the sound of clothes being washed. When she got there, she came across a plump old lady dressed in a red skirt and a *purrutxeta* [headscarf], and next to her was a young girl who was watching attentively. When the Bedaio Barrena girl saw the two strangers she had a fright and ran home. At home, when her mother asked her what the matter was, she answered: "There are two strangers washing clothes in our Edar Spring." When her mother heard this she said that was impossible but that they should go there anyway and send them away.

The mother and daughter went to the spring but found nobody there, nor was there so much as a trace of the witches. Afterwards, the girl from Bedaio Barrena washed her clothes and when she was heading back home, the witches shouted after her: "We will be here next time too!"

A fortnight later, the girl went back to Edar Spring to wash clothes. She was frightened but she made the sign of the cross and got to work. This time she didn't see anybody.

Thus, while witches frighten and seemingly threaten the girl, she easily wards them off by making the sign of the cross. José María Aguirrezabala of Gipuzkoa[83] told a similar story to Barandiaran in 1926. A man comes upon a woman washing some clothes as he travels with his cattle in the middle of the night. He helps her wring something out; the woman—who turns out to be a witch—mocks him when he finds gorse with thorns in his hands. In this story, then, the witches seem more interested in teasing the man than harming him. In text 3.8 below, collected by Barandiaran from Juan Miguel de Aguirre from Ataun (Gipuzkoa) in 1919, witches do mete out a punishment to a young woman for another kind of infraction:

Text 3.8: *"Neska Gazte 'Atzuuk . . ."*[84]

Neska gazte 'atzuuk etxe 'atea biltze ementzien jostea. Bein alkarren arteen izpiittu: batek ez dala sorgiñik; besteek, baietz. Sorgiñik etzala ziona, illuntze 'ateen etxea ementzijoon eta nun agertzen zaion berealdiko sorgin-talte 'at esanez: "Ez geala baiño ba-***gaittun***. Maripetraliñ ez beste guztiik emen ***gaittun***."

Eta bakoitzek ille-izpi 'at buruti ataa ementzion, eta neskea ille bae geittu ementzan.

"Some Young Girls . . ."

Some young girls used to meet in a house to sew. One day an argument started, one claiming that there were witches, others that there was no such thing.

The one who claimed that there were no witches was on her way home one night when all of a sudden a crowd of witches appeared to her and said: "You say we don't exist, but we do. We are all here except Maripetraliñ."

And each of them tore out a hair from her head and the girl lost all her hair.

While the girl likely did not appreciate being left bald by the witches, her "punishment" certainly does not rise to the level of evil promised to witches' enemies or detractors in the *Malleus Maleficarum* or witch trial testimonies. Other stories suggest that even if witches wish to cause humans harm, humans can easily foil such plans:

Text 3.9: "Etxe batetan bi ahizpa zütüzun"[85]

Etxe batetan bi ahizpa zütützun. Bata belagile. Bestiak erran ziozun: "***Ezpaitun*** aizo hortan deuse egiten."

"Ez ***diñat*** ahal: eun oroz ezartzen ***dine*** zopan ahamenta."

"Abilua olako olhaala. Ardiak han ***diñee***."

Juan züzun eta artzanhoa ardien artian zuzun besuak kouutxe. Etzizun deus ee egin ahal üken. Eta arra juan züzun. Ordian artzaña kreduaen kantatzen ai. Eta ez deus ee egin ahal üken.

"There Were Two Sisters in a House"

There were two sisters in a house. One of them was a witch. The other sister said to her: "Why, you don't do anything in that neighborhood!"

"I can't: they put mint in the soup every day."

"Go to that shed. That is where they keep the sheep."

She went but the mastiff was there among the sheep, with its arms folded in the shape of a cross, so she couldn't do anything. And she went back there. That time the shepherd was singing the Creed, and she couldn't do anything.

These simple remedies—putting mint in the soup or reciting the Creed—contrast with the elaborate rituals and talismans against *sorginak* described in witch investigations.[86] Indeed, to the extent that Basques believed in or feared witches, they have had other accessible antidotes at hand, such as fastening thistle to the front door or saying "Jesus" aloud. In a slightly different version of this story reported by Dueso, "The Witch's Misfortune," the witch eventually gives up: she "grew weary of going back and forth, and decided to stay at home. And she vowed that she would never again take notice of what her half-witch sister said."[87] In "A Cross Shoos Away the Witches" (*Gurutzeak Sorginak Uxatxan Du),* told by Ramona Otamendi Jauregi of Bedaio (Gipuzkoa), a young girl evades witches when a priest simply makes a cross on the road she needs to take on her way home. In "The Witch Who Was Unable to Walk,"[88] told by sixty-six-year-old Josefa Antonia Agirrezabala (also of Bedaio), two sisters pass by a man lying on the ground; he cries out to them: "Ukitu ***nazan***" ("Touch me!"). The girls just run away and when they tell their mother what had happened, she tells them they would have gone away if they'd touched him, for he was a witch (the only male witch in my corpus).

Other stories suggest that human cunning and bravery alone can defeat a witch's power. In "The Story of the Stealing Witch" (*Sorgiñ-Lapurren Ipuie*), a father and his three sons own an orchard from which someone steals apples night after night. The two oldest brothers take turns watching the orchard overnight but fall asleep. The youngest brother brings a sickle when his turn comes. Seeing a black shape along the orchard wall, he strikes it with his sickle, but the apple thief escapes. The next day, the three brothers find a black hand beside the wall and follow a trail of blood to a large stone, which covers a huge cave. The youngest brother volunteers to descend into the cave, where he finds a beautiful princess whom a witch has kidnapped and imprisoned. He vows to rescue her and she gives him a scapulary for protection. He ties a rope around her waist and his brothers hoist her out of the cave—only to abandon him still inside:

Text 3.10: *Sorgiñ-Lapurren Ipuie*[89] (continued)

T' alakoaten billatzen do sorgiñe, katu aundi'at aldamenen dola, aulki aten eseitta illek orrazten. Ikusi zon urduko, saltatzen zaio aurpegia katue, ta ekitten dio atzamarka motilleeri.

Katu ue erretiazitteko geo, onik nai bazon, otseitte ementzion motillek sorgiñeri.

"Ezetz" sorgiñek, ta gañeara siñuka mingañe ataz asi emenzitzaion.

Baitta jutentzaio motille ondoa ta bik alkarri eldu ta ekiten dioia burrukan.

Beize sorgiñek siñuka mingañe eakuste' ementzion. Baño motillek ittaiekiñ mingañe moztu ta polsillon gorde.

Baño ez ementzion orreatio sorgiñek ogeitzen, ta urdun motillek eskupelariok buriti bera sartu ementziotzan.

"**Kenduiatzak**" nei ok," deadar eitte ementzion sorgiñek.

"Ez, ez ***ditzenat*** kenduko, ni emendi atatze ***ezpanaun***."

"Atako aut ba." T'artu matxiko t'aiden leizen gora ata ementzoon.

Geo andi motil ori leizeko neskagazte aren aite-erregen erria jun ementzan. T' an aittu ementzon erregen alaba sorgiñen mendeti motill bate kata ementzola, eta motill ori beakiñ urrungo euen zijola ezkontzea.

Geo ostatu batea sartu t'ango apusuntu 'aten burnizko maillu txiki 'atekin kax-kax-kax leio joz zerbaitt eitten ai balitz bezela, eunguztie pasau ementzion.

Urrungo goizen jarri ementzan leioti beida noaiz ezkongaiek agertuko ote zien. T'alakoateen nun ikusteitun, jende saill baten erdiñ, be anaie zarrena ta erregen alaba ezkontzea dijotzela.

Artu eskutan sorgiñen mingañe ta 'miari, miari, emen urduko an *ize*'ari' eitte ementzion.

Onekin, sekulako, danak eaman bearreko aize'at irten ementzon. Ta egoaldi txarra zeola ta urrungo euneako ezkontzea atzeatu emetzoen.

Ostatuko motill orrek eun guztie be apusuntun, maillukin kax-kax-kax leiota joz pasau ementzon.

Urrengo goizen badijotz beize ezkongaiek een ezkontzea eittea.

Baitta ostatuko motillek artu eskutan sorgiñen mingañe ta 'miari, miari, emen urduko an *ize* ari" beizee aurrekon bezela.

Onekin sekulako aizea irten da besta eun batez ezkontzea atzeatu bear ize ementzoen.

Ostatuko motill orrek lenaukotan bezala eun guztie leiondon maillukiñ kax-kax-kax eiñez pasau ementzon.

Irugarren unen irteten die ezkongaiek, ta beize besteek 'miari, miari, emen urduko an *ize*'ari' ta ezkonzaik eziñ eiñ.

Bazellala erri artan parte txarrrekon bat ta bila asi mentzien.

Belexe zaldu ementzan iñork zer zeabillen antzik emate'etzion motill arrotz bat ostatun antxe zeola.

Artu ta erregen aurrea eaman ementzoen. Baño ez ark ezer esan nai erregeeri. Bakarrik erregeen alabari azaldu nai ziokeela zeiñtzan.

Deittu dioia ba erregeen alabari. Ta motillek urdun eskupelariok ata ta ea ak ezautzen zittun esa'ementzion.

Baietz, ezautzen zittulla. Baitttan motill gazte uexe zala sorgiñeen mendeti ue ata zona.

Geo bik ezkondu t'aurrea oso ondo bizi ize' ementzien.

Ori ala bazan sartu deilla kalabazan.

The Story of the Stealing Witch (continued)

. . . Eventually he came upon a witch sitting on a bench with a big cat next to her, combing her hair. As soon as the cat saw the boy, it jumped on the boy's face and scratched it. The boy screamed at the witch to call the cat back if she did not want to have trouble.

"No," the witch replied, and stuck her tongue out mockingly.

The boy approached her. They started to fight. The witch stuck her tongue out once more, but the boy cut out her tongue with his sickle and put it in his pocket. Even so the witch did not give up, so the boy put the scapulary on her.

"Take these things away," screamed the witch.

"No. I won't remove them unless you get me out of here."

"I'll get you out, then."

She put him on her back and flew him out of the cave. Then the lad went to the land of the father-king of the girl in the cave. And there he learnt that a boy had freed the king's daughter from a witch, and they were getting married the next day. Then he went to an inn, and once in his room, spent the whole day tapping on the window with a small iron hammer as if he were busy.

The following morning, he watched through the window for the moment when the bride and groom would show up. At last, there in the middle of a big crowd of people, he saw his own eldest brother and the king's daughter, about to be wed.

He grasped the witch's tongue and addressed it in this manner: "Tongue, tongue, as soon as you are here, be there."

No sooner had he spoken these words than it grew so windy that it seemed as if the wind would sweep everybody away. The wedding was postponed until the following day on account of the bad weather. The boy in the inn spent the day in his room once more, tapping on the windows with his hammer. The following morning the couple again came out to get married.

The boy in the inn grasped the witch's tongue again and addressed it as the day before: "Tongue, tongue, as soon as you are here, be there."

No sooner had he spoken these words than it grew windy and the wedding had to be postponed once more. As before, the boy in the inn spent the day by the window tapping on it with his hammer.

On the third day, along came the couple, and again the boy said the magic words to stop the wedding from taking place: "Tongue, tongue, as soon as you are here, be there."

People suspected someone was casting a spell, and a search party was organized. Soon the rumor spread that there was a young stranger at the inn who was up to something or other. They went to get him and he was brought before the king, but he did not want to talk to the king. He only agreed to reveal his identity to the king's daughter. The king's daughter was called. Then the boy took out the scapulary and asked her if she recognized it. She admitted that she did, and said that this young boy was the one who had freed her from the witch.

They got married and lived happily ever after.

If this story is true, let it go into a pumpkin.

While in this story the witch engages in maleficent activities such as apple stealing and kidnapping, so too do the two older brothers by abandoning the youngest in the cave and absconding with the girl he saved—actions they take without any prodding from the witch.[90] This flies in the face of inquisitors' reports' suggestions that humans do evil at the behest of the devil or his minions like witches. Not only does text 3.10 imply that wrongdoing stems from human nature itself, it also shows that counterforces in human nature—goodness and ingenuity—can overcome evil, whether caused by supernatural or human beings, or some combination thereof.

In another set of stories, collected primarily by Barandiaran in the southern Basque Country, witches visit harm upon humans in the guise of animals or forces of nature. He collected one such story, "In Sorgintzu and Arrantzu,"[91] from Juan Iruretagoyena of Zarautz (Gipuzkoa) in 1921. Two women who sell sardines between Zarautz and Hendaia—twenty miles apart—stop for the night in the woods when they see a light from a house in the distance. They find two children alone in the house and ask to stay there that night instead. The next morning, the children's mother arrives in the form of a donkey; their father, as a thundercloud. Rather than accept payment for the lodging, they ask (now back to their human form) the sardine sellers to deliver a message to a nun in a neighboring town, the last stanza of which says, "she won't forget/the night we both met/at the witches' coven/where we were last night!"[92] But when the sardine sellers come upon people from the town on the road, they learn that witches had pushed the nun down the stairs and broken her neck.[93]

While the witches go unscathed for killing the nun in the story above, *sorginak* rarely go unpunished for their crimes. In "The Wicked Witch" (*Sorgin Gaiztoa*), a happy young couple have a baby boy. While the wife sits with the baby in the father's absence, an old woman insists upon brushing the wife's hair. When the wife finally allows her to do so, the old woman sticks her with a pin and turns her into a dove. The old woman convinces the husband that a witch has made her ugly and old, but that she remains the wife he loves. They live this way for many years, until the husband captures the dove and removes the pin, and his real wife reemerges: "The witch was burnt in the town square. The couple lived happily ever after, and no witch came near them again."[94]

Kontxi Altuna Garmendia of Amezketa (Gipuzkoa) narrated "The Witch-Wife Who Appeared To Her Husband as a Horse" (*Sorgin Andrea Bere Gizonari Zaldi-Tankeran Azaldu*),[95] in which a shepherd strikes his son with his cane as they make their way home from the mountain. They find a horse blocking their way home soon after; but the shepherd, who knows his wife is a witch, recognizes her: "You're still here, what the hell, you're still here" (Hemen al *hago* orain ere, mila arraioa, hemen al *ago*). Upon confronting his wife when he gets home, his witch-wife more than holds her own: "If you hit my son again, I'll think of something to do to you."

Like many other cultures, the most common animal stand-in for witches is the cat. In "Burning a Cat-Witch" (*Katu Sorgina Erre*),[96] told by Ramona Otamendi Jauregi (Bedaio, Gipuzkoa), a cat keeps bothering a mother when she attempts to feed her baby some mush. In desparation, the mother throws some hot oil in the cat's face—and the next day she sees her elderly, female neighbor with a burnt face. "Old Woman With a Broken Leg" (*Atso Anka-Ausia*)[97] deviates from this plot slightly: the husband breaks the leg of the cat-witch that is bothering his wife, and the next day he finds the old woman next door also has a broken leg. In "A Witch Who Looks Like a Cat" (*Sorgina Katu Itxuran*), narrated by Errosario Salzedo Aretxaga of Bizkaia, a cat appears in front of the washing stone some women used to wash their clothes. When a woman attempts to hit the cat with a stick and misses, "the cat said, 'Hit me again' [Berriz jo ***nezan***]. When she heard that, the woman realized that because the cat was a witch, it must not be struck an even number of times."[98] A similar rule prevails in "The Witch of Gorriti"[99] (*Gorritiko Sorgina*), although this time the witch does not appear in disguise. When a shepherd shoots her in fear, she asks him to shoot her again but he refuses: "'Bat aski ***don***,' errantzun zion artzaiak. Bigaŕena tiratu balio, sendatuko zan" ("'One time is enough,' the shepherd answered. If he had shot a second time, she would have recovered").

In other stories, humans defeat witches without suffering any negative consequences:

Text 3.11: *Mus de Zaro . . .*[100]

Mus de Zaro zen Zaro-ko kuntia. Gamen beitzen beste bat, Eiezkia etxian. Mus de Zaro han izan zizun. Eta erretiatzian ilhuntuik, emazte bat jauzi ziozun bere zamaian bridara.

"*Ehiz* juanen aitzinago," erran zeon emaztiak.

"Utzi ***nezan***."

"*Ehiz* juanen."

Ordian Mus de Zaro'k tiro bat tiatu zizun. Eta emazteak erran ziozun: **Emak** beste bat, **emak** besta bat.

"Aski ***badun***, aski ***badun***."

Etxia zenian, kuntiak mütilari erran ziozun: Beha **dük** bihar jeiki argizeñiak gabe, nun entzuentian hilzeñiak. Barda belagile bat eho **diat**.

Eta mütilak Sibos'en entzun zizun hilzeñiak. Sibose'ko belagile bat zen. Kuntiak eman baleo bi tiro, belagilia etzen hilen; hilen zen kuntia. Erraiten die belagiler ez dela eman behar kolpe bat edo hiru baizik bea ehaiteko. Biga emaiten bada, emailia hiltzen dela.

The Master of Zaro

The Master of Zaro [in Baxe Nafarroa] was the count of Zaro. There was another at Game, in the house called Eiezkia. The Master of Zaro visited there. On his way home at night, a woman pounced onto his horse's reins.

"You shall not go further," she said.

"Leave me alone."

"You shall not go."

However, the count of Zaro fired a shot at her.

And the woman said: "Shoot me again, shoot me again."

"It's enough, it's enough."

And he left her there.

When the count got home, he said to the servant boy: "You must get up before the bell rings for the *Angelus* to see where you hear the death knell. Last night I killed a witch."

And the boy heard the death knell at Sibos. It was a witch from Sibos. If the count had fired twice, the witch would not have died, the count would have died. It is said that to kill a witch, it must be struck once or three times. If it is struck twice, it is the person who strikes her who dies.

Thus, despite the fear the *Malleus* and witch trial transcripts would instill about *sorginak*, they can be defeated with the same weapons used against humans and animals.

The final example of witches-as-mother-nature bridges the worlds of witches and sirens. In "The Three Waves" (*Hiru Olatuak*), three sailors find they cannot catch any fish while other boats fill with them. The skipper's nephew, Bilintx, stands watch one night and claims that two ghosts—shaped like women—had made their ship rise above the clouds at great speed, eventually landing on an olive tree. Even as his fellow sailors snicker at him, Bilintx continues with his harrowing tale:

Text 3.12: Hiru Olatuak (excerpt)[101]

Handik gutxira emakumeak azaldu ziren, eta ontzia airez aire hegan joan zen berriro. Eta halaxe, atzera hona etorri ginen. Ontzitik alde egin aurretik, hala esan zion emakume haietako batek besteari: "Gaur gauerako ontzi horretako marinelak urazpira joanak izango ***ditun*** gaztiak, holaxe erakutsiko ***zienat*** zenbaterainoko indarra daukadan. Orain arte, arrantza ondotik uxatu besterik ez ***zienat*** egin, bainan errematea jotzeko ordua heldu ***zaigun***. Arrangatziko puntatik aurrerago pasa baino lehen, beldurgarrizko hiru olatu altxaraziko ***ditinat***: esnezkoa lehendabiziko, malkozkoa bigarrena, odolezkoa hirugarrena. Aurreneko biak aise gaindituko ***ditizen***, baina ez ***diten*** hirugarrena menderatzeko indarrik izango, ni neu izango bainaiz olatu hori. Modu bakarra ***zagon*** horri aurre egin eta bizirik ateratzeko: odolezko olatuari sabelera arpoi bat jaurtitzea. Hori, ordea, ez ***diten*** sekula jakingo." Handik gutxira bi emakumeak barre-algara zoroak eginez ezkutatu ziren.

The Three Waves (excerpt)

After a short while the women came and the boat flew through the air again. And that is how we got back here. Before they disembarked, one woman said to the other: "By tonight the sailors on that boat will have drowned and I'll have shown them how powerful I am. Until now all I have done is to scare away the fish, but the time for our big day has come. Before they have sailed past Arrangatzi Point, I shall cause three terrific waves to rise up: the first of milk, the second of tears, the third of blood. They will manage to ride out the first two without difficulty, but they won't be strong enough to withstand the third, because I will be that wave. There is only one way to confront it and survive: by throwing a harpoon at the belly of the wave of blood. But they will never know that!" Soon afterwards the two women disappeared, laughing like maniacs.

When Bilintx takes out an olive branch, his fellow sailors finally believe him: some calling them sirens; others, witches. They continue their journey at the skipper's insistence, but the first two waves come upon them as predicted before landing on shore. When the third wave of blood comes at them, the sailors strike it with their harpoons. They believe they have won the day, for the sea becomes calm and they have the biggest catch of fish ever. But when they reach the shore, the skipper finds his daughter dead and his wife dying—for they had been the ghosts on their ship. Despondent, the skipper dies of a broken heart. Bilintx sets sail for America.

Thus, we have seen that Basque *sorginak* in these folk stories deviate from seventeenth-century stories about witches in many ways. While they do apply a special ointment to travel to their *akelarres*, in only one Basque story does the devil even appear and he receives poor treatment rather than worship. Despite frantic accounts of the evil they do—destroy crops and people with their powders, or feast on babies or offer them to the devil—Basque witch tales never mention infants or small children, and only one person (the nun) is killed—but so is one witch. In these stories, then, Basque witches do not unremittingly do evil to hapless humans in their path. For the most part, *sorginak* play tricks on humans and sometimes do them some (not irrevocable) harm, but humans often retaliate in kind.

Indeed, "The Egg and the Serpent" (*Arroltzea eta Herensugea*) features what can only be described as a good witch, who uses her powers to defeat an evil snake-like figure called the "*herensuge*."[102] Every day the snake emerges from his cave to feed on the "best girl in the village." An old woman, who is a witch, provides counsel to one such feast-for-the-day: "Take this egg and hit the serpent with it five times on his forehead" (Eraman ***ezan*** arroltze bat eta Herensuge jo ***ezan*** bost aldiz arroltzearekin kopetan). The village girl heeds the witch's advice and kills the snake.

Thus, we see that the *sorginak* in Basque folktales do not, for the most part, live up to their terrifying reputations. As we shall see below, neither do most Basque sirens.

"Sirens" and *Noka*

Sirens and fairies, infamous for entrapping young men with their beauty and song, abound in European folklore. Ironically, given the Basques' penchant for singing (see chapter 4), Basque sirens (*laminak*) do not sing—nor are they always beautiful, young, or female. These deviations from the usual "beware the beautiful mythical female creature lest she ensnare you" script parallel similar deviations from sociolinguistic norms when it comes to pronouns, as indicated in table 3.4.

Table 3.4: *Noka* Stories about "Sirens" (N = 32)

	Title	Provenance	*Noka*
1.	The Andretto Siren	***Isabelle Laphaillet*** (Z)	2
2.	"The Comb-Loving Sirens . . ."	No informant indicated	3
3.	Ea and Natxitua	No informant indicated	5
4.	Elantxobe	No informant indicated	1
5.	Equal Measure Doesn't . . .	***Martine Lapitchet*** (Z)	4
6.	"A Farmwife in the Lamindao"	Bizkaia	1
7.	"Hey You from Karatxe!"	Bizkaia	3
8.	The Humiliation in Landabero	Amaiur, Nafarroa	7
9.	"In Abaurrepea . . ."	Bizkaia	3
10.	"In a Neighborhood of Arratia"	No informant indicated	1
11.	The Labors of Linen	No informant indicated	4
12.	A Midwife at Eilalamiarte	Bizkaia	3
13.	"A Midwife Was Needed . . ."	Bizkaia	1
14.	"Once Upon a Time a Man . . ."	Bizkaia	5
15.	Seeing the Cave	No informant indicated	3
16.	A Siren and Cyclops	Luzaide, Nafarroa	16
17.	The Siren and the Shepherd	No informant indicated	11
18.	The Siren Beaten (Altzuruku)	Jean Salaber (Z)	2
19.	The Siren Beaten (Behorlegi)	"Hargindegui" (Behorlegi, BN)	2
20.	The Siren Beaten (Gotaine)	***Gratieen Etxekopar*** (Gotaine, Z)	13
21.	The Siren Beaten (Sara)	Lapurdi	5
22.	The Siren from Ogoño	***Luciana de Zabala*** (Elantxobe B), 1960	3
23.	The Siren Giving Birth"[103]	No informant indicated	11
24.	The Siren in Labor (Gotaine)	***Martine Laichet*** (Gotaine, Z)	1

25.	The Siren of Ogoño	No informant indicated	3
26.	A Siren's Labour Pains	***Martine Lapichet*** (Gotaine, Z)	3
27.	The Sirens' Lake	No informant indicated	2
28.	The Sirens of Okamika Cave	No informant indicated	6
29.	"The Sirens . . . Come Down"	No informant indicated	6
30.	The Siren Who Did Not Want . . .	No informant indicated	1
31.	The Three Waves[104]	Joan Benanzio Arakistain, 1866	18
32.	The Woman Spinner	No informant indicated	4
		TOTAL	**153**

Before diving into the details of those stories, a brief discussion about the origins of "*lamina*" might be informative. Basques took the term from the mythology of the Romans, with whom they had had contact;[105] but the Romans had themselves borrowed the term from Greek mythology. Indeed, "various types of female monsters called Lamias"[106] feature in many European cultures. Given their far reach into European myth and history, it should perhaps not surprise us that Basque folktales portray *laminak* in a variety of ways. Gallup, in his classic *A Book of the Basques,* considered the *lamina* "a cross between the fairies of Celtic legend and the English goblins or Scandivanian kobolds."[107] His close friend and collaborator Veyrin described *laminak* as "merely imps, a kind of hairy and extremely nimble homunculus, who live sometimes under riverbeds and sometimes in caves."[108] In some legends culled from the Bizkaian coasts, *laminak* "appear with the bust of a woman and the tail of a fish . . . [but] in the highlands of Gipuzkoa they appear with bird feet (chicken, duck) or talons."[109] *Laminak* vary in size as well as appearance: "[i]n one or two [stories] they appear to be as big as human beings, while in others they are as small as the orthodox fairy, that is to say, almost small enough to pass through the holds of a sieve."[110]

When it comes to representations of *laminak*, however, scholars agree about one thing: they are decidedly not Christian.[111] Indeed, Veyrin argues that while folklorists' methods for collecting *lamina* stories may be unsystematic, the "lessons" of the stories point in the same direction: to allow the ingenuity and ready wit of Christians to triumph over mysterious powers."[112] But my analysis below will show that Christians do not always triumph over the "mysterious powers" of the *laminak*—and humans in their midst would do well to cut their losses.

Laminak and *Noka*

Several stories about *laminak* have analogs in other cultures and can be categorized according to the Aarne-Thompson-Uther (ATU) classification system,[113] the main index of world myths used by scholars to organize, classify, and analyze folk narratives. For example, among the most common plot lines in Cerquand's 1875 *Légendes et Récit Populaire du Pays Basque*—the first volume of folktales published in *Euskera*—involves those in which a pregnant siren needs a human midwife to deliver her baby. Known as "Midwife in the Underworld," these tales are classified as Migratory Legend 5070 or ATU Type 476.[114] Cerquand collected the following tale from Martine Lapichet in Gotaine, Zuberoa:

Text 3.13: Lamina Haur Minetan[115]

Gotaine Sorzabüriaren khantian igaraiten da erreka bat, eta erreka haren üthür geia ez da handik hürrün. Uthürri haren saihetsean bazen botxü zilo bat, eta han laminak.

Egün batez lamina bat haur minetan agitzen da. Sorzabürüko etxenko anderea, emagin beit zen, beharten die lagünetako. Juaiten zaie eta iruski jin zen haurra. Biharamenean emagina berriz ützültzen da haurraren trotxatzera, eta lana egin ondoan lamina batek eskentze dero, phakütako, bi thipinatarik haitia: bata zen ürhez gorderik eta bestea eztiz. Sorzabürüko anderea haitatzen da ürhez gorderik zenaz. Hain sari laminak erraiten dero:

"A! Ez ***dün*** khausitü. Urhez gorderik denak barnea estiz betheri ***din***, eta eztiz gorderik denak, aldiz, ürhez betherik ***din*** barnea."

A Siren's Labor Pains

A river flows through the area of Gotaine Sorzabüria, and its source is not far away. Beside the spring is a rock where sirens gather. One day, a siren happens to be in labor. They get the farmwife from Sorzabüria farm, who was a midwife, to assist her, so she comes and the baby was born without mishap. The midwife returns the following day to change the baby, and when she has finished a siren offers her a choice between two vessels as payment, one of which was covered with gold and the other with honey. The woman from Sorzabüria chooses the one covered with gold. The siren immediately says to her:

"Ah! You didn't get it! The one covered with gold is full of honey inside, whereas the one covered with honey is full of gold."

In a version of this story collected by Azkue, "In Abaurrenea," sirens provide this counsel to the midwife: "Look, only ask for a carding comb [used to clean wool] in payment. Anything else that you ask for will turn into coal. On your way home, do not look back."[116] Of course the woman does turn around, to close the door when she gets home, and "somebody threw a stone which made a big hole in the doorway, where for years cats and little dogs loitered constantly, quite fearless of the sirens."[117] In another version, "A Midwife Was Needed," half the midwife's card disappears into the siren's den when she turns around.[118] Kalzakorta[119] includes another version of this story from Zuberoa which uses *noka* eleven times, suggesting that this pronoun was quite routine for female-centered activities like childbearing.

These stories, I suggest, portray the relationship between the supernatural and human as not only interdependent but one that should be based on fairness and respect. The siren needs the woman to bring her child into the world, and the woman can expect to be fairly compensated for doing so. Because of her greed for gold, she receives only honey in payment. Or, because the midwife violates the terms of her reward, the sirens take it back. In "The Sirens of Okamika Cave" (*Okamikako Leizeko Lamiak*), the sirens show the midwife gratitude by inviting her to a "sumptuous spread"[120] for lunch. When the midwife asks where the sirens have procured the delicious food, one siren explains:

Text 3.14: Okamikako Leizeko Lamiak (excerpt)[121]

"Ikusten ***dunan*** guztia ukoaren emaitza ***dun***," azaldu zion lamia batek. "Adibidez, artzain batek berrogeita bost ardi izan, eta hurkoari ez laguntzegatik berrogeita bost besterik ez ditula esaten badu, guk geuretzat hartzen ***ditinagu*** isildutako bost horiek. Eta beste hainbeste egiten ***dinagu*** beste edozer gauzarekin."

The Sirens of Okamika Cave (excerpt)

"Everything you can see was obtained as a result of a denial. For instance, if a shepherd who owns fifty sheep gets out of helping his neighbor by claiming only to have forty-five, the five that he didn't mention are ours. And we do the same thing with everything."

The midwife does not immediately take in this lesson about fair dealings. She attempts to take home a piece of a pure white loaf of bread, but cannot stand up when she attempts to leave. The sirens warn her: "Woman, leave whatever you have taken on the table, otherwise you will never be able to stand up!" (Emakumea, ***utzan*** hartu ***dunana*** mahai gainean, gainerakoan ez *haiz* sekula altxatu ahal izango aulkitik!). The embarrassed midwife does as bidden and is able to stand up; "the sirens then gave her a whole loaf of white bread as a present before she left, so that she could show it to her whole family."[122]

The forgiveness the sirens extend the midwife in this text contrasts sharply with how a woman-of-the-house ("*etxekoandre*") treats an errant siren in a story collected by Cerquand in Gotaine, Zuberoa, from Gratienne Etxekopar. The most common kind of siren story that uses *noka*, "The Siren Beaten" exemplifies ATU Type 1137: "Self Did It:"

Text 3.15: Lamina Kolpatua (Gotaine)[123]

Gotaine Sorzabürüko etxearen khantian, erreka arte, edireiten da Thartazia deithürik den etxea, zuin etxe laminen aizo ere beit zen.

Negüko gai lüzetarik batez, Thartazüko etxenko anderea ari zen berantian ürüten, sü ondoan, nuiz ere tximinian behera iküsten beit dü erasiten lamina bat, zuin khantian ttottatzen beit zaio erraiten derolarik:

"Ez *hadila* lotsa, ez ***nün*** deus gaiztotara jiten, *ari* adi aitzina ürüten."

Eta besteagorik gabe, kota gibeleti goititürik, üzkia berotzen dü. Elhestatü ziren lüzaz; galthatü zeron laminak khotxüta bat ezne; edan zian eznea eta jun zen berantian, jin ber bideti, erraiten zorolarik:

"Bihar arratsen ützüliko ***nün***, begira ***izadan*** eznea, eta ez erran ihuri ni heben izan nizala."

Emazteak hitz emaiten dero. Bena, lotsatü beit zen, erraiten dero senharrari zer agitü zaion.

"A! Hola da?" dio senharrak. "Bihar arratsen nahi ***dinat*** nik egürüki."

Gaia heltu denean, gizon horrek ezarten dütü suinean emaztearen phildak, hasten da ürüten bere gisa suthondo xokhoan, eta ezarten dü sü-phala gorritzen aska murran.

Hantik laster ikusten du lamina eraisten tximinian behera. Jarten zaio khantian, eznea galthatzen dero, edaten dü eta erraiten dero:

"*Hi* barda prim prim, eta gaur larri larri?"

"Bai, behar ***ditinat*** khandera errezinen binbaletak egin."

"Nula deitzen *haiz*?"

"Nihau."

Eta bezpera gaian bezala laminak kota goititzen dü eta üzkiaren berotzen hasten da. Hain sarri gizonak sü-phala gorritürik hartzen dü eta gibel aldian ezarten dero. Heiagoraz hasten da lamina, ezkapatzen da tximinan gora, eta lagün saldo bat jiten zaio galthatzera min hori nurk egin deron. IIhardesten dü:

"Nihau(k)."

"A! *Hihauk* egin ***düna***? ***Ihauk*** gein ***badün***, ***ihauk*** goza ***ezan***.

Ez zian seküla enthelega erazi ahal ükhen lagüner nurk egin zeron min hura, eta ez zen haboro ützüli Thartazialat."

The Siren Beaten (Gotaine)

By the stream that runs past Sorzabüria farm in Gotaine there is a house called Thartazia, and this house is in a place where there are sirens.

One long winter evening, the mistress of Thartazia sat spinning late into the night by the fire, when she sees a siren coming down the chimney. The siren sits down next to her and says to her:

"Don't be afraid, I haven't come to do you any harm; carry on spinning."

And without further ado she holds up the back of her skirt and warms her behind. They chatted for a good while. Then the siren asked her for a bowl of milk. She drank it and as she was leaving the same way she had come in she said:

"I will be back tomorrow evening. Save some milk for me, and don't tell anybody I was here."

The woman promises she won't, but out of fear she tells her husband what has happened.

"Ah! Is that so?" the husband says. "Tomorrow night I will wait up for her."

The next evening arrives and the man puts on his wife's clothes and starts spinning in his own fashion by the fire, and he places the poker in the embers to make it red hot.

After a short while, he sees a siren coming down the chimney. She sits next to him, asks for her milk, drinks it, and says:

"How come last night you were spinning so nicely and today you barely can?"

"Yes, I have to make wicks for the candles."

"What are you called?"

"Myself."

And like the night before, the siren raises the back of her skirt and starts warming her bottom. Suddenly the man takes the red hot poker and puts it on her back. With a scream, the siren dashes up the chimney, and some of her friends come and ask her who has done this to her. She replies: "Myself."

"Ah! You did it yourself? If you did it yourself, enjoy it yourself!"

Cerquand collected three other versions of this story deviating primarily in the punishment allotted to the pestering siren. In one version gathered from Sara (Lapurdi),[124] the "wife" strikes the siren with hot pokers rather than scalding her with fat.[125] In another from Altzürükü (Zuberoa),[126] the siren dies from her injuries. In only one does the siren get some measure of revenge, by undoing all the furrows in the "spinner's" field.[127] Azkue collected three versions of this story which end with the same "Me, Myself'" punchline: "from a Scotsman who ha[d] learnt Basque in the Markina area" in Bizkaia; "A Siren and Cyclops" from the village of Luzaide (Nafarroa)[128] and "The Humiliation of Landaboro"[129] from Amaiur, Nafarroa. The most unusual version of this story is "The Woman Spinner,"[130] in which the woman consults with her mother rather than her husband in regards to how to handle the pesky siren, and she gets rid of it, by throwing soup in the siren's face.

Even so, Azkue claims that "[m]ost often the Basques of old employed other means to defend themselves against the sirens, other than boiling fat":[131]

Text 3.16: "Bein Laminaranen Barna Gizon Bat"[132]

Bein Lamiaranen barna gizon bat bidez zijoan. Itsaondoan Erosape deritzaion zubitxo-ondoko latsean ere Lamiak bizi ziran; eta aietako batek, gizon bidezti hura ikusita, uluka ta garasiz itz auek esan zizkion goialdeko lagun bati:

"A Laminarangoa!"

"Zer gura ***dona***, Erosapekoa?" eranzun zion Laminarendik lagunak.

"Or ***doan*** oreri bota ***eiona*** lakiriao."

"Zelan botako ***dotsanat*** lakirioa? Gabonariz egina ***daroiana*** soinekoa."

"Once Upon a Time . . ."

Once upon a time a man was making his way through Lamiaren ["Of the Sirens"]. There were also sirens living in the stream by the small bridge by the sea called Errosape, and one of them saw the man on his way past, and shouted to a friend who was higher up:

"Hey, you from Lamarain!"

"What do you want, you from Errosape?" called back her friend from Lamiaren.

"Trap that one who goes there."

"How can I trap him? He's wearing a suit of Christmas thread."

These stories, I would argue, emphasize the importance of hard work and respecting those that do it. The story below, told to Cerquand by sixty-year-old Martine Lapitchet from Gotaine, Zuberoa, also chides those who do not fulfill their side of work obligations:

Text 3.17: Ber Izaria Ez Da Ber Pizua[133]

Beste aldi batez Sorabürüko ber etxenko anderea juan zen ber laminetara gunka erdi bat ogiren jesaitera ogi berriak egin artino. Laminek hola arrapostu emaiten dere.

"Bai, ükhenen ***dün*** ogi gaithatia, bena ordaria nahi ***dikeñagu*** ber izari eta ber phezütako.

Etxenko andere horrek hitz emaiten dere eta ogia etxerat eremaiten dü.

Ogi berriak jin zirenean eramaiten dü ordaria laminer. Horiek ediren zien ber izaria bena ez ber phezia, Etxenko andereak nahi ükhen zeren emendatü izaria ber pheziaren emaiteko, bena laminek ez ziren hatü nahi ükhen haborokina, eta erran ziren:

"Nahi ***badün*** gero ekharri ber izaria eta ber phezia, erein ezan ogia Abentüko estiapenean."

Equal Measure Doesn't Make Equal Weight

On another occasion the lady of the same house in Sortzabürü went to the same sirens to borrow half a bowl of wheat to tide her over until the new wheat was ready. The sirens replied as follows: "Yes, you may borrow the wheat, but we want it returned to us measure for measure and weight for weight."

The housewife promises and goes home with the wheat.

When the new wheat was in, she took her payment to the sirens. They found it to be the same measure but not the same weight. The lady wanted to add a measure to produce the same weight, but the sirens refused to accept the top-up and told her:

"If you want to bring the same measure and the same weight, sow the wheat at the waning of the December moon."

Cerquand collected two similar versions of this story. In neither do the sirens seem particularly upset by the farmwoman's omission. As I do not know whether the advice regarding the waning December moon constitutes good or bad advice, perhaps the sirens do intend this advice as a kind of punishment after all. The sirens may have secret knowledge about the workings of nature. The story recounted by Isabelle Laphaillet of Zuberoa, "The Andretto Siren" (*Andrettoko Llamina*), suggests as much. An unspecified "they" seize two sirens bathing in a spring. One of them says to the other (first in Bearnaise, then in Basque): "Whatever they tell you, yeah or nay, you will never mention the virtue of the alder, nay!" (Zernahi erran ***dizeña***, bai ala ez, seküla haltzaren berthütea ez ***dün*** erranen, ez).[134] And indeed, despite a rigorous interrogation, the siren only reveals this obscure piece of information: "I have seen the place where Oloron is all overgrown with weeds, and the area of Dona Mari all full of seeds."[135]

Dueso's collection of siren stories more closely resembles the "beware the seductive siren" narrative commonly seen in other cultures. In "The Siren Who Did Not Want To Live On Behorlegi Mountain" (*Behorlegui Mendian Bizi Nahi Ez Zuen Lamia*)[136] a blond siren with a dark complexion convinces a mesmerized shepherd to carry her on his back to a location she has specified in return for money and pleasure, even though "frightening things were said about sirens."[137] As they make their journey, ever more fearsome creatures (many of them incarnations of the devil) meet them on their path: a billy-goat with a man's face, seven-headed snakes, two-headed cats, and "other kinds of creatures . . . what kinds they were [the shepherd] could not say, but he could tell their looks did not express friendliness."[138] Despite the siren's assurances that the creatures will do them no harm, and none of them do, the shepherd's legs eventually give out and he drops the siren. He flees into the forest, never to go back to the cave—where the siren herself eventually returns, in exhaustion.

The besotted young man fares much better in "The Siren and the Shepherd in Love" (*Lamia eta Artzaina Maiteminduak*). In this version, a young man tends his flock near a cave when he sees "an extremely beautiful lady with a bright face and dark complexion, wearing a golden dress."[139] The siren tells the shepherd she wants to marry him. Amazed that such a creature would wish to marry a "lowly" and "humble" man like him, the shepherd enthusiastically agrees. Before he can do so, the siren tells him he must guess her age. The shepherd consults an old woman reputed to have the ability to tell fortunes. She promises to have the answer by nightfall, for a small sum. She goes to the siren's cave, gathers up her skirt, opens her legs, bends forward and puts her head between her legs. When the siren sees her, she exclaims: "In my one hundred and five years I never saw anything like it!" The old woman tells the shepherd what she has learned, and the shepherd decides against the marriage.

Sometimes the man in such stories has the wherewithal to best the siren on his own. In "The Labors of Linen" (*Lihoaren Penak*), a man tries to prove his bravery by crossing a path in front of the sirens' cave between midnight and two o'clock in the morning—a time the sirens have explicitly forbidden. As one of the sirens grabs him by the neck and drags him into the cave, the man cries out: "I will come, alright, I will come with you to the cave of my own accord, only allow me to recite the labors of linen first" (Joango ***naun***, lasai, neure borondatez joango ***naun*** *hirekin* haitzuloraino, baina utz ***nazan*** lihoaren penak esan artean).[140] The man does so laboriously, despite the siren's exortations to hurry up, until a rooster begins to crow: "[H]er hair stood on end as if she had been startled and she fled to the cave like lightning, letting the man loose and leaving him to his own devices. But before she ducked into the cave she cursed the untimely rooster thus: 'Ah Okabio's red wood-grouse rooster, you took away the big fish that was to be my dinner! May the evil fox destroy you!'"[141]

We saw above that Mari has a penchant for combs made of gold; sirens share this predilection, and they do not take kindly to humans who steal them. In "The Sirens' Lake" (*Lamien Aintzira*), a good-looking hunter named Summer comes upon a lake and spies twelve beautiful women playing there, completely naked. They vanish upon noticing Summer, but the vision transfixes him to the spot until nightfall. His stepmother, despite her misgivings at the trouble the sirens will cause Summer, gives him a golden comb with which he lures the most beautiful of the sirens by saying: "In exchange for the comb, be mine!" (Orraziaren truke, neurea izan behar ***dun***!).[142] What the stepmother had perhaps feared transpires: after "unit[ing] again [and again] in the sweetest of embraces"[143] the young hunter falls asleep. When he wakes the siren, now looking at him with an "evil glare" as she combed her hair with the golden comb, tells him this terrible truth: he will be her captive forever now that she has her comb back. And his stepmother had been a siren all along, forced to take on the form of a Christian woman. But now she, too, had returned to Sirens' Lake.

Sirens mete out a different kind of punishment to women who steal their combs, taunting them with bodily harm: "Bring me my comb/Otherwise I will give you/Aching bones your whole life long" (***Ekartzan*** nere orrazea/bestela emango ***diñet/*** ere biziko ezurretako onazea)[144] or worse: "Mari Iñasi/Bring my comb here/If you don't/Your end will be near" (Mari Iñasi/***Ekan*** ona nire orrasi/Ezpabere gaur ***dona/****Ire* azkasi).[145]

Taken together, we can see these stories about Basque sirens are more complex and their meanings much more nuanced than previous scholarship has acknowledged. These stories cannot be reduced to tales of Christian triumph over pagans. Indeed, the *lamina* and human being each have powers the other does not have. Basque sirens can make gold and silver, grant wishes, and provide sensual pleasures. Yet *laminak* need humans to carry out mundane tasks such as bringing their children into the world, for which they rely on midwives, and to transport them from one location to another, for which they require men's assistance. These stories present *laminak* and humans (especially females) in symbiotic—but simultaneously, potentially antagonistic—relationships with each other.

I suggest that these stories illustrate a fundamental cultural concept in Basque culture: "*auzolan*," or "neighborhood work." When a family needed assistance with an agricultural task, it would call upon its neighbors to carry out the work, with the understanding that the favor would be returned when needed.[146] As discussed by Sandra Ott in her classic work, *A Circle of Mountains*, the "'neighborhood' consists of all those households for whom one is obliged to perform certain agricultural and ritual services and from whom one is entitled to receive the same."[147] In these stories, *laminak* and humans engage with (and against) each other in such tasks. As such, the tales discussed exemplify "*alkharr laguntza*" (mutual help) and "*ordari*" (reciprocity)[148]—key to survival in rural areas of the Basque Country, where in remote areas "*auzolan*" entailed the building of mountain roads even into the twentieth century.

Conclusion

In this chapter, I have shown that depictions of "witches" (*sorginak*) in Basque folktales differ markedly from the "witches" persecuted by de Lancre and at Logroño in the early seventeenth century. The latter portray "witches" as handmaidens of the devil engaging in nefarious activities such as Black Masses, feasting on unbaptized babies, and causing bodily harm or death to humans. In contrast, Basque folklore depicts *sorginak* as tricksters whose ploys humans rather easily can subvert; and they take no cues from the devil. Similarly, rather than the beautiful temptresses human men cannot resist (at their peril), Basque sirens ("*laminak*") collaborate with humans in carrying out tasks important to both parties. Human midwives deliver siren babies and human men carry sirens to far away destinations; if all goes well, the humans receive a reward.

These differences are important not only for their own sake—as a native Basque speaker, it saddens me that I was deprived of these stories for so long—but also because representations have real world consequences. It wouldn't matter how witches (or sirens) were depicted if they remained just in the imagination. World literature is full of evil characters and monsters that provide cathartic experiences, life-lessons, and enjoyment for those who read or listen to them. However, for centuries Christian dogma alleged that witches actually existed and engaged in the heretical activities detailed in tracts like the *Malleus Maleficarum* and de Lancre's *Tableau de L'Inconstance*. Worse, the leading questions and intimidating tactics of inquisitors resulted in innocent people (primarily women) being persecuted, tortured and executed as witches. Even if the threat of witch burnings has waned (one would hope), "witch" is still a common epithet wielded against "untraditional" women and derogatory terms still abound for women and girls who supposedly use their "feminine wiles" to entrap men, as sirens reputedly did. To the extent that the witches and sirens of Basque folklore counter and complicate those stereotypes, all to the good.

These stories are also important for what they suggest about gender. The translators of the biblical texts discussed in chapter 2 were all male, notwithstanding Queen Jeanne d'Albret's role in commissioning the 1571 Protestant New Testament. In contrast, women told twenty-two of the seventy-five tales discussed here for which attribution was made; men told eleven. This represents 26 percent of the total corpus. While still not parity vis–à–vis male storytellers in Basque culture writ large, it far exceeds the zero representation of the weighty biblical materials discussed in the previous chapter. The percentage might be greater still, as some of the "anonymous" sources were likely female, given the role women play transmitting folktales in other cultures. As such, these tales represent the underappreciated and important roles women have played in transmitting Basque culture.

This is particularly true when we consider the use of *noka*. We saw in chapter 1 that *noka* is disappearing from contemporary speech. Even native Basque speakers rarely use it, and those who do feel much less comfortable using it than they do its male counterpart, *toka*. But in these tales, we see sophisticated uses of *noka*, many by women, including the allocutive forms considered so complicated to master. These stories can be told without employing familiar forms of address. In fact, the majority of the folktales in my wider corpus use the gender-neutral *zuka* instead of *hika*, including variations of the tales discussed here. Hence, the use of *hika* in these texts represents a choice made not only by the teller, but also by the transcribers and compilers.

At one level, the choice is "merely" a linguistic one. In order to use *noka* in these tales, both the storyteller and transcriber/compiler would obviously need to be familiar with the forms. One could argue that the prevalence of *noka* in some texts just reflects the storyteller's natural speech patterns; that is, they used *noka* in the stories because they used *noka* in everyday speech. This may or may not be true, and in the case of Cerquand's informants from 1875, we have no way of finding out. However, we know that speakers do not just use language to speak "for themselves"; even those who only speak one language use different registers, accents, pacing, pitch, and other strategies to "voice"[149] opinions not their own, or perform disparate identities. In my research among high schoolers, for example, I found that even speakers who did not know *hika* would use it—along with other cues, like slowing down the pace of their speech—to mimic the voice of the country bumpkin.[150] I would suggest, then, that while the frequent use of *noka* in some stories might reflect the prevalence of *noka* in their tellers' own speech, it might also demonstrate those tellers' attempts to "voice" the characters in the stories, whether or not they use *noka* with any frequency in their own lives.

This evinces a sophisticated sociolinguistic awareness indeed. In chapter 2, we saw that Protestant texts use *noka* in complicated and varied ways in interactions involving personages ranging from slaves and handmaidens to ancestresses and the Mother of God. Similarly, the folktales discussed in this chapter use *noka* in the mouths and ears of every kind of female: from the divine or supernatural (Mari, witch, and siren), the royal (king's daughter), and the humble (sardine seller, seamstress, and peasant). Basque folktales use *noka* not only to curse or do harm, but also to carry out domestic activities such as spinning or washing clothes as well as more specialized tasks such as midwifery. These stories use *noka* for a variety of conversational purposes, from the mundane to the magical. Basque folktales widen the sociolinguistic scope of *noka* in that they broaden the kinds of interactants—human and supernatural—who use or receive *noka.*

In the next chapter, we shall see that Basque folksong pushes the sociolinguistic boundaries of *noka* further still.

Notes

1 Henningsen, *The Witches' Advocate,* 391.
2 Ibid., 198–200.
3 Henningsen, *The Salazar Documents,* 403.
4 Henningsen, *The Witches' Advocate,* 393.
5 Ibid., 193–197.
6 Ibid., 209.
7 Ibid.
8 Ibid., 227–235.
9 Ibid., 304.
10 Ibid., 488–489.
11 Ibid., 7–8.
12 Ibid., 8.
13 Ibid., 9n9.
14 Ibid., 9n10.
15 Henningsen, "Basque Country," 94.
16 Ibid., citing Indoate, *La Brujería en Navarra y sus Documentos,* 18.
17 Henningsen, *The Witches' Advocate,* 22.
18 Lea, *A History of the Spanish Inquisition,* 219.
19 Henningsen, *The Salazar Documents,* 372–373.
20 Barandiaran, *Diccionario de Mitología Vasca,* 12.

21 Henningsen, *The Witches' Advocate,* 57.
22 Ibid., xxvi.
23 Discussed in chapter 2.
24 Scholz Williams, *On the Inconstancy,* xxvii.
25 Ibid., xxiv.
26 Henningsen, *The Witches' Advocate,*24.
27 Ibid., 25.
28 De Lancre, *Tableau de L'Inconstance,* 2.1.61. Translation from the French by Alan R. King.
29 Ibid., 1.4.118. Translations from the French by Alan R. King.
30 Ibid., 3.4.207.
31 Ibid., 2.4.129.
32 Ibid., 6.4.465.
33 Ibid., 2.3.125
34 Ibid., 3.4.2009
35 Ibid., 1.4.118.
36 Ibid., 5.3.398.
37 See www.sacred-texts.com/pag/mm.
38 See Jan Ziarnko, *Description et Figure Du Sabbat Des Sorcieres* (1613), for an elaborate engraving of an *akelarre* that accompanied de Lancre's text.
39 Henningsen, *The Witches' Advocate,* 7.
40 Ibid., 83.
41 Ibid.
42 Henningsen, *The Salazar Documents,* 132.
43 Henningsen, *The Witches Advocate,* 30–32.
44 Ibid., 383.
45 Trask, *The History of Basque,* 13.
46 Ibid.
47 Ibid.
48 Barandiaran, *A View From the Witches' Cave,* xi.
49 Ibid., 95.
50 Wentworth Webster's 1879 *Basque Legends* (in English) also includes stories from the northern Basque Country. A version in *Euskera,* based on Webster's original handwritten notes, was not published until 1993.
51 Caro Baroja, *The Basques,* 277.
52 Dueso, *Lamiak eta Sorginak,* preface.
53 Caro Baroja, *The Basques,* 277.
54 Ibid; Barandiaran, *Diccionario de Mitología Vasca,* 27–38, 131, 143.
55 Baroja, *The Basques,* 277.
56 Ibid.
57 Information about provenance is provided in as much detail as notated in source material.
58 Dueso, *Lamiak eta Sorginak,* 14–15. Unless otherwise indicated, English translations of folktales done by Alan R. King.

59 Caro Baroja, *The Basques,* 277.

60 Etxebarria Ayesta, *Bizkaialdeko Ipuin-Esaundak,* 261–262. Domingo Arroita was a 77-year-old man from Orozko who had been living in Basauri for a long time when he told this story in 1982. This story was translated by Begotxu Olaizola.

61 Ibid..

62 Ibid., *Bizkaialdeko Ipuin-Esaundak,* 331.

63 Ibid., 293-294.

64 Arriaga, *Euskal Mitologia,* 103; cf. Azkue, *Lamiak Euskalerrian,* 23 for another version of this story.

65 Etxebarria Ayeste, *Bizkaialdeko Ipuin-Esaundak,* 331. This story was translated by Begotxu Olaizola.

66 When no title was provided, I quote the first few words in the story.

67 Gender of narrator is not specified.

68 Kalzakorta, *Lamia, Sorgin eta Tartaroen Erresuma Ezkutua,* 177–178.

69 Ibid., 71.

70 Henningsen, *The Salazar Documents,* 116–117.

71 Barandiaran, *Brujeria y Brujas,* 93. Spanish title in the original.

72 Ibid., 94.

73 Ibid., 92–93.

74 Dueso, *Lamiak eta Sorginak,* 149–153. His source: Barandiaran, *Tradiciones y Leyendas.*

75 Other versions of this story include: "The Story of the Muleteer" (*Mandazainen Ipuina*), in Dueso, *Lamiak eta Sorginak,* 189–192 for which he credits Barandiaran, *Folklore en la Montaña Alavesa*; and "A Mule Driver from Sakana Valley . . ." ("Napar-Sakaneko Mandazai Bat . . .") in Barandiaran, *Brujeria y Brujas,* 84–86.

76 Barbier, *Légende du Pays Basque: d'après la tradition,* 134.

77 Dueso, *Lamiak eta Sorginak,* 189–192. His source: Vinson, *Literatura Popular.*

78 Ibid., 193–198. His source: Vinson, *Literatura Popular.*

79 Ibid., 195.

80 Garmendia Larrañaga, *Jentilak,* 18–19.

81 De Lancre, 161, 403.

82 Garmendia Larrañaga, *Jentilak,* 28–29.

83 Barandiaran, *Brujería y Brujas,* 112–113.

84 Ibid.,109.

85 Barandiaran, *Brujería y Brujas,* 133.

86 See Henningson, *The Witches' Advocate.*

87 Dueso, *Lamiak eta Sorginak,* 148. His source: Barandiaran, *Tradiciones y Leyendas.*

88 Garmendia Larrañaga, *Jentilak, Sorginak eta Beste,* 33-34.

89 Barandiaran, *El Mundo I,* 83–87.

90 A slightly different version of this story, "The Thieving Witch" (*Sorgin Lapurra*) appears in Dueso, *Lamiak eta Sorginak,* 207–213. His source: Barandiaran, *Brujería y Brujas.*

91 Barandiaran, *El Mundo I*, 101–103.
92 Ibid.
93 A slightly different version of this story is in Dueso, *Lamiak eta Sorginak*, 159–161. His source: Barandiaran, *Brujería y Brujas: Eusko-Folklore. Obras Completas II*, 76–78.
94 Dueso, *Lamiak eta Sorginak*, 220–223.
95 Garmendia Larrañaga, *Jentilak*, 17.
96 Garmendia Larrañaga, *Jentilak*, 38.
97 Azkue, *Euskaleriaren Yakintza II*, 381.
98 Garmendia Larrañaga, *Jentilak*, 20.
99 Azkue, *Euskaleriaren Yakintza II*, 406.
100 Barandiaran, *Brujería y Brujas*, 134–135.
101 Dueso, *Lamiak eta Sorginak*, 97–102.
102 See Barandiaran, *Diccionario de Mitología Vasca*, 77-78.
103 Kalzakorta, *Lamia, Sorgin eta Tartaroen Erresuma Ezkutua*, 68
104 Dueso, 97–102. This is a version of the "The Three Waves" in table 3.3 above which features sirens rather than witches in the menacing waves.
105 Caro Baroja, *The Basques*, 276.
106 Trask, *The History of Basque*, 324.
107 Gallup, *The Book of the Basques*, 169.
108 Veyrin, *The Basques of Lapurdi*, 289.
109 Caro Baroja, *The Basques*, 276–277.
110 Gallup, *The Book of the Basques*, 170–171.
111 Veyrin, *The Basques of Lapurdi*, 289; Caro Baroja, *The Basques*, 276.
112 Ibid., 286.
113 Uther, *The Types of International Folktales*, 2004.
114 See also Carthaigh, "Midwife to the Fairies," 133–144.
115 Cerquand, *Ipar Euskal Herriko Legenda II*, 43.
116 Azkue, *Lamiak Euskalerian*, 15–16.
117 Ibid.
118 Ibid.
119 Kalzakorta, *Lamia, Sorgin eta Tartaroen Erresuma Ezkutua*, 68.
120 Dueso, *Lamiak eta Sorginak*, 61–62.
121 Ibid., 61.
122 Ibid.
123 Cerquand, *Ipar Euskal Herriko Legenda eta Ipuinak II*, 58–60.
124 Cerquand, *Ipar Euskal Herriko Legenda eta Ipuinak II*, 54–55.
125 Cf. Barandiaran, "The Siren from Ogoño," for a version of this story from the southern Basque Country; also, "Salabarren" and "Sorginen Katu Itxuran," though the pestering supernatural figure is a witch disguised as a cat.
126 Ibid., 62–63.
127 Ibid., 57–58.
128 Azkue, *Euskaleriaren Yakintza I*, 214.
129 Ibid.

130 Kalzakorta, *Lamia, Sorgin eta Tartaroen Erresuma Ezkutua,* 64.
131 Azkue, *Lamiak Euskalerrian,* 23.
132 Azkue, *Euskaleriaren Yakintza . . . I,* 327.
133 Cerquand, *Ipar Euskal Herriko Legenda II,* 44.
134 Ibid., 53.
135 Cerquand, *Ipar Euskal Herriko Legenda eta Ipuinak,* 53.
136 Dueso, *Lamiak eta Sorginak,* 65–68.
137 Ibid.
138 Ibid.
139 Ibid, 54-59.
140 Dueso, *Lamiak eta Sorginak,* 92–95.
141 Ibid.
142 Ibid., 94.
143 Ibid.
144 Arriaga, *Euskal Mitologia,* 35.
145 Ibid., 103.
146 Caro Barojo, *The Basques,* 208.
147 Ott, *The Circle of Mountains,* 64.
148 Ibid., 69.
149 Bahktin, *Discourse in the Novel.*
150 This is an example of Goffman's "say for," or "the practice of projecting mimicked words into the mouths of figures that are present" (535). Urla also discussed how free radio programmers use *toka* and *noka* and other vernacular resources as a way of "'performing' a voice that is other than their own" (187).

4

Don't Know Much about Her Story

Noka in Basque Song

The Basques are the people who sing.

—French saying, quoted in Trask, *The History of Basque*

We complete our sojourn into *noka*'s social history where the introduction into Basque culture and language often begins: song. Basques have a long history of singing about all aspects of the human experience: life and death, history and war, daily life and work, religion, friendship, family, and love.[1] The oldest songs date to the fifteenth century and include all varieties of Basque, including the Roncal dialect that went extinct at the death of its last speaker, Fidela Bernat. She died in 1991.

However, few women have been allowed to opine through song. The 1452 *Fueros de Bizkaia* (legal charters) forbade women from improvising verses or participating as they traditionally had as hired mourners (*hiltariak*) or "*profazadas*," women who traveled from town to town "invent[ing] couplets and ballads with the intention of defamatory libel."[2] Several other factors contributed to the construction of Basque song as a male domain. First, Basque singing took place in cider houses or taverns, where men looked askance at women in their midst. Second, songs usually cast women and girls in secondary or passive roles, providing little insight into their own perspectives. Third, much of the song corpus stems from ritual verbal dueling (*bertsolaritza),* several variants of which involve only two participants who, until recently, have been exclusively male—although the female versifier Maialen Lujanbio Zugasti won the championship in 2009 and 2017. But the androcentric nature of this verbal art form historically is linguistically marked by the frequency of familiar second-person pronoun for a male addressee (*toka)* in its verses.

As a long overdue correction to this androcentric song narrative, this chapter focuses on songs that use *noka*, as these by definition have a female addressee[3]. I will show that while songs in *noka* are few and far between, their uses and meanings are wide ranging. That is, individuals from disparate social stations use *noka* in these songs for various interactional purposes, to construct a variety of identities, and to express many emotions and perspectives. In this sense, these songs resemble the folktales discussed in chapter 3; they provide interactional role models for how *noka* could be (re)used in contemporary speech. The *noka* interactional models in song might be the most accessible of the literary genres discussed thus far, as they express quotidian concerns and were composed (and sung) primarily by "ordinary" people rather the educated elites who composed or transcribed the biblical and folkloric texts. Further, the songs that use *noka* relate stories about women and girls that rarely circulate otherwise. Songs in *noka*, therefore, provide us with important counter narratives about female identity and possibility—for good or ill.

Sources

Basque song has been a main conduit of Basque culture for centuries and comprises an important part of the Basque language and literature curriculum. In this chapter, I examine songs from every variety of Basque, written between the fifteenth and twentieth centuries.[4] Many of these songs were collected by R. M. Azkue (1884–1951), whose folktale compilations were discussed in chapter 3, and the musicologist, composer, and priest José Gonzolo Zulaica (1886–1956) better known as Aita (Father) Donostia, as he was born in the city of Donostia (San Sebastian). The Jesuit priest Antonio Zavala (1928–2009) carried on this tradition through the end of the twentieth century. Combined with anthologies edited by scholars such as Patri Urkizu and the *bertsolari*, musician and translator Xabier Amuriza, these efforts produce a voluminous corpus of several thousand pages. I scoured every page, looking for songs in *noka*, outlined below.

Findings

Despite the large number of songs in Basque, I only found 125 songs that use *noka* specifically, as indicted in table 4.1.

Table 4.1: Songs in *Noka*

	Songs	*Noka*	Female Narrators
R.E.S.P.E.C.T.	16	84	4
All The Single Ladies	35	222	3
Love and Marriage	22	139	4
Stairway to Heaven	13	64	2
Ding, Dong! The Witch is Dead	6	30	2
Girls Just Wanna Have Fun	13	48	1
These Boots Were Made For Walking	15	42	4
My Country 'Tis Of Thee	4	35	0
	125	**664**	**20**

The table above shows that only sixteen of these songs (R.E.S.P.E.C.T)—or 13 percent—use *noka* for unambiguously negative purposes, to chide or mock a female addressee, consonant with the Catholic uses of *noka* discussed in chapter 2. The remaining songs use *noka* for a far wider range of interactional purposes and contexts. Thirty-five ("All The Single Ladies") concern finding suitable husbands for girls and unmarried women. Another twenty-two ("Love and Marriage") recount married life; and the perspectives of the girls and women who populate these songs often differ considerably from the more well-known songs on these topics. Similarly, the nineteen songs that use *noka* to relay tales of religion ("Stairway To Heaven") and witchcraft ("Ding, Dong! The Witch Is Dead!") construct more encompassing images of women (human or supernatural) than those projected by the oft-sung prayers to the Virgin Mary. The thirteen songs about women enjoying themselves

("Girls Just Wanna Have Fun"), usually by drinking and/or gambling, draw even more divergent kinds of female identity still. Fifteen songs ("These Boots Were Made For Walking") use *noka* for a variety of pedestrian purposes on a miscellany of themes; another four ("My Country 'Tis Of Thee") concern the Basque Country or war.

Below, I examine illustrative songs from each category in table 4.1. When dialects had more than one song in each category, I narrowed the possibilities to those based on their contextual information and understandability to me. That is, some songs not only use archaic language but also have difficult-to-decipher historical clues. In addition, documentation about the songs varies widely. For some, no documentation exists except the text itself. For others, the compiler provided information about provenance—not only the province whence it comes, but sometimes even the city or village, the reciter or author, as well as its historical context and cultural significance. When deciding upon songs in the same dialect opining on the same theme, then, I chose those whose linguistic, cultural, and historical context I understood best. Unless otherwise indicated, all translations are my own.

Before examining these counter narratives in *noka* songs, the section below provides some examples of songs that use *noka* in ways consistent with its uses in the Catholic materials discussed in chapter 2, that is, for negative interactional purposes.

Noka Songs of Many Notes

I began this book with the linguistic puzzle my fieldwork had uncovered: if *noka* equals *toka* linguistically, as "just" a familiar singular pronoun, why has it retreated from speech at a faster rate than has *toka*? Why do contemporary language ideologies ascribe *noka* with so many more negative associations than *toka*? I argued in chapter 2 that much of *noka*'s semantic derogation stems from its use in Catholic texts, which use it for exclusively negative purposes, usually to "apostrophize" inanimate addresses (metaphorically cast as female) for faithlessness to God. But Basque songs also provide examples of *noka* used to chide or berate the female addressee—and in these cases, that addressee is an animate human being.

R.E.S.P.E.C.T: *Noka* Songs of Disrespect

Of the 125 songs, 16 use *noka* to to mock or chastise a girl or woman for "inappropriate" behavior or appearance (***female narrators are italicized and bolded***; male narrators are underlined).

Table 4.2: *Noka* Songs of Reproach (N = 16)

Song Title	English Gloss	Provenance	*Noka*
1. *Andere Gazte Eder Bat*	A Beautiful Young Woman	***Josefa Latasa*** (N)	2
2. *Andren Aphainduraz*	About Women's Clothing	Jean Robin (L)	13
3. *Astea Luze*	A Long Week	Eusebio Santxotena (N)	6
4. *Atso Zarra Belendrin*	Old Hag	Mariano Azkue (G), 1912	7
5. *Atzo Ttun Ttun*	Yesterday, We Were Stupid	Ignacio Perez (G)	6
6. *Bi Etxek Andere*	Two Women-of-the-House	P. Topet Etxahun (Z), 1786-1862	11
7. *Ezpeletako Katalin*	Catherine of Ezpeleta	***Josefa Latasa*** (N), 1920	2
8. *Gormant Haundi*	A Big Glutton	J.B. Larralde (L), 1804-1870	4
9. *Hartzen Dit Ofizioa*	I Take A Job	IparANON	1
10. *Khilo-Egilearen*	The Spinners' Song	Joanes Otxalde (BN), 1878	4
11. *Maria Peliz*	Maria Peliz	BizkaiANON, 1922	1
12. *Mari Trapuzar*	"Old Rag" Maria	***Josefa Iturbe*** (B)	3
13. *Ortzirale Arratsean*	On Thursday Afternoon	IparANON	2
14. *Purra, Maria*	Here Chick-Chick, Maria	Irurita (N), 1918	2
15. *Trumon-Euria*	Thunder and Rain	BizANON, 1902	16
16. *Zaharrak, Beti . . .*	The Old, Always Old	***Catalin Guarda*** (Ipar)	4
			84

[B = Bizkaia; BN = Baxe Nafarroa; G = Gipuzkoa; L = Lapurdi; N = Nafarroa; Z = Zuberoa; Ipar = *Iparralde*; IparANON = *Iparralde*, anonymous author; BizANON = Bizkaia, anonymous author][5]

Four of these songs criticize women or girls for their appearance. "*Ezpeletako Katalin*," by Josefa Latasa of Nafarroa, uses *noka* to mock a girl named Catherine of Ezpeleta (a village in Lapurdi): "You are unattactive and you know it" (Ederra ez eta ***badakin***).[6] But "*Andren Apainduraz*"[7] (About Women's Clothing) written by Jean Robin (1738–1821) of Lapurdi uses *noka* to criticize girls for dressing up in fancy clothes to look "better" than their station. "*Trumon-Euria*"[8] (Thunder and Rain) chastises women for speaking Castilian instead of Basque to do so. "*Maria Peliz*"[9] sounds a similar theme, criticizing a woman for dressing up in an elegant skirt, meandering, and doing nothing.

Donostia collected a song in this vein from Amaiur, Nafarroa. (*Gender-neutral familiar forms used with a female addressee are italicized*; ***noka forms with transitive verbs, a female indirect object or allocative conjugation are italicized and bolded;*** gender-neutral familiar forms used with a male addressee are underlined; **toka forms with transitive verbs, a male indirect object, or allocutive conjugation are underlined and bolded**.):

Text 4.1: *Atso Zarra Belendrin* ("Old Hag")[10]

Atso zarra belendrin	Old Hag
Ire bentak egin ***din***	You have done your shopping
Ortzak ere juan ***zaizkin***	You have no teeth
Eta diabru zarra ***dirudin***	And you look like an old devil
Txirulin, brinkulin,	[onomatopaeic wordplay]
Brinkulin, brinkulin	[onomatopaeic wordplay]
Txirulin, brinkulin atsua	[word play] Old Hag
Su ondoan *agoenian*	When you're by the fire
Ez ***daukan*** moxkor gaiztua	You're not a bad drunk
Ez ***daukan*** moxkor gaiztua	You're not a bad drunk

Another subcategory of *noka* songs ridicules behaviors deemed unattractive. "*Maria Trapuzar*,"[11] gathered by Donostia from Josefa Iturbe from Arati (Bizkaia), comments upon a whole family for not attending to their chores and spending time indulging their vices instead:

Text 4.2: *Maria Trapuzar* ("Old Rag" Mary)

Mari Trapuzar iñarartеko	"Old Rag" Mary of the heathers
Sasi artean yaioa:	Born in the bramble bush
Egundo bere ***ezton***	You've never seen
Ikusi *eure* garian gorua	A distaff in your time
Aita ta seme tabernan dagoz	Father and son are in the tavern
Amata alaba yokuan:	Mother and daughter are gambling
Ostera bere egongo ***ditun***	In the restaurant will hang
Abarka zarrak kakuan	Your leather shoes, on a hook

While the lyrics of this song do not explicitly criticize the family for having so much time on their hands, other songs clearly regard such leisure activities with opprobrium. In "*Khilo-Egilearan*" (The Spinners' Song) by Joanes Otxalde, a mother uses *noka* to rouse her daughter: "Wake up, child! Isn't the night long enough for you?" (Jeiki *hadi* haurra/Ez deia aski luze *hiretako* gaua?).[12] The daughter replies that she'd rather go to the market than work outside; the mother bemoans that "Girls today are/too soft to work the land/nothing but lazy!/Soon there will be no farmers."[13] "*Andere Gazte Eder Bat*"[14] (A Beautiful Young Woman) collected from Josefa Latasa from Imotz (Nafarroa) by Azkue, rebukes a young woman for not attending to her domestic chores as dutifully as she had in the past. Similarly, the male narrator of "*Astea Luze*"[15] (A Long Week), collected from Eusebio Santxotena (Bozate, Nafarroa), uses *noka* to chide a woman for not attending to her chores. The woman proffers one excuse after another; the narrator ultimately concludes: "You are a better drinker than a weaver/woman, much better" (Irule baino edale azkar/Azakarrago *aiz*, emaztea). Finally, the father in "*Hartzen Dit Ofizioa*" (I Take A Job) levels a vague yet menacing accusation at his daughter: "Where have you been, notorious one?" (Nun ebiltzen *hiz*, laidogarri?).

Another six songs remain in this category. "*Gormant Haundia*" (A Big Glutton), written by Jean Baptiste Larralde (1801–1879), criticizes a female addressee for eating "my apple . . . you devoured it . . . do you also eat cat remains?" (***hik*** jan ***baitun*** nere sagarra . . . ***heorrek*** iretsi . . . gatuen ondarrak ***baitiun*** iresten?).[16] "*Purra, Purra, Maria*", collected by Donostia in 1918 in Irurita (Nafarrua), informs addressee Maria that "everyone is laughing at you at your news" (mundu guzia irriz ase ***dun/ire*** berriak jakintza).[17] That "*purra, purra*" translates roughly as "here, chick, chick, chick"—as if calling out to chickens—emphasizes the mean intent of this song. In "*Ortzirale Arratsian*" (On Thursday Afternoon), a mother and son host the narrator (whose gender is not specified) overnight, then berate that person for breaking the pot that held the soup they had given. In the penultimate verse, the narrator uses *noka* to plead: "Leave me in peace!" (Utz ***dautan*** pazientzia). The addressee is unspecified: it might be the mother, or it might be that the pot-breaker, whose gender is indicated thereby as female. "*Atzo Ttun Ttun*" (Yesterday, We Were Stupid) asks plaintively: "Stupid yesterday, stupid today, always stupid: We have spent all our money. Who will want us?" (Atzo ttun ttun, gaur ttun ttun/Beti ttun ttun ***gaittun*** gu/Gure diruak ***gaittun*** eta/ Nork naiko ***gaittun*** gu?). In "*Bi Etxek Andere*,"[18] a woman-of-the-house ("*etxekoandre*") kicks her daughter-in-law out of the house they share, burdening the "miserable old one" to do the work of two people. Finally, Catalin Guarda's "Zaharrak, Beti Zaharrak" dismisses a "hunted, old woman" to bed.

As we shall see below, mean-spiritedness infuses many a song about unmarried women and girls as well. They do not always take the insults lying down.

All the Single Ladies

Of the 125 *noka* songs, 35 concern unmarried women and girls—whether they will marry and, if so, whom:

Table 4.3: *Noka* Songs About Unmarried Women (N = 35)

Song Title	English Gloss	Provenance	*Noka*
1. *Adizan Gabriela*	Listen, Gabriela	Bera (N), 1921	13
2. *Agur Maiteño*	Good-bye, My Love	Nafarroa ANON	2
3. *Ai Mari Miguel*	Oh, Mari Miguel	Felipe Abasolo (B)	2
4. *Aita Tun Tun*	Foolish Father	Roncal (Nafarroa)	2
5. *Aitak . . . Dio Alabari*	Father Tells His Daughter	Nehor & C. Dufau (Ipar), 1921	3
6. *Aita Nuen Saltzaile*	Father Was My Seller	Juan Ramon Arburua (N)	2
7. *Ama Alabak*	Mother and Daughter	IparANON	10
8. *Ama-Alabak Daude*	Mother and Daughter Disagree	Amezketa (G)	25
9. *Amak Dio*	Mother Said	Hasparen (L)	1
10. *Amak Dio Alabari*	Mother Tells Her Daughter	Sara (L), 1913	5
11. *Amak Ezkondu . . .*	Mother Married Me Off	***Aurekoetxea & Bengoechea*** (B)	6
12. *Artzai Nindogoenian*	When I Was a Shepherd	Lekaroz (N)	2
13. *Atarratze Xauregian*	In Atarratze's Palace	Maule (Z)	3
14. *Basabila Hortan*	On That Wild Path	IparANON	4
15. *Begitarte Egidazu*	Make a Face	Antonio Elizalde (N), 1944	11
16. *Behin Batez*	Once Upon a Time	***Graziosa Zabalo*** (BN)	3
17. *Bi Ahizpak*	Two Sisters	Pierre T. Etxahun (Z), 1786-1862	12
18. *Brodatzen Ari Nintzen*	I Was Embroidering	IparANON	3
19. *Dama Gazte Batentzat*	For a Young Woman	Gipuzkoa	2
20. *Ermuko Mutila*	A Boy from Ermua	Ermua (B), 1908	2
21. *Errekaldeko Alhaba*	Daughter of Creekside	Arrute	5
22. *Etxe Aundi Eder Bat*	A Big Beautiful House	Euloji Gorrotxatea (N), 1932	4
23. *Ezkontza*	A Wedding	Manex Etxamendi (BN), 1924	3

24. *Ezkontza Baten . . .*	About a Marriage	Tolosa (G)	38
25. *Gazte Naiz eta Lorios*	I Am Young and Happy	***Adrianne Dibarassarry*** (L), 1917	5
26. *Gure Bordaltian*	In Our House	Pierre Etxas (Z), 1927	7
27. *Lau Lagun Tabernatik*	Four Friends From the Tavern	Zarautz (G)	1
28. *Naranjaren Gisako*	Like an Orange	Gipuzkoa	3
29. *Neskatxa Batek Amari*	A Girl to Her Mother	Irun (G)	8
30. *Nurbaiteki Ezkunti*	Wanting to Marry Someone	IparANON	6
31. *Oi Pello Pello*	O, Pello Pello	IparANON	17
32. *Orai Negu-Txoriak*	Like a Winter Bird	Leoncio Iturralde (N)	3
33. *Pasacalle*	Pasacalle (A Dance)	Jose Iribarren (Eugui, G)	3
34. *Primaderako Florian*	In the Flowering of Spring	IparANON, 18th-19th century	2
35. *Usoak*	Doves	Bizkaia	4
			222

[BN = Anonymous Author, G = Baxe Nafarroa; R = Roncal]

In two songs in this category, an unspecified person dispenses general advice to an unmarried girl. "*Aita Tun Tun*" (Foolish Father),[19] collected by Aita Donostia in the Roncal Valley of Nafarroa, suggests that finding the daughter of a particular household a mate may not be very easy: as she and her parents are stupid (*tun tun),* she would need to find a stupid husband so he would fit in: "Oro tun tun izaiteko/Tun tun bear ***dun*** senara." ("Pasacalle" is a variation on this theme). "*Errekaldeko Alhaba,*"[20] collected by Aita Donostia in Arrute (Bizkaia) in 1923, chastises "the Daughter of Creekside" for not wanting to marry a laborer's son, when she herself is just a basketmaker's daughter (***Hik*** ez ***duna*** nahi senhar laboraria?/Eta *hi* zer *hiz*?/Saski-egile baten alhaba *baihiz*!").[21] We shall see below that Basque songs do not suffer snobbery gladly. In "*Basabila Hortan*" (On That Wild Path), a new bride uses *noka* to confront an old widow who encouraged her to marry an old widower, a marriage that evidently did not end up a happy union. Indeed, that the bride deigns to use *noka* to an older woman asymmetrically, violating sociolinguistic norms against its use by younger speakers to older addressees, further speaks to the young woman's outrage.

Most songs in this category involve parents trying to convince or coerce their daughters to marry someone other than the man she herself would like to marry. For example, in "*Artzai Nindagoenian*"[22] (When I Was A Shepherd), a father chastises his daughter for flirting with a shepherd in Mass; she can do better. But in "*Aitak Erran Dio Alabari*"[23] (Father Tells his Daughter), when a father threatens to disown his daughter if she marries a particular boy, she defies him. The remaining two songs regarding fathers and daughters relate darker tales. In "*Etxe Aundi Eder Bat*"[24] (A Big Beautiful House) collected by Zavala from Euloji Gorrotxate in 1932, a father tells his daughter about the rich husband he has chosen for her—who turns out to be abusive.

The worst of these songs is perhaps "*Aita Nuen Saltzaile*,"[25] collected by Zavala from Juan Ramon Arburua from Etxalar (Nafarroa) wherein a girl's entire family colludes to literally sell her off to the highest bidder:

Text 4.3: *Aita Nuen Saltzaile* ("Father Was My Seller")

Aita nuen saltzaile	My father was my seller
Ama diruen artzaile	My mother, the money taker
Nere anaia Bernardo	My brother, Bernardo
Moru-errira entregatzaile	Manager of the village Moors
Saldu nenduen dirutan	They sold me for money
Dirutan ere aunitzetan	A lot of money
Neunek pisa-ala urretan	As if I had my weight in gold
Bi ezti kupeletan	And two barrels of honey
"Neure alaba Miarrez	"My daughter, Miarrez
Zer ***dun*** orrela nigarrez?	Why do you cry like that?
Ire yauntziak eginik tziauden	Your clothes will be made
Urrearekin zilarrez"	Of silver and gold"

A bad end also awaits the twenty-two-year-old narrator of "*Primaderako Florian*"[26] (In the Flowering of Spring), who announces in the first verse that she will die soon. Pining for her beau of four years, her parents promise her hand in marriage to a rich Marquis' son instead. Heartbroken, she takes to bed and no doctor can cure her; the doctor who attends her is a "barber," sometimes a euphemism for doctors who attend to unwanted pregnancies.

However, at times the daughter wins the day in appeals to a parent about her marital wishes. In "*Gure Bortaltian*"[27] (In Our

House), a father agrees to marry his daughter off in the next year so he will have peace in his house. In "*Usoak*"[28] (Doves), a daughter rejects all the suitors her parents offer her—a carpenter, a baker, and a butcher—until they offer her a soldier. Things do not turn out so well in "*Nurbaiteki Ezkunti Nahi*"[29] (Wanting to Marry Someone). When a daughter pleads with her mother to marry her off, believing that her dowry will fetch her a handsome young husband, she ends up with a husband who wastes all her money on drink while she spends all her time carrying for their many children.

Perhaps not surprisingly, mothers more often than fathers provide daughters with romantic advice. In "*Amak Dio*,"[30] a mother tells her daughter that she will lose her dowry if she marries her current beau. In the similarly titled, "*Amak Dio Alabari*" (Mother Tells Her Daughter)[31] the mother warns her not to go out with so many "aitonen seme" ("grandfather's sons"). Both "*Ama Alabak*"[32] (Mother and Daughter) and Adrianne Diharassarry's "*Gazte Naiz eta Lorios*"[33] (I am Young and Happy) take these warnings one step further: a mother advises her daughter not to run around with too many men or she will end up in trouble; in the case of the former song, the mother knows whereof she speaks. Similarly, in "*Neskatxa Batek Amari*" (A Girl to Her Mother)[34] a young girl ignores her mother's warning not to wear such provocative clothes to a dance, only to find her skirt torn by one of her partners. And "*Lau Lagun Tabernatik*"[35] (Four Friends from the Tavern) tells the story of four men fined or imprisoned for sexually harassing women at a bar. Even so, the mother cautions her daughter that if she does not like the kinds of games men play in bars, she should not get married.

However, daughters sometimes prevail in their marital choices. Zavala collected three similar songs on this theme. In "*Ama Alaba Daude Diskordiarekin*" (Mother and Daughter Disagree)[36] a mother tries to dissuade her daughter from marrying a young man fond of partying and getting into fights and choosing instead an older man—who is rich, hardworking, and honest. The discussion continues for twenty-three verses (the mother using *noka* twenty-five times, with the daughter responding with the formal, *zu*) with the daughter still determined to marry the young partier. "*Ezkontza Baten Gainean*" (About a Marriage) essentially recounts the same story, though the names of the girl's suitors differ. In fact, Zavala notes that it appears to have been written, by hand, by the same author as that of "*Ama Alaba Daude Diskordiarekin*."

"*Amak Ezkondu Ninduen*" (Mother Married Me Off) remains popular today, appearing in many anthologies and sung around the table throughout the Basque Country and the diaspora. Azkue spliced together the version below. He notes that Juliana Aurekoetxea of Zugaztieta (Bizkaia) recounted the first verse; Cristostema Bengoechea of Lekeitio, Bizkaia, supplied the remaining verses:[37]

Text 4.4a: *Amak Ezkondu Ninduen* ("Mother Married Me Off")

1. Amak ezkondu ninduen	When I was fifteen
Amabost urtekin	My mother wanted me to marry
Senaŕak bazituen larogei beŕakin	An eighty-year-old man!
Oi ai neskatila gaztea	A young girl like me
Agure zarrakin	With such an old man?!
2. Ama, zeŕtarako det nik	Mother, what good is
Agure zar hori	An old man like that?
Aŕtuta leyotikan	I'll take him to the window
Jauŕti beaŕ det nik	And throw him out?
Oi, ai! Neure leyotikan	That's right
Jauŕti behar dut nik	Throw him out the window!
3. Neska: *ago* isilikan	Daughter, be quiet!
Aberatsa ***den*** hori	That man is very rich
Epez igaro itzan uŕte bat edo bi	Just be patient a year or two
Ori ilezkeroztik	When he dies
Biziko *aiz* ongi	You will live well
4. Deabruak daramala	But the devil got into me
Oilar urtetsua	The old rooster:
A baino nayago't nik	But I would rather have
Nere aukerekoa	One of my own choosing:
Oi, ai! Ogei bat uŕteko	Oh, my! A twenty year old
Gazte lorekoa	In the flower of his youth!

Azkue notes that, in addition to the song "seeming modern," it appears to originate from Gipuzkoa despite his having heard it in the Bizkaian villages of Ondaroa and Gorozika as well as the towns indicated above. Further, I have come across a version (written in the Gipuzkoan variety) with an additional, penultimate verse:

Text 4.4b: *Amak Ezkondu Ninduen*

Neska, ***etzanala*** hartu	Don't take someone
Dirurik gabea	Who has no money
Bestela izango ***dun***	Or you will have
Nahiko lanbidea	A lot of hard work to do
Oi, ai, txorrakerik utzita	Don't be so silly
Harzan agurea	Marry the rich old man!

Thus, in this subcategory of songs, girls often vehemently negotiate with their parents over whom they should marry; even if they do not always get their way or their choices do not turn out to be as wise as they had thought.

Another group of songs tells many a varied tale about the goings-on of unsupervised girls and unmarried women. In "*Oi Pello Pello*,"[38] a woman repeatedly asks a man to accompany her to bed, advances which Pello fends off by giving her task after task to complete. In "*Ermuko Mutila*,"[39] a boy from the village of Ermua (Bizkaia) provides a litany of wrongs done to him by his former fiancée—whom he calls "old furniture" and compares to a witch—though this should not have surprised him as she'd mistreated nine fiancés before him.

In some of these songs, things go quite badly indeed for the girl in question. In "*Brodatzen Ari Nintzen*"[40] (I Was Embroidering) a mother sends her daughter to invite some sailors to their home for dinner. The sailors kidnap the girl instead; she kills herself rather than lose her virtue. The fate of the girl in "*Dama Gazte Batentzat*"[41] may be no better:

Text 4.5: *Dama Gazte Batentzat* (For a Young Woman)

1. Bertso berri batzuek	Some new verses
Dudarikan gabe	Without a doubt
Dama gazte batentzat	For a young woman
Komeni dirade	She deserves them
Irun'en serbitzalle	As a waitress in Irun
Zeguan mirabe	She worked
Bana Naparrua'ko	But she was
Alaba zerade	A daughter of Nafarroa
2. Ogei ta zortzi urte	Twenty-one years old
Zure edadia	Your age
Oraindik juiziyorik	Her judgment

Etorri gabia	Still had not come
Esplikatzera nua	I will explain
Enfermedadia	Her illness
Ganera orrek daukan	As well as
Abillidadia	Her cleverness
3. Paketa bat bazuen	She had a package
Nagusiayagandik	From her boss
Gurasoen etxera	To take to her parents' house
Eraman du andik	When she brought it
Amak esaten diyo:	Her mother said:
Alde ***idan*** emendik	Get out of here
Bestela jipoien bat	Otherwise I will give you
Emango ***dinat*** nik	Such a beating
4. Paketa ori zuben	She had received the package
Irun'en artua	In Irun
Berez naparra baña	It was Navarrese
Frantzia'n partua	But birthed in France
Orren arbolatikan	From that tree
Datorren frutua	Comes the fruit
Apaiz egin liteken	The priest may have done it
Ez da ziertua	Though that is not certain
5. Lenbizi Donosti'ra	First she went to Donostia
Gero Donijuana	Then to Donijuana
Barbero ta mediku	To the barber and the doctor
Adituengana	To those who had heard of it
Ikusi zutenian:	When they saw her, they said:
Zer daukazu, dama?	What is it, woman?
Operaziyo on bat	A good operation
Egin biar dit, jauna	Is what I need, Sir
6. Au da mediku jaunak	This is what the doctor
Esandako itza:	Said to her:
Erremediyo billa	Why are you looking
Zertako zabiltza?	For a remedy?
Barrengua galtzeko	To lose what's inside you
Etsaiak dabiltza	Is the devil's idea
Laister sendatuko da	Soon you will be healed
Zuk daukazun gaitza	From what ails you
7. Dama ori egun batez	One day, that woman
Irun'dik galdu zen	Lost her way from Irun
Semia egin omen du	And had a son
San Juan de Luz'en	In San Juan de Luz
Azia bota eta	The wind blew
Fruta eldu zen	And in came the fruit
Ori konserbatzera	Let us try
Saiatu gaitezen	To protect him

Thus, we do not know the fate of this young woman; indeed, the song expresses more concern for the son she has left behind than the whereabouts or welfare of the young mother herself.

However, in Graziosa Zabalo's "*Behin Batez*"[42] (Once Upon a Time), the girl fares much better: she fends off the advances of a man pursuing her. He offers to "assist" her to the mill and to the schoolhouse, but she retorts that she already receives all the assistance she needs from her parents and her priest. In "*Naranjaren Gisako*" (Like An Orange)[43] two women debate the potential of a handsome—but impoverished—object of desire.

Several other songs convey the importance attached to the institution of marriage. More specifically, they reveal its importance for women by mocking those who do not achieve this marital state. Collected from Antonio Elizalde of Amaiur (Nafarroa) in 1934 by Aita Donostia, "*Begitarte Egidazu*"[44] (Make a Face) ridicules an older woman for not having married while still young. "*Ai, Mari Miguel*"[45] mocks a woman for not having any romantic prospects: "Where is your boyfriend? When is your wedding day?" (Nun ***don*** senargei hori? Noiz ***don*** eztegua?).

Collected by Aita Donostia in Madrid from a "young man from [the village of Bera] of the Bidasoa" Valley in Nafarroa in 1921, "*Adizan Gabriela*"[46] demonstrates the tall tales two unmarried women will tell to fend off the stigma of spinsterhood:

Text 4.6: *Adizan Gabriela* ("Listen, Gabriela")

1. ***Adizan*** Gabriela zenbat urte ***ditun***	Hey, Gabriela, how old are you?
Ogei ta amasei nik geia ***baditun***	I'm thirty-six; you're older than me
Baldin oraingo txandan ezkontzen ez ***bagaitun***	If we don't get married this time
Geren bizi guziko neskazaharrra ***gaitun***	We will forever be spinsters
2. Nereak oita amalau ***ditun*** onezkero	I am thirty-four
Baña neskazahartzerik ez ***diñat*** espero	But I don't expect to be a spinster
Mutillak ezkontzeko ain zebiltzan bero	The guys are hot to marry me
Beintzat nik ***badizkiñat*** zazpi zapatero	At least seven shoemakers
3. Nik ere ***badizkiñat*** lau txikiatzaile	I also have four ram castrators
Zazpi barkilero ta bi piper-saltzaile	Seven waffle vendors, two pepper salesmen
Eta gañera iru kale-garbitzalle	And three street-cleaners
Bi kabo primero ta lau arpa jotzaile	Two corporals and four harpists
4. Nere bizi moduaz nion ernegatzen	I curse my life
Mutil guztokorikan ez ***diñat*** billatzen	I don't attract the guys I like
Gorputza asi zaidan pixka bat torpetzen	My body is going to pot
Neskazarra naizena zidaten igartzen	It looks like I'll be a spinster
5. Soñekorik onena egin ***diñat*** jantzi	I wore my best skirt

Gañera eskutikan sonbrilla ta guzi	With a parasol and everything
Oingo mutil gaztiak ainbeste malezi	Today's guys are cruel
Ni ikusi orduko ziazten igesi	They run away when they see me
6. Oso itxusia ***den*** neskazar izena	Spinster is such an ugly word
Aditu utsarekin artzen ***diñat*** pena	It pains me to hear it
Oraiñ edukirikan sasoirik onena	When I am at my peak
Au da lastimagarri gu biok gaudena!	Our situation is pitiful

A song written by Zuberoa's Piarres Topet Etxahun (1786–1862) describes sisters in a similar squabble:

Text 4.7: *Bi Ahizpak* ("Two Sisters")[47]

1. Katalina entzün ***diñat*** egia segürki	Katalin, I surely heard the truth
Maitia ***deitañala hik*** nahi ideki	You want to steal the one I love
Segretik behar ***dütün*** bai utzi hareki	You better leave him alone
Nahi ***ezpalinbatün*** olhuak eraiki	If you don't want to be hit
2. Maider, ***enün*** ebilten ez ihuren ondun	Maider, I'm not chasing anyone
Ez eta huna jiler nahi ihesi jun	Or trying to get away with anything
Ust'ukhen ***balindadün hirik*** diel'en'ondun	If you think those near me belong to you
Eztitzañala ützi ebiltera kanpun!	Don't let them out!
3. Ai ahizpa falsia! Ai lotsagarri!	Ai, untrustworthy sister! You are shameful!
Ene zopa hunen jaten bethi izan *hiz* ari!	You are always eating of my soup!
Sorthü *hintzan* axuri izateko ardi	You were born a lamb, to become a sheep
Bena beldür ***nün*** egin *hizala* ahari!	But I fear you are a ram!

Thus, even sisters will steal each other's boyfriends to avoid remaining unmarried. However, in the song below from 1564—one of the oldest on record—two sisters conspire to keep one of them from having to marry a man she does not wish to wed:

Text 4.8: Atarratze *Xauregian*[48] (In Atarratze's Palace)

1. Atarratze xauregian, zitroina da loratzen	In Atarratze's castle, a lemon flowers
Dongarayeko primiak batño du galdetzen	Dongaray's heir asks for one
Respostia izan emendu, eztirela ondu	It is not ripe, was the answer
Ontzun direnean batño izanen du	When it is, he will get one
2. Aita, zuk saldu nuzu idi bat bezala	Father, you have sold me like an ox
Baita abandonatu ez izanik bezala	And abandoned me like I don't exist
Ama bizi uken banu, aita, zu bezala	If Mother were living, Father, like you
Eninduzu, ez, juanen Espainian barna	She wouldn't send me to Spain
Bano bai ezkonduren Atarratze Salala	But marry me off in Atarratze
3. Aizpa, xantzi ***dezan*** xarpa[49] berdea	Sister, put on your green cloth
Nik ere xantziren ***diñat*** mosolin xuria	I will wear white
Engoitik ina ***duken*** gure jaun gaia	And we will fool your fiancée
Abil eta erran izozu eri nizala	"Go and tell him I am ill
Zazpi urte untan oyean nizala	That I have been in bed for seven years"

4. Nik erranagatik eri zinala
Bera zinen duzu, bai, zu ziren lekura
Jinko onak dagizula egun on maitea
Baita eta zuri ere, Dongarayeko primia
Bidean entzun dizit eri zirela
Eri izateko sobera, eder zira
5. Aita, goazen goazen, alegerarik
Etxera jinen zira begiak bustirik
Begiak bustirik eta ni tonban sarturik
Atarratzeko ezkilak beren donez sonatzen
Eta andere Klara erritik partitzen
Ango txipi-aundiak beltzez dira bestitzen
6. Aizpa, goazen, goazen, goyen goyen salala
Andik so eginen *iagun den* iparra ala egoa
Iparra baldin bada, Salarri goraintzi
'ta egoa baldin bada Dongarayeko primiari

Because I said you were ill
He went to where you were
Good day, my dear Klara
Same to you, heir of Dongaray
I heard on the road that you were ill
You're too beautiful to be very ill
Father, let's go, joyfully
You will go to the house, teary-eyed
With teary eyes and me in the tomb
Ararratze's bells will toll
And Lady Klara's illness will pass
Young and old are dressing in black
Sister, let's go to the upstairs room
See if he comes from north or south
If from the north, we will greet the room
If from the south, Dongaray's heir

This use of *noka* can be seen as a marker of solidarity, akin to other *T* forms: the one sister uses the familiar form when she suggests the other fake her death to avoid the unwanted marriage. While it is unclear from this text if the plan works or not, this song certainly shows the sisters as actively attempting to control their fate. Interestingly, then, most songbooks which feature "*Atarratze Xauregian*" omit this verse—I only recently came across it, even though I've sung the song for many years—thereby obscuring this kind of usage as a possible linguistic resource for female assertiveness. Further, most versions of this song blame the mother rather than the father for selling the daughter off as if she were cattle (verse 2).

I would like to conclude this section with two songs of heartbreak told from the point of view of the lovers themselves. In "*Orai Negu-txoriak*" (Like a Winter Bird)[50] a young man asks his girlfriend why she has become as silent as birds in winter: "I used to hear you say every night: "I love no one but you" ("Len gabero entzuten ***ninan ireganik***/'Ez **tiat** bertze maiterik.'" Alas, the girl fell silent because her beau has allowed his mother to choose someone else for his bride. The couple in "*Agur, Maiteño*"[51] (Good-bye, My Love) uses similar words of love to each other. The young woman tells her beau: "I love no one else/You are my only master/If you do not have my heart/May this cold ground take me soon" (**Eztiat** neor bertze maiterik/Yoa herori aut yabe bakar/Nere biotz au, ik izan ezik/lurr otzak laxter bekit ar). But the cold ground does not take her; when he leaves to herd sheep in America, she finds someone else:

Text 4.9: *Agur, Maiteño* (Good-bye, My Love)

Ni Amerikan *izaz* oroitzen	When I was in America, I thought of you
Gainalde aietan taldezain	As I watched my flocks on those hills
i aldiz nizaz antzia emen!	While you forgot about me here!
Agur, maiteño, *banoain*	Goodbye, my love, I am leaving

Heartbreak and betrayal aside, these two songs make a pronominal point as well: the young woman and man express their love to each other by using mutual *hi* (the man uses *noka* with the woman, and she *toka* with him). As will be clear by the end of this chapter, this pronominal usage between lovers is very unusual in Basque.

In sum, many *noka* songs about "the single lady" portray women and girls in negative terms because of their unmarried state, or present daughters as mere pieces of property to be sold to the highest bidder in marriage. Yet a fair number of *noka* songs also show unmarried girls and women vigorously negotiating their marital choices and getting their way (for good or ill). In some cases, they reject outright their marital options or have the upper hand when it comes to the men who would be their suitors. We do see, then, girls and women playing active roles in romantic terrain allotted them. Having fought so hard to have their wishes respected in matters of the heart, how do women fare once married? The section below provides a glimpse.

Love and Marriage: Go Together Like a Horse and Carriage?

The second most common theme among *noka* songs—22 of 125—concerns the vagaries of marriage. This should not surprise us, given that in "traditional" Basque society, "marriage was considered to be the desirable state for both women and men."[52]

Table 4.4: *Noka* Songs about Marriage (N = 22)

Song Title	English Gloss	Provenance	*Noka*
1. *Agur, Ama Neuria*	Hello, My Mother	***Eusebia Grajinea*** (N), 1934	1
2. *Andria, Jetxi*	Wake up, Wife	Burundia (N)	1
3. *Antton eta Maria*	Antton and Maria	Banka (BN)	2

4. *Apexa eta Lorea*	The Bee and the Flower	J.B Elizanburu (Sara, L), 1862	10
5. *Argi Daritzanari*	To the One Who Is Light	Arnaud Oihenart (Z), 1592-1668	21
6. *Arranuak Bortietan*	Eagles at the Door	Atharratze (Z)	3
7. *Beltxanari*	To the One Who Is Black	Arnaud Oihenart (Z), 1592-1668	16
8. *Bi Ama Alhaba*	A Mother and Daughter	Etxahun (Z), 1786-1862	7
9. *Ene Emaztia Jeiki*	By the Time My Wife Awakes	IparANON	5
10. *Ene Hauzotegian*	In My Neighborhood	C. Becas (L), 1847-1911	8
11. Ezkontza	Marriage	Manex Etxamendi (1924)	4
12. *Gazte Soltero Nago*	I Am a Young Bachelor	BizaiANON	2
13. *Joan Behar*	Must Go	IparANON	3
14. *La, la, la*	La, La, La	IparANON	3
15. *Londresen, Senarra*	I Have a Husband in London	***Maria Josefa Izpirua*** (Gabika, B)	3
16. *Martin eta Katalin*	Martin and Katalin	Gratien Adema, 1851 (Senpere, L)	4
17. *Oro Poz Pozik*	Thoroughly Happy	***Juliana Izagire*** (Segura, G)	11
18. *Peru Gurea*	Our Peru	Toribio Iriondo (Elgoibar, G)	1
19. *Santsin*	Santsin	C. Becas (L), 1847-1911	9
20. *Senarra Degu*	We Have a Husband	***Josefa Treku*** (Orio, G)	1
21. *Xo, Mariano*	Sh, Mariano	Elizondo (N)	2
22. *Xuria Daritzanari*	To the One Who Is White	Arnaud Oihenart (Z), 1592-1668	22
			139

Of the five songs featuring a man pining for a woman—"*Argia Daritzanari*"[53] (To the One Who is Light), "*Beltxaranari*"[54] (To the One Who is Black), and "*Xuria Daritzanari*"[55] (To the One is White)—three appear in *O'ten Gaztaroa Neurtitzetan* ("Measuring the Youth of O") by Arnaud Oihenart (1592–1667). He was a poet, lawyer, and historian from Maule, Zuberoa:

Text 4.10: *Argia Daritzanari* (To the One Who is light)

1. Gauik, egunik	By night, by day
Eztinat hunik	I have nothing good
Hireki ezpaniz, Argia:	Unless I am with you, Light:
Hireki ezpaniz	Unless I am with you
Itsu hutsa niz	I am merely blind
Zeren *baihiz* en'argia	For you are my light
2. *Hirekil'*aldiz	If I am with you
Bederak'aldiz	Every time
Bazter lekutan baturik	I find myself out of the way
Nonbanago	Anywhere
Nun botzenago	I rejoice more
Ezi Errege gertaturik	Because I am become King
3. Lagun artean	When I come
Hel naidean	Among friends
Elhaketan, erhogoan	Talking, conversing,
Ez ***nun*** dostatzen	I do not enjoy it
Ez ***nun*** minzatzen	I do not speak
Hi beti, beti *aut* gogoan	I am always, always thinking of you

4. Nik dudan lana	The work that I have
Ezin errana	Unspeakable
Zer koeinta dudan *higati*	What worry I have because of you
En'ixil, eta	My secret and
Maiz pensaketa	Frequent thought
Egonak ***ziotsan*** nigati	Being informs it of me
5. Kadran-orratzak	Compass needles
Burdin-aitz latzak	Sharp magnets
Hunki-eta buztan mehea	Slender-tailed
Xuxen, han hara	In a straight line
Eguerditara	Southwards
Diadukan punta xehea	Points your minute tip
6. Ni, hala hala	I, just so
Tiraz bezala	As if pulling
Hik joz geroz bihotzean	When you touch my heart
Hiri gorpitzez	With your body
Beti, ed'orhitzez	Always, or when remembering
Narrain, bait'are lotzean	You follow me, even when asleep
7. Bana herabe	But timidly
Estakuru gabe	Without excuse
Dinat, Argia, jitera	I say, Light, come
*Hir'*etx'irira	To your village
Leku agerira	To the open place
Jenten mintz'erazitera	To cause people to talk
8. Beraz *higanik*	So, when I
Egin, jadanik	Run from you
Noiz ***nakiduna dakidan***?	Trying to escape from you
Jin, eta nura	Come along
Gorde-lekura	To the hiding-place
Eta *hi* han bat ***akidan***?	And join me there

The longing expressed in this song might be directed to Juana d'Erdoy, a widowed noblewoman Oihenart married in 1627. Interestingly, only three of his romantic poems use *noka* in addressing the female beloved; the other fourteen (including the elegy he wrote for Juana) use the formal pronoun *zu* instead. It might seem odd for a pining lover or husband to thus use a formal form of address with the object of his love. As we saw in chapter 1, however, in Basque culture the relationship between spouses supposedly "preclude[s] solidarity between husband and wife"[56] rendering familiar forms of address between them inappropriate. Why does Oihenart use *noka* at all in these verses? Unfortunately, the documentation about his oeuvre provides no explanation. Nonetheless, these three poems illustrate *noka*'s use to express unbridled passion, a rare usage we see only in the Song of Solomon (see chapter 5).

Indeed, the bulk of the *noka* songs about married couples portray them as unhappy. In "*Ene Emaztia Jeiki,*"[57] a man beats his wife with his cane for getting up too late for his liking. "*Arranuak Bortietan*"[58] (The Eagles at the Door) portrays a man cheating on his wife, though he expresses regrets about it at the end. In "*Apexa eta Lorea*"[59] (The Bee and the Flower) written by Jean Baptiste Elizanburu (Lapurdi) in 1862, a "flower" ultimately cannot abide the flitting around done by her "bee":

Text 4.11: *Apexa eta Lorea* (The Bee and the Flower)

1. Neguaz primadera zenean jabetu	When winter becomes spring
Sasi baten hegian apexa zen sortu	A bee was born in a bramble bush
Leku berean baitzen lorea gertatu	A flower happened to be there too
Gaixoek elgar zuten bihotzez maitatu!	How the two loved each other!
2. Iguzkiak ihintza pizten duenean	When the sun kisses the morning dew
Apexa doa beti hegalez airean	The bee always flies up in the air
Nahi luke loreak segitu bidean	The flower would like to follow
Girthoinak zertako du gelditzen lurrean?	Why must the stem stay on the ground?
3. Nere besoak ditik ihintzak zerratzen	The dew closes my arms
Ondikotz! iguzkiak goizean urratzen!	Then the sun wakes the morning
Zertako haiz hi beti nitarik urruntzen?	Why do you always leave me?
Hi guan eta **badakik**, nigarrez **nauk** urtzen	When you leave, I weep
4. Zertako nigar egin, o lili maitea?	Why do you cry, my love?
Egunaz iguzkia ***dun*** nere jabea	At night, you own me
Goizetik lorez lore ***dinat*** nik bidea	I flit about all day
Iguzkia sartzean beti ***naun*** hirea . . .	When the sun goes down, I am yours
5. Goiz guziez adio, arratsean agur	Each morning goodbye; each evening, hello
Egunak luze **dituk**, gauak aldiz labor	But the day is long and the night is short
Nere nigarrez, otoi, ez hadila samur	Remember my tears and do not be angry
Zeren hire galtzeaz beti **nauk** ni beldur . . .	For I worry about losing you
6. Iguzkiak, goiz batez, zenean agertu	One day, when the sun arose
Lorearen besoak zituen urratu	She opened the flower's arms
Bi maitek zutenean elgar besarkatu	And found the two lovers embracing
Apexak haizeari hegalak hedatu	But the bee flew away
7. Haize bihotz gabea zertako herritik	Why is there a heartless wind
Ereman **duk** apexa mendien gainetik?	That takes the bee over the mountains?
Zertako **duk** urrundu maitearen ganik?	Why do you leave your love?
Hegaztin gaixo horrek ez **zian** hobenik	You will find no one better
8. Apex hegal flakoa, geldi hadi, geldi	Lightwinged bee, stay, please stay
Utziz bozkarioa, doluan sar hadi:	Leave your repast
Zertako haiz fidatu haize gaixtoari?	Why do you trust that evil wind?

Lorearen gainera lurra **duk** itzuli! . . .	Return to your flower!
9. Maitea, kausitzen *hut* lurrez estalia!	My love, I find you covered in dirt!
Jainkoak bereganat deitu *hau*, lilia!	God has called you to himself
Hi lurreko *hindudan* sosegu guzia	Leaving you at peace on earth
Hil *haiz*! . . . Orai neretzat deus ez ***dun*** bizia	Life is nothing to me, now you are dead
10. Oraino iguzkia *zoan* inguruan	The sun still surrounds us
Apexa zenean hil bere sorlekuan . . .	The bee died where it was born
Izan baitzuen aski zorigaitz munduan	For he suffered enough in this world
Agian Lorea du kausitu zeruan! . . .	Perhaps he will find the bee in heaven

Lest we think that *noka* songs only present women as the wronged party in marital infidelity, other songs suggest otherwise. In "*Bi Ama Alhaba*,"[60] a daughter confronts her mother with the rumor that her godfather is actually her biological father. The mother tries to deny it at first, but finally (almost) admits the truth:

Text 4.12: *Bi Ama Alhaba* (A Mother and Daughter)

Hire egüzaita	Your godfather
Zer gizun xarmanta!	What a fine man!
Hareki bürüz bürü ***diñagu*** zopa	Together we ate soup
Ordin danik ***badinat*** bai nik bethi lotsa	Ever since then I have feared
Hunki zietan kota	That he touched my skirt

We can infer the sexual allusion of "eating soup" as Piarres Topet Etxahun used the same euphemism when he wrote "*Bi Ahizpak*" ("Two Sisters"; text 4.7). Four other songs in this category feature philandering—or at least, extra-marital flirtations—by wives. In "*Antton and Maria*,"[61] written by Arnaud Haranburu in 1855, Antton returns to his village after an absence to learn his wife had borne a son the night before. He does not greet this news with the joy we might expect; he has been gone for two years.

The wife in the song below also finds ways to amuse herself in her husband's absence. Azkue collected this song in the village of Gobika (Bizkaia) from his "excellent" eighty-year-old informant, Maria Josefa Izpirua:[62]

Text 4.13: *Londresen Dot Senarra* (My Husband is in London)

1. Londresen dot neuk senarra	My husband is in London
Zirin-bedarrak ekarten	Bringing purging herbs
Bera andik dan artean	While he is there
Gu emen dantza gaitezen	We can dance here

Oi au egia!	O, that's the truth
Daigun jira bi Maria	Let's take two spins, Maria
2. Kapoiak dagoz erreten	The capons are roasting
Oilaskotxuak mutiltzen	The chickens are growing
Orek ondo erre artean	While he is among them
Gu emen dantza gaitezen	We can dance here
Oi au egia!	O, that's the truth
Daigun jira bi Maria.	Let's take two spins, Maria
3. Neure oilanda nabarra	My multicolored hen
Txikarra baina zabala	Small but wide
Zetan *oa i* auzora	Why are you going out
Etxean oilarra ***donala***?	With a rooster in the house?
Oi au egia!	O, that's the truth
Daigun jira bi Maria	Let's take two spins, Maria
4. Neuk ugazaba nekusan	I see my master
Izurdiako zubian	On the bridge of Izurdia
Ori zestorik urten artean	While he is there
Gu emen dantza gaitezan	We can dance here
Oi au egia!	Oh, that's the truth
Daigun jira bi Maria	Let's take two spins, Maria
5. Neure mutiltxu txoria	My little boy, my little bird
Ik esan **eustan** egia:	You told the truth
Gaur gabean dantzauko zala	That my wife would
Nire emazte Maria	Dance tonight
Oi au egia!	O, that's the truth
Iretzat mando zuria	For you, a white mule

While this song uses *noka* in a playful rather than mean way, this exchange occurs not between husband and wife, but between the wife and her "dance partner" (at the very least) other than her husband. The corpus includes two other variations of this song, "*Peru Gurea*" (Our Peru)[63] and "*Senarra Degu*" (We Have a Husband)[64] the latter attributed to Josefa Treku of Orio, Gipuzkoa.

Several songs portray husbands and wives bickering or fighting with each other. Similar to the songs above censuring daughters for their snobbiness, in "*Andria, Jetxi*"[65] (Wake Up, Wife) a husband tells his wife to "get off that blue horse"—that is, her high horse—as she must live with him on the ground where he lives. In most of these songs—"*Joan Behar*" (Must Go),[66] Juliana Izagirre's "*Oro Poz Pozik*" (Thoroughly Happy),[67] *La La La*,"[68] "*Santsin*,"[69] and "*Xo, Mariano*"[70]—a wife protests her husband's excessive drinking. "*Ene Hauzotegian*,"[71] written by Charles Becas (1847-1911), spews the most vitriol of them all:

Text 4.14: *Ene Hauzotegian* (In My Neighborhood)

1. Ene hauzotegian bi senhar emazte	A husband and wife in my neighborhood
Bakean bizi dira hasarratu arte	Live in peace until they argue
Goardia elgarrekin behin samurtzetik	Once that happens
Heien xuxentzaileak lan ona behar **dik**!	Heaven help us!
2. Lehenik intzirinka, gero deihardarka	They yell, they scream
Gero berriz eskainka, azkenekotz joka	They plead, they fight
Horra zer bizi modu duten maiz segitzen	They'll come to a bad end
Dudarik gabe gostu diote kausitzen	If they don't change their ways
3. Gizon etxe galgari, arno edalea	You drunken home-wrecker
Ahalke behar huke hola bizitzea	You should be ashamed of yourself
Haizen bezalakoa arraila goizetik	Running around at the crack of dawn!
Hoakit, higuin tzarra, begien bixtatik	Get out of my sight, you disgusting old thing!
4. Nere andre gaixoa, ez bada hasarra	A dear wife, who doesn't get angry
Hi bezalako baten ***badinat*** beharra	That's what I need
Emazte baliosa eztia, ixila	A wife who's sweet and quiet
Holako bakhar batek balio ***tin*** mila	Is worth a thousand others"
5. Gizon alfer-tzar, gormant, zikin itsusia	You lazy, old, gluttonous, dirty, ugly man!
Aspaldien **nauk** hitaz asetzen hasia	I am sick of you!
Bethi gerla gorria sekulan bakerik	Always picking fights
Infernuan bide **duk** hi baino hoberik	They behave better in Hell!
6. Othoi, *ago* ixilik, ene emaztea!	Watch your mouth, woman!
Indan, bai, laster gero, biarten bakea	Or you'll start something you'll regret
Zer nahi ***dun*** enekin gerla irabizi	What do you want? To pick a fight?
Lehen ere ***badakin*** nola *hautan* hezi	Remember what I taught you the last time
7. Emazteak orduan hartzen du erkhatza	The wife picks up a broom
Eta ximiniatik gizonak laratza	The husband, a poker from the fireplace
Batek uma-ahala bertzeak: ai! ai! ai!	Both throw tantrums
Oi zein eder guduan holako bi etsai!	A war between two enemies!
8. Eltze, zertain, gathilu, oro nahasteka	Pots, pans, dishes, glasses
Lurrerat arthikiak dabiltza jauzteka	All over the floor
Joaiten naiz jaun andere haien bakhetzera	I tried to make peace between them
Urmaturik hor naute igorri etxera	But they sent me home!

Interestingly, Gratien Adema ("Zalduby")'s version of this song, *"Martin eta Katalin"* uses *noka* only four times. Though the relationship between husband and wife is no less antagonistic than that of the couple in *Ene Hauztegian*, Martin addresses Katalin in *noka* in only the final verbal invetive he throws at her, while Katalin berates Martin in *toka* throughout.

Aptly titled *"Ezkontza"* (Marriage) suggests that discord—even of a less dramatic sort than suggested by *"Ene Hauzotegian"*—is par for the marital course and must ultimately be borne by couples. Written by Manex Etxamendi of Ezterenzubi (Baxe Nafarroa) in 1924, in this song a daughter complains that people blame her for impoverishing her husband. Her mother provides her this advice, in *noka*:

Text 4.15a: *Ezkontza* ("Marriage") (excerpt)[72]

Amak: Zer uste ***dun*** dela, haurra	Mother: What did you think, child
Ezkontza hortan sartzea?	Getting married like that?
Ala kaderan jarri eta han	That you would sit around
Kantuz kitarra jotzea?	And play guitar?
Ez ***dakina hik*** arrosak ere	Don't you know
Baduela arantzea?	That even roses have thorns?
Estatu guzietan gizonak	Men from every station
Badin bere kurutzea!	Have their crosses to bear!

Ultimately, the young bride and groom reconcile themselves to their marital lot. They work hard and learn that "all sorrows must be borne with meekness," and are rewarded with long life. The last line brings home the song's lesson:

Text 4.15b: *Ezkontza* (continued)

Espos horiek etsenplu on bat	This couple is a good example
Guri emaiten dute hor:	For us all:
Penarik gabe gertatzen denik	There is no one on this earth
Lur huntan ez baita nehor	Who lives without sorrow
Bat bestiaren huts guzietan	Let us bear each other's faults
Izan gaiten bai jasankor	With patience
Ongi eginen saristatzeko	God does not forget to reward
Jinkoa ez da ahazkor	Those who have done good

This last song notwithstanding, most of the songs about marriage give a woeful representation of the institution indeed. Given this, perhaps we should not be surprised to find "*Gazte Soltero Nago*" (I Am a Young Bachelor) who, after using *noka* to reel off a litany of burdens experienced by married couples, concludes "it's better/to stay free/be always happy/as a young bachelor."[73]

The final *noka* song in this section, related by Eusebia Grajirena of Sunbila (Nafarroa), tells the most ominous cautionary tale of all about how high the cost of marriage can be:

Text 4.16: *Agur, Agur Ama Neuria*[74] (Hello, My Mother)

1. Agur, agur, ama neuria	Hello, my mother
Ongi etorri zarela, seme neuria	Welcome, my son
Ezkondurik edo ezkongai eldu zara, semia?	Are you married or engaged, my son?

Ezkondurik eldu naiz, ama neuria
2. Frantzesa edo española duzu andria?
Frantzesa dut bañan da guziz noblia
Mortura guan eta ill egin biar **dik**
Nik **eztiet** kusi nai frantzes erreinarik
3. Andikan guan nitzen apezarengana
Apezarengana eta anaiarengana
Arek ere esan ziran amak bezala
Mortura guan eta ill egin nezala
4. Andikan guan nitzen arrebarengana
Arrebarengana eta gaztenarengana
Aretxek erran zidan biar zen bezala
Etxera karri eta maitatu nezala
Estimatzen zuela koñata bezala
5. Andria, igesi, igesi zaldien ganera
Mortura guan eta ill egin biar ***dun***
Andriak eldu dira andik eta emendik
Nere arreba Juana ezta ageri iñondik
6. Senarrak eman ziran lenbiziko kolpia
Bereala koñadu apezak aldamenetik bertzia
Oi kanabitaren puntaren zorrotza!
Usua arrapatu dio nere amari biotza

I am married, my mother
Is your wife Spanish or French?
French, but of noble blood
Take her to an isolated place and kill her
I cannot abide French royalty
I went to a priest
A priest who was also my brother
He said the same as our mother
To take her to an isolated place and kill her
Then I went to my sister
The youngest of us all
She said what should be said
To take my wife home and love her
That she will love her as a sister-in-law
Go, woman, on that horse to escape
They are going to kill you
Women are coming from here and there
My sister Juana is nowhere to be found
My husband gave me the first blow
His brother, the priest, the second
O, the sharp point of the knife!
A dove brought the heart to my mother

Powerful and vindictive, the mother in "*Agur, Agur Ama Neuria*" comes the closest Basque song gets to featuring a female antiheroine.

Overall, if we consider "All the Single Ladies" and "Love and Marriage?" together, we see that unlike the pining between lovers ("Romeo, Romeo, wherefore art thou, Romeo?") we find in English literature and in other languages, the familiar form of address rarely expresses love in Basque song. Rather, *noka* sounds the note of command with regard to whom a daughter must marry or a note of discord for what a woman or girl does or looks like. Within the marital unit, men use *noka* to express their complaints to or argue with their wives—who reciprocate in kind with *toka*. *Noka* addresses women not necessarily satisfied with their marital lot or narrates stories of women not behaving like "The Good Wife:" making merry with other men while her husband travels elsewhere or even making a cuckold of her husband and bearing a child with her lover. No dupes, these husbands know of their wives' indiscretions. Yet none can control or change his wife's behavior.

Stairway to Heaven

As discussed in chapter 2, while Roman Catholicism has reigned supreme in the Basque Country since the tenth century, its ascendency has been hard won. Protestants—Calvinists called Huguenots, more specifically—won converts in the French Basque Country (*Iparralde*) beginning in the sixteenth century, though Catholics drove them out by the end of the eighteenth. Some scholars read Basque folk tales as remnants of a matriarchal indigenous religion, given the predominance of Mari, *sorginak*, and *laminak* in these stories.[75] The priest and ethnologist José Miguel Barandiarian admitted that "the Basque Country has been evangelized and Basques are good Christians. . . . There exists, even so, cults behind the scenes, small powerful deities."[76] Unfortunately, few historical records such as diaries or personal communication exist that illuminate the interior lives of "ordinary" people. Thus, Basque song may be the genre that hews most closely to the spirituality of the average Basque. And Basque songs indicate that religious conflicts and spiritual struggles weighed heavily on the Basque soul indeed.

Table 4.5: *Noka* Songs about Christianity (N = 13)

Song Title	English Gloss	Provenance	Noka
1. *Eguen Zuri Gordetan*	Observing "Fat Thursday"	Ramona Apoita (B)	4
2. *Eihartxe eta Miñau*	Eihartxe and Miñau	Piarres T. Etxahun (Z)	10
3. *Erreginetan*	The Queen of May	Valley of Baztan (N)	3
4. *Iturengo Arotza*	The Carpenter of Ituren	Nafarroa	3
5. *Konpai Komaiak*	Godparents	IparANON	2
6. *Lheille*	Lheille	Pierre T. Etxahun (Z)	3
7. *Mendi Gaineko Aithor-Minak*	Testimony from the Mountain	Manex Etxamendi (1895)	1
8. *Oi Mirakuili Guztiz* . . .	This Tiresome Faith . . .	IparANON	6
9. *Otso Saindu*	The Wolf-Saint	IparANON	1
10. *Protestantea eta Belle Marie*	The Protestant and Lovely Marie	IparANON	6
11. *Sarako Martira*	The Martyr of Sara	Joanes Otxalde (BN), 1894	7
12. *Txulufrina Ta*	With Carnations and . . .	Francisca Irigoyen (N)	3
13. *Zelestin eta Zecilia*	St. Cecilia & St. Celestin	IparANON, 1808	15
		TOTAL	**64**

Thirteen songs use *noka* to discuss explicitly Christian topics. Most recount themes one could find in any culture steeped in the Roman Catholic tradition. Like medieval French religious dramas, "*Eihartxe eta Miñau*"[77]—a man's and woman's name, respectively—is part of a farcical song cycle sung during Carnival which precedes Lent. Piarres Topet Etxahun uses language deliberately in this parody: priests use Latin; lawyers and civil authorities use French; Satan speaks Castilian; hurlers of insults and curses uses Bearnese (a variety of Gascon spoken in southwest France). In half of the twenty verses, a man uses *noka* ten times while exchanging barbs with a woman. In "*Oi Mirakuilu Guztiz Sinheste Nekea*"[78] (This Tiresome Faith), a girl goes to pay respects to her mother's memory on the anniversary of the latter's death, only to hear the voice of her departed sister in purgatory, who advises her living sister not to take vows (for the convent) too readily.

Several of the songs in this category discuss the lives of the saints or their devotees. On "Fat Thursday," the Thursday preceding Lent, Bizkaians go house-to-house singing songs like "*Eguen Zuri Gordetan*"[79] soliciting alms. Azkue collected the words of this song from an old blind woman named Ramona Apoita of Beriz (Bizkaia). It uses *noka* to berate a woman too poor to give any alms: "***Hik*** ez ***don*** asko emango" (You won't give much). "*Erreginetan*"[80] (The Queen of May) similarly uses *noka* to dismiss "the woman who does not give alms," adding "an old dog is near her/full of white lice." This theme extends to Francisca Irigoyen's "*Txulufrina Ta*," intended to gather items for a bride's dowry; singers use *noka* to reproach a poor woman: "***Utzan utzan*** isilik/Orek ***eztin*** dirurik" (Leave her alone/She has no money).

Another subgroup of songs takes saints as their topic. "*Zelestin eta Zecilia*"[81] features a dialogue between Saints Cecilia and Celestin. "*Otso Saindu*"[82] (The Wolf-Saint) describes a parable in which a wolf transforms into a saint. And "*Iturengo Arotza*" (The Carpenter of Ituren)[83] takes a more irreverent stance on this topic: a wife chastises her husband for melting down a Saint Christopher medal (worn to protect the wearer while traveling). In a familiar pattern, the spouses use mutual *hi* while sparring. Three other songs extol Christian virtue or provide instruction in its direction. "*Konpai Komaiak*" uses birds and flowers as allegories to delineate the responsibilities of godparents. In "*Lheille*,"[84] a dying man lives after he sees an apparition of the Virgin Mary in some flowers. And in "*Mendi Gaineko Aithor-Minak*"[85] (Testimony from the Mountain), a girl's Christian parents save her from her vanity and pride.

However, the corpus also includes two songs that provide insight into the religious conflicts that beset the Basque Country in particular. "*Protestanta eta Belle Marie*,"[86] written in 1924, details a "miracle" that supposedly occurred in the Basque Country in 1829: dazzled by the wealth of a Protestant who has come to her home town of Ezpeleta (Lapurdi), the beautiful Maria "thought she was in heaven's glory" and marries him. But the songwriter makes clear that when the couple marries in "the Protestant temple/they threw their souls into hellfire."[87] The song admonishes other girls of the village to "take courage . . . don't be greedy, but beware . . . or at least marry a Catholic."[88] For "awful incidents occurred to 'those who favor Protestantism'": "seven or eight were condemned" and "they hanged a woman in Ezpeleta."[89] Returning to Belle Marie in particular, the twenty-fifth verse condemns her:

Text 4.17: Protestantea eta Belle Marie[90] (excerpt)

Neska urgulutsua, Mariaren sustengua	The girl's pride sustained Maria
Protestanten maseientzat satanez hautatua	To choose Satan like the Protestants
Zerk *habil* da zoratua, infame arnegatua	What made you crazy for such blasphemy?
Finkatu nahiz Luterren begia zer ***dun*** buruan sartua	Have Luther's views gone to your head?
Ifernutik jen munstroa	That monster from Hell
Dudarik gabe kasatu nahiz gure lege saindua	No doubt he wants to shatter our holy laws
Hik egin obren pagua Luziferrek ***zaukan*** hautatua	Lucifer will punish you for what you have done

Another song, "*Sarako Martira*,"[91] extols the bravery of a Basque girl who makes a religious choice quite the opposite of Belle Marie's. Based on a true story and written by Joannes Oxalde in 1894, it tells of fifteen-year-old Madalena Larralde of Sara (Lapurdi) who submitted to the guillotine rather than renounce her Catholic faith. French soldiers ambush Madalena when she goes for confession to Bera (in the southern Basque Country, about eight miles from her hometown); they demand (in *noka*) to know why she had gone to Spain. She tells them the truth, and they somewhat surprisingly caution her to "be quiet with that declaration . . . it would be a shame to kill someone so young."[92] She remains steadfast: "were I dead, I would say the same thing/I went to confession in Bera, that is the truth/I will not be shamed into denying it."[93] This angers the soldiers, who then tie her up and berate her for "laughing at [their] laws."[94] They mock her in *noka*:

Text 4.18: *Sarako Martira*[95] (The Martyr of Sara) (excerpt)

Saratik Donibanera, soldaduek burlaka	From Sara to Donibane, the soldiers mocked her
Badabilkate gaixoa xizpa-zurekin joka	Hitting the poor thing with the rifle butt
"Oihu egin ***zan***, ergela: Biba nazionea"	"Say it, fool: Long live the nation!"
Madalenak aldiz beti: "Bib' erlisionea"	But Madalena responded: "Long live my religion!"

Even when condemned to the guillotine, Madalena stays brave: "Everyone cried, but she sang joyfully/Her eyes facing heaven, the Salve Regina."[96] The song concludes with a lesson: "Let us, with you, learn to love the truth/In all things, whatever happens, to be aware of lies."[97] Although reminiscent of Joan of Arc, the historical Madalena was thirty-five, not fifteen.

We see that these two songs take opposing positions vis-à-vis the women around which they focus: text 4.17 condemns "Belle Marie" for becoming a Protestant, while text 4.18 celebrates Madalena for remaining Catholic. Even so, their detractors use *noka* to them in similar ways: to condemn them—to death, in Sara's case—for the religious choice they have made. Whether considered brave or cowardly, both Belle Marie and Madalena certainly exhibit personal agency, which would be lost to us if we did not seek out songs in *noka*. However, both songs ultimately favor Roman Catholicism over Protestantism. Below I examine *noka* use in songs about another belief system that possibly competes with Catholicism: witchcraft.

Ding, Dong! The Witch Is Dead

In this section, I examine *noka* songs about Mari, witches ("*sorginak*"), and sirens ("*laminak*"). One might expect a plethora of songs about these female personages given their ubiquity in Basque folklore and their propensity to use *noka* amongst themselves and to human females, as we saw in chapter 3. But table 4.6 suggests otherwise.

Table 4.6: *Noka* Songs about Witches (N = 6)

Song Title	English Gloss	Provenance	*Noka*
1. *Atzo Bilbon*	Yesterday in Bilbao	***Engracia Lazkano*** (A)	3
2. *Jaiki, Jaiki Maria*	Wake Up, Maria	Valley of Baztan (N)	1
3. *Lau Andren Besta*	Four Women's Party	J.B. Elizanburu (L), 1897	18
4. *Sardin Zestuan*	In a Sardine Basket	BizkaiaANON	2
5. *Sei Mila Demoniok*	Six Thousand Devils	***Juana Xoxua*** (Zumaia, G) 1922	2
6. *Sorginkeria*	Witchcraft	Nicolas Ormaetxea (B), 1888-1961	4
		TOTAL	30

[A = Araba]

Indeed, while some Basque songs feature *sorginak*, most in fact do not use *noka*. The one song I found that mentioned a *lamina*, a contemporary song written and recorded by Benito Lertxundi, uses no *noka*. And only one song in the entire corpus, written by Nicolas "Orixe" Ormaetxea, is about Mari. In "*Sorginkeria*" (Witchcraft), a priest suspects his maid, Katalin, of being a witch; he purposely leaves his lectionary open on the altar after Mass, for "everyone knows witches cannot leave the church when [the lectionary] is open."[98] However, Katalin tricks the altar boy into closing the book and engages in some suspicious activity upon reaching home:

Text 4.19: *Sorginkeria* ("Witchcraft")[99]

1. Katalin onek, etxera eta	This Katalin went home
Garbitzen du zartagia	Cleaned the frying pan
Debruk ere ez luke jakinen	Not even the devil knows
Zertaz egin ***dun*** basia	Of what she made her sauce
Gatz, piper, ozpin, ardangazi ta	Salt, pepper, vinegar, sorrel
Tipula-buruz josia	Mixed together with onion
Soillik palta da—ark baititu	Only one thing missing;
Sorginak—baratzuria	what witches fear—A clove of garlic
2. Jan-ondoren igurtziko du	After eating, she kneads
Aurreguneko taloaz	Into the corn tortilla from the day before
Ikatz eta kez, kedar eta autsez	Charcoal and smoke, soot and ash
Biziro mindutakoaz	To cause great harm
Aizean barna jun bear baitu	For she must fly in the wind
Axolik ez du txerloaz	Without a worry in the world
Goizeko orraztu-legea aski du	The morning wind is enough

Bost zarpillago ba doaz
3. Orraztokia berekin baitu
Pentsa-orduko, Txindokin
Sorgin guzien amari aitor
Zerk biotzean dion min
Apeza jaunak agertu dula
Meza-liburuarekin
Ortaz errian jakinen dela
Zer oillianda dan Katalin
4. Arri-jasa bat eskatzen dio
Ordubiak alderako
Esku-al ori duena baita
Mari Aundi Txindokiko
Ba ***dun***, alaba; bainan apez jaunak
Ez ***din*** itzik aterako.
Jenden aurren len bezala *adi*
Ez *au* inork usmatuko
5. Sorginen ama au, eder; buruan
Urre gorrizko orrazea
Ikatza baino beltzago ilea
Zuri-gorri larrupea
Begiak lauso detzakena da
Aren lepoko katea
Gorputza lerden, eskuak legun
Ez basajaunen andrea
6. Seda-mataza ariltzen ari da
Ari baten adarretan
Urre-adarrak zitun, azkazal
Urre-gorriak anketan
Bein edo beste nasi-bereizten
Arkitzen bazan neketan
Berak, adarrak onera ta ara
Laguntzen zion benetan
7. Ola zeudela, Donamartiko
Atsoa arri-jasa-billa
Eiheramendin Etxegaraiek
Bai omen andre abilla
Aren mendeko sorgintto bati
Autsi baitio orkatilla
Ostu nanean joan zaiola
Seaskan zeukan mutilla
8. Emezortzika seme-alaba
Emazte kaskoin aundia
Izketa adituz nor-naik usteko
Euskaldun dala garbia
Ark omen-zeukan ate-ondoan
Gorderik baratzuria
Andik anka autsi sorginak, eta
Bial zezola azurria

To carry five more like her
She has her needlecase with her
Before you know it, she's on Txindoki
And tells the mother of all witches
What her heartaches are
That the priest arrived
With the lectionary
And now the whole village will know
What a precocious young girl is Katalin
She asks for a torrent to come
Around two o'clock
As that is in the hands of
"Big Mary" of Txindoki
You shall have it, daughter, but the priest
Will have nothing to say
If you act like before with the people
No one shall suspect you
How beautiful this witches' mother:
Red-gold brush in her hair
Hair blacker than coal
With rosy skin
Eyes can be blinded
By the shine of her necklace
With her svelte body and smooth hands
She is not the wife of the Man-of the-Forest
She threads silk
Sitting on a ram
His horns made of gold
Red-gold claws on his feet
When she errs in threading
When she gets tired
The ram helps her
By tilting his head to and fro
That's how they were, when Donamarti's
Old woman came, hoping for a torrent
From Eiheramendi to Etxegarai
She is a skillful woman
Under a witch's command
For she broke her ankle
When she went to steal
A baby boy from his crib
Eighteen sons and daughters
Has the big Gascon woman
When she speaks
You'd think she was a pure Basque
She apparently has hidden
Garlic by the door
The witch broke her leg
Send her a punishment

9. Mari Aundiri oinetan musu
Emanez, gure Katalin
Orraztokia sakelan dula
Esan bino len Uitzen
Eultzi-lekura, joan ta asi da
Mintza batekin, bestekin
Nork sumatuko goiz artan bertan
Izana dala Txindokin?

Having kissed "Big Mary"'s feet
Our Katalin
Needlecase in her pocket
Goes to Uitzi
To the threshing place and begins to speak
To one person, then another
Who would have guessed that that morning
She'd been in Txindoki?

Thus, the song confirms the priest's doubts about Katalin: indeed a witch, she visits Mari—in her guise as the "Lady of Txindoki" (a mountain in Bizkaia)—who tells her how to evade the priest's suspicion in the future. So too in the song below, women are not always what they seem:

Text 4.20: *Lau Andren Besta*[100] ("Four Women's Party")

1. Iragan besta bigarrenean
Berek dakiten xoko batean
Lau andre, hirur mutxurdin
Bat alarguna, jarriak itzalean
Harri xabal bat belaunen gainean
Ari dire, ari dire trukean
2. Zer othe duten nik jakin nahi
Pitxarrarekin bertze jaun hori
Zorroa du biribila, moko mehea
Tente xutik egoiki
Xahako bat othe den nago ni
Hanpatua, hanpatua ederki
3. Jes! nik oraino zer dut ikhusten?
Zer hegalpean dute gordetzen?
Egoitza goxo hortarik, burua alto
Xahakoaz trufatzen
Bihotzez azkarrago zeren den
Kuiattoa, kuiattoa ari zen
4. Handik, ximiko, hemendik irri
Haurrak bezala jostetan ari
Gogotik ematen dute begi kolpe bat
Hegal pean denari
Hitz bat erran gogo diote sari
Beharrirat, beharrirat kuiari
5. Seira truk dira zazpietarik
Tantoz orobat bi aldetarik
Xahakoa eroria da, mokoz iphurdi
Naski odol husturik
Kuiattoa han dago etzanik
Azken hatsa, azken hatsa emanik

On the second day of the village festival
In a corner that they know
Four women, three spinsters
And a widow, sit in the shade
A flat stone across their knees
They are gambling
What wouldn't I like to know
About that man with the pitcher
With the round bag, thin beak
Standing there like a fool
I'm wondering if that's a bota bag
Nicely filled up
Jesus! What do I see now?
What's hiding in the wings [skirts]?
From that nice place
Head held high, joking
With all their hearts
Because the gourd was stronger/faster
Teasing there, laughing here
Playing like children
Taking a peek
At what's under the wings [skirts]
They'll say something later
To the gourd's ears
The seven trumps the six
Both sides get a point
The bota bag falls, upside down
Emptying its blood [wine]
The gourd is laying there
Breathing its last

6. Gezurrik gabe goazen, Maria
Eman jokoan ezti-eztia
Hurbil ***zan*** untzi beltz hori
Dezagun edan trago bat edo bi
Bihotza ***dinat*** epeltzen hasia
Harek zuen, harek zuen grazia!
7. Zahagiaren seme joria
Nun **duk** axtiko zorro lodia?
Gaizoa, lehen birundan zurgatu **dautek**
Odolaren erdia!
Orai hor ago zimurrik arpegia
Kokoriko, kokoriko jarria
8. Nahiz zeraukan azken eskua
Mariak zuen hasi gudua:
Truk, jo ***zan***! Mariak xango
Katixak xaldun, Marixunek hirua
Mari-Martin, xoratu ***zain*** burua
Lauarekin hiruaren keinua!
9. *Ago*, Maria, otoi, ixilik
Ez ***dun*** ikhusi nere keinurik
Xorta bat edanez geroz begiak ñir-ñir
Zer! Ez ***dun*** ahalkerik?
Edan ***bezaken*** azkarren hortarik
Gatilua, gatilua beterik.
10. ***Bazakinagu***, tresna makurra
Ezdunala bik hatsa laburra
Ez ***dun***, ez, ***dionan*** bezala
Huna xurgatuz
Biribildu muturra
Ez eta ere gorritu sudurra
Milikatuz, milikatuz elhurra!
11. Apho mutxurdin moko biphila
Zeren ondoan othe *habila?*
Hatz ***badun*** gibel aldean, ikhusiko ***dun***
Zenbat naizen abila
Xuhur ***badun***, *ago*, neska xirtxila
Ixil, ixil, ixil, ixil, ixila
12. Kartak utzirik, eta tantoak
Han zituzten han gero saltoak
Bakharrik hiruen kontra
Zer eginen du, Mari-Martin gaizoak?
Nahiz izan azkar zango besoak
Hartu ditu, hartu ditu paloak
13. Herriko besta arrats aphalian
Lau gatu zahar anjelusean
Bat mainguz, hirur saltoka
Sorginak pujes! zoatzila bidean
Ikusi ditut nik amets batean
Akelarre, akelarre gainean

"Let's go, Maria, no lies:
Give the sweet game
Bring me that black container
So we can take drink or two
My heart is warming up
That was tasty
Abundant son of the wineskin
Where do you keep the fat bota bag?
You poor thing, after your first turn
You drank half the blood [wine]
Now, there you are, with your wrinkled face
All curled up
At the last hand
Maria started a fight
"I trump you!" Maria had a jack,
Kathy had a horse [jack], Maria a three
Mari-Martin goes crazy
Winking with her four and three
Be quiet, Maria
Didn't you see my wink?
After taking a drink, your eyes blink
Have you no shame?
You should be able to drink
From a full glass
We know this thing's not working
Don't hold your breath
No, don't do as you say
Sucking this here
Don't turn up your snout
Or redden your nose
By licking the snow
Unmarried toad, brave beak
What are you after?
You have a finger behind you
You'll see how smart I am
If you're stingy, silly girl
Be quiet, be quiet
Leaving the cards, and the points
Later, things got jumping
One against three
What will poor Martin do?
Though his legs and arms are strong
He took his hits
Late afternoon during the village festival
Four old cats at the chiming of the angelus
One limping, three jumping—"pujes!"
—Witches going down the road
I saw them in a dream
About a coven

The women in this song engage in more pedestrian activities than Katalin in text 4.19: they drink and gamble as they play *mus*, a card game not unlike poker that involves passing signs (thus the winking and blinking). Usually played at table, players often drink during the game; success depends upon one's ability to attend to the rules and pass signs and (sometimes) hold one's liquor, simultaneously. However, several women other than the ordinary play this time: they do not play out in the open but in the shade, perhaps to stay out of view; they drink from a "black container" which could possibly be a reference to a cauldron. The tenth verse may suggest that one of these women has been transformed into some kind of animal; "*muturra*" refers to an animal's snout—although the next lines uses "*sudurra*" ("nose" for humans), indicating the temporary nature of any transformation into an animal. This reading conforms with medieval and early modern witchcraft texts that claimed the devil could transform witches into animals at will, then turn them back into their human form.[101]

By the final verse, the women transform completely: they have been turned into cats, a common manifestation for witches in Basque folklore as elsewhere. The three spinsters jump and the widow limps at the sound of the church bell chiming the "*angelus,*" "a devotion that honors the Incarnation three times a day."[102] The term "*puyes*" refers to a way to ward off witches by "crossing the fingers on both hands ("*hacer la higa*" in Castilian)."[103] The narrator softens the ominous connotations of the song by suggesting that perhaps this *akelarre* occurred only in a dream. The Holy Office provided the Spanish inquisitors of the Logroño "witches" with a questionnaire with which to interrogate suspected witches; "several of the questions were aimed at establishing whether the experiences of the witches were dreams or reality."[104] In "*Jaiki, Jaiki, Maria*,"[105] a father tells his daughter he sees a witch in the corner. She dismisses it as a dream, claiming only a kitten is there, playing. A "crazy cat" also features in Engracia Lazkano's "*Atzo Bilbon*"[106] (Yesterday in Bilbao), in which a "fancy girl/subordinate to the goat" (neska farandona/ akeran bekoki) goes into the forest to search for her husband.

However, "*Sei Mila Demoniok*"[107] (Six Thousand Demons), related by Juana Xoxua of Gipuzkoa, suggests that a girl's alliances with the devil may not always be of her own doing: six thousand demons take Katalin, "a capable girl" in a red skirt. "*Sardin Zestoan Sardine*"[108] accuses a sardine-carrying woman wearing a blue skirt of looking like a witch. It would seem that attire must be chosen carefully. When the demons hear a bird chirping and a sword being drawn, they flee for some reason to Saint Vincent.

Girls Just Wanna Have Fun

The songs in this section suggest that when girls and women engage in recreational activities their male counterparts partake in without notice, they can be accused of witchcraft.

Table 4.7: *Noka* Songs about Partying and Play (N = 13)

Song Title	English Gloss	Provenance	*Noka*
1. *Ai, Ai, Buruan Min*	Oh, I Have a Headache	M. Baluyan (Iparralde), 1858	4
2. *Aurten Arnua Merke*	This Year's Wine Is Cheap	Amantzi Urriolabeitia[109] (B), 1941	2
3. *Dantzaria*	The Dancer	Leon Elizanburu (L)	3
4. *Emakunde*	Womanhood	Nicolas Ormaetxea (B), 1888-1961	1
5. *Emazte Edalea*	A Woman Who Drinks	Jean Baptiste Elizanburu (L)	3
6. *Erri Koskor Batian*	In a Small Village	J.M. Ugalde (G)	6
7. *Gizakunde*	Incarnation	Nicolas Ormaetxea (B), 1888-1961	3
8. *Gure Gelariak*	Our Waiters	Amikuze (BN), 1922	3
9. *Kauserak*	The Bakers	IparANON	3
10. *Mendekoste Pestetan*	On Pentecost	Juan Etxamendi (BN), 1782-1879	2
11. *Nafartar Edaliak*	Drinkers from Nafarroa	BN ANON	8
12. *Orakunde*	Carnival	Nicolas Ormaetxea (B), 1888-1961	1
13. *Salbatore-Aratsean*	On St. Salvador's Afternoon	Tristan Manex (L)	9
		TOTAL	**48**

Of the thirteen songs in this subcategory, three tell stories of women who drink—usually, to excess—on religious feast days. In "*Nafartar Edaliak*,"[110] (Drinkers from Nafarroa) five young girls and a married woman goad each other to drink from the "red cup" on Saint Salvador's Day, toasting that the drink may renew them. In "*Salbatoren-Aratsean*,"[111] a mother also encourages her daughter to enjoy libations on the afternoon of Saint Salvador's day. The imbiding on this feast day is particularly ironic as Saint Salvador was renown for his austerity and fasting.

But "*Mendekoste Phestetan*,"[112] taken from a collection of songs written in the northern Basque Country, suggests that more than drunken revelry might be afoot:

Text 4.21: *Mendekoste Phestetan* (On Pentecost)

1. Mendekoste phestetan	At the festival of Pentecost
Aurthen Arneik'errekan	This year, at Arnei's river
Ixtorio bat gerthatu da	Something happened
Kasik ezpeitiot erran:	I can barely speak of it:
Bost emaztek edan dituzte	Five women drank
Hamar pint'arno betan	Ten full pints of wine
Jokhaturik kartetan	As they played cards
2. Jokua zuten florian	The game was on
Arnei Madrilenian	Arnei in Madrid
Atso gaixoek uste zuten	And the poor old women thought
Zirela zeruko lorian	They were in heaven
Saindu ororen erdian	In the midst of the saints
Bere botoilak aldian	Their bottles at their sides
Bai eta plazer handian	Having a great time
3. Batek zion bertziari:	One said to the other:
Haurra, *hire* graziari	Child, to your health
Arnono hunek alegrantzen	This little wine
Ditan bihotznua niri	Makes my heart happy
Ene plazerra hola luken	It would please me more
Banu zonbeit ogi poxi	If I had a little bread
Arno ezti huneki	With this sweet wine
4. Katrina eta Katalin	Katrina and Katalin
Auzo biak elgarrekin	Two neighbors, together
Arno edaten ari ziren	Drinking wine
Kuraia handi batekin	With gusto [with a lot of courage]
Gero ondoan bazuten	Afterwards their sides hurt
Gibel aldian zer egin	So much they knew not what to do
Bere fanfarreriekin	Because of all their partying
5. Hirugarrenak ederki	The third one
Tanteatzen omen daki	Knows well how to score points
Hamarrekuak harek zituen	She had a ten
Omen markatzen orori	She told everyone about it
Ondarrekotz nahasi zen	Then she got confused
Eta lurrerat erori	And fell to the ground
Orduan etzen egarri	Then she wasn't thirsty anymore
6. Laugarren hori zer pheza	The fourth one, what a card
Maria zapatainesa	Maria the shoemaker
Untsa esplikatzen zituen	She explained very well
Eskuara eta frantsesa	In Basque and French
Bai eta ere aisa egiten	And she easily
Bide handian esa	Travels that road
Horixe da haren letra	That is her signature

7. Bostgarren hori zoin othe da?	The fifth one, which is she?
Pentsatzeko ez da phena	To think of her is not a shame:
Garaxane gaizo horrek	That poor Garaxe
Nola ezpaituke lehena	Since she would not have the first one:
Benedika dakiola, dio,	She says she knows the blessing
Mahatsari aihena	For the one who brings
Arno ekartzen duena	Wine to the table
8. Ahuntzez jokatu eta	They played like goats
Hasi ziren kolpeka	Then started to fight
Gaston deitzen zen guarda bat	A policemen called Gaston
Kanpotik jinik lasterka	Came in from outside
Hak partitu izan zituen	He separated them
Ez uste bezain aisa	Not as easily as he'd expected
Arrazoinik ezin pasa	Unable to let it go
9. Zuk' ere, etxek' anderia	You, too, woman-of-the-house
Erran beharzu egia	You must tell the truth
Solas hortan zu othe zinen	Were you the one
Horien buruzagia?	Spreading such rumors?
Bost emaztek egiteko	For five women
Horixe da komedia!	To cause such a ruckus
Hurran baitzen zahagia!	That was quite the wineskin!

"*Mendekoste Phestetan*" resembles "*Lau Andren Besta*" (text 4.20) in several ways. It too, narrates the verbal jousting, drinking, and ribbing between women and on Pentecost, no less, "popularly regarded as the birthday of the [Catholic] church" as it commemorates the "descent of the Holy Spirit upon the Apostles."[113] The final verses strongly hint at witchcraft: one of the women "says she knows the blessing/for the one who brings wine to the table"[114] and then they play "like goats,"[115] which could be an allusion to witchcraft even though "*ahuntza*" (female goat) is used rather than "*akerra*" (male goat). One of the participants in this drinking fest is named Katalin, a common name given to witches in Basque song, as we saw in text 4.19 above.

Another song suggests that accusations of witchcraft are not the only possible outcomes of excessive drinking:

Text 4.22: *Aurten Arnua Merke Da*[116] (This Year's Wine Is Cheap)

Erranen ***diñat***, erranen,	I will say it, I will say it
Enun ixilik egonen:	I will not be quiet:
Dupela pian zortzen den haurra	A child born under a wine vat
Ez dela aguador jinen	Will not become a water carrier
Zeren aitak eta amak ere	Because the father and mother too
Afizione baitzuten	Had a liking [for drink]

Other songs about women drinking, however, do not cast such aspersions. Three songs describe girls flirting with boys at village festivals: "*Gizakunde*",[117] "*Emakunde*",[118] and "*Orakunde*" (these constitute part of the "Carnival" cycle, alongside "*Sorginkeria*"[119] (text 4.18; written by Oxobi). "*Gure Gelariak*"[120] (Our Waiters) expresses concern about the virtue of girls who enjoy drinking and dancing too much. Yet "*Erri Koskor Batean*"[121] (In a Small Village) portrays four women drinking while playing *mus*, without suggesting they are witches. Other *noka* songs in this category feature girls or women who drink when they should be doing something more productive. "*Ai, Ai, Buruan Min*"[122] (Oh, I Have a Headache) and "*Dantzaria*"[123] (The Dancer) call on girls to drink or dance, even though they had used headaches to avoid work that morning. In "*Kauserak*" (The Bakers)[124] three sisters party together while their husbands are away; the "drinking woman" of "*Emazte Edalea*"[125] does so as well, seemingly indifferent to the fact her husband and children starve while she imbibes.

These Boots Were Made for Walking

Alcoholic beverages appear in more mundane contexts as well; they are among the many items in daily life that some *noka* songs discuss.

Table 4.8: Pedestrian Uses of *Noka* in Song (N = 15)

Song Title	English Gloss	Provenance	*Noka*
1. *Agur Marie*	Hail, Mary	***Francisca Iribaren*** (Baraibar, N)	2
2. *Ahizpa Nahi Duna*	Sister, Do You Want to Trade?	(Ligi, Z) ANON	2
3. *Alarguntza . . .*	Widowhood . . .	Mañex Etchamendy (BN)	3
4. *Aldaztorrean*	In the Tower of Aldaz	***Guillerma Akaregi*** (B*)*	6
5. *Aldean Degu Eguna*	A Day to Ourselves	BizkaiANON	1
6. *Ama, Ene Anaiak*	What's Wrong With My Brother?	IparANON	11
7. *Ardiak Yo Nau*	A Sheep Kicked Me	***Carmen Mendiluze*** (G)	1
8. *Dugun Edan eta Edan*	We Drink and Drink	Piarres Ibarrart (L), 1921	4
9. *Eztinat Iruin*	I Cannot Manage . . .	Azpilkueta (N), 1919	3
10. *Gure Etxean Lakaraz*	Tough Times at Home	***Francisca Irigoyen,*** (N)	1
11. *Hauzeko Anderia*	The Neighbor Woman	IparANON	1
12. *Katalin Tirun*	Catherine: Ring, Ring	***Mauricia Agare*** (N)	2
13. *Maitenaren . . . Kexu*	Maitena's Complaints	IparANON	2
14. *Sail Au Egin*	Do This Task	ANON, 1922	2
15. *Zinzikitrun*	Zinzikitrun	***Mme. Harambure*** (BN)	1
		TOTAL	**42**

Songs in this category portray women engaging in everyday activities at the market or at home. "*Aldean Degu Eguna*" (A Day to Ourselves)[126] describes a family gathering, in Castilian as well as Basque, to welcome an uncle who has been traveling abroad. In Guillerma Akaregi's "*Aldaztorrean*" (In the Tower of Aldaz)[127] a pregnant woman loses most of her family in a shipwreck; she rushes to claim the dowry hidden in the ship's cupboard. "*Ahizpa Nahi Duna*,"[128] (Sister, Do You Want to Trade?) from Ligi (Zuberoa), asks a woman if she will give the speaker wine in exchange for some piglets yet unborn. In "*Katalin Tirun*" (Catherine: Ring, Ring),[129] courtesy of Mauricia Agare of Nafarroa, two women negotiate the prices of sardines and headscarves. In "*Dugun Edan eta Edan*,"[130] (We Drink and Drink) a man asks a woman for a drink to "cure" his hangover. In "*Sail Au Egin*" (Do This Task)[131] a man asks a woman to console him for some unspecified trouble as they carry out some task. "*Zinzikitrun*,"[132] written by Madam Harambure from Donibane Garazi (St. Jean de Luz, Baxe Nafarroa), simply laments, perhaps to herself: "This Year's Wine Is Pricey" (*Haurten Arno Onak Sosak Balio* ***Tin***).[133] Three other songs use *noka* to express distress. "***Eztinat*** *Iruin*" (I Cannot Manage) from Nafarroa makes the general complaint that "I'm having some tough times today."[134] "*Ardiak Yo Nau*,"[135] by Carmen Mendiluze of Gipuzkoa, specifies the cause of a complaint: a sheep kicks a woman and she fears she will die from her injuries. And in Francisca Irigoyen's "*Gure Etxean Lakaraz*" (Tough Times at Home), a woman rues the money she has squandered but then admits she has saved a few coins no one else knows about. Finally, "*Maitenaren Etxekuak Kexu*" (Maitena's Complaints)[136] enumerates a woman's grievances about her household, including the death of her mother twenty years before.

Two other songs use *noka* in unusual ways. As demonstrated in chapter 2, Catholic texts use *noka* almost exclusively to metaphorically accuse cities of harlotry for their disloyalty to God; certainly, *noka* never addresses the most holy female personage in

Catholicism: the Virgin Mary. So it was quite a surprise to find this gem, recounted by Francisca Iribarren of Nafarroa:

Text 4.23: *Agur Marie*[137] (Hail, Mary)

Agur Marie	Hail Mary
Ederra ***den*** arie	The thread is beautiful
Graziaz betie	Full of grace
Dena orapiloz betie	Full of knots
Jauna dago zurekin	The Lord is with you
Atorra ederra ***din*** berekin	The fine shirt is with Him

Alas, a closer look reveals that this *noka* song does not glorify the Virgin Mary, which would have been a radical departure from Catholic pronominal norms indeed. Rather, according to Azkue who collected this song in 1922, this song about weavers uses *noka* to crack wise at an ill-formed thread.

I would like to conclude this section with songs that use *noka* to portray human mothers in everyday contexts. "*Alarguntsa Errekardia*" concerns a hard-working widow who travels far from town to town to provide for her children. When a snowstorm delays her return home, her youngest daughter worries about her:

Text 4.24: *Alarguntsa Errekardia* (Widowhood of 'River-sheep')

Ah! Bidea luze ***dun***	Ah! The road is long
Gaua ere ilun!	And the night, dark
Amaren harrabotsik	The capture of a mother
Ez entzuten nihun!	Is unheard of
Bortuak gora ***ditun***	The doors are high
Han paretik legun	The walls, smooth
Elurretik bizirik	From the snow, alive
Jalgiko ahal ***dun***	Will you emerge?

At first blush, it might seem that the daughter uses *noka* to her mother, which would be very unusual usage. However, it is also possible that the young girl uses *noka* in thinking these thoughts to herself.

Finally, the song below uses *noka* by a mother to a daughter not to chide her about some misbehavior or misguided choice of beaux, as we have seen throughout this chapter, but rather to console her daughter for quite another kind of misfortune:

Text 4.25: *Ama, Ene Anaiak Egun Zer Othe Du*[138] (Mother, What's Wrong with my Brother?)

1.Ama, ene anaiak egun zer othe du	Mother, what's wrong with my brother?
Begitarte guzia baitzaio ilhundu?	His face has darkened
Sehaska huni buruz kantu eta kantu	I'm singing away by his crib
Irri baten aiduruz astia dut galdu	I've been waiting for him to smile
2.Ama, gure Battitak deus eztu erraiten	Mother, our Battita says nothing
Orai geldi-geldia hortxet da egoiten	Now, he lies there without moving
Hatsa urbildik ere ez diot entzuten	I do not hear him breathing
Hila dela diote, nik ez dakit zer den	I am not sure but fear he is dead
3.Ama, zer dut ikusten? Zu ere nigarrez?	Mother, do I see you crying too?
Zorigaitza etxerat jin zaiku arabez?	Has misfortune come into our house?
Ez dakit nigar egin behar diotanez	I don't know if I should be crying
Zuk erradazu, Ama, garbiki bai'al'ez	Tell me, Mother, yes or no
4.Ez haurra, ez ***dun*** behar nigarrik ixuri	No child, do not shed tears
Zorigaitzik ***etzaion*** gertatu nehori	No misfortune has struck anyone
Hire anaia orai zeruan ***dun*** ari	Your brother is now in heaven
Kantatzen errepikan ospe Jainkoari	Singing praises to God
5.Sehaska hotz hunetan gorphutz huts bat baizik	There's only a body in this crib
Ez ***dun*** orai gelditzen; ez ***dun*** bertze fitsik	Nothing else is here
Arima ilki zion Jaun goikoak goizik	His spirit has gone up to God
Aingeruen gorthean hartu ***din*** jagoitik	Taken up by angels
6.Haurra, ikusi ***dun*** joan den egunean	Child, the other day did you see
Pinpirin-arroltze bat zur horren gainean	A cocoon on that piece of wood?
Kuxkua hor utzirik apexa beha zan	From that cocoon, a bee was waiting
Hegaldaka johaki ederrik airean	To fly out into the air
7.Hala hala Battittak gorputza utzi ***din***	Just so did Battita leave his body
Gero joan ***dun*** zerurat eder eta arin	And go to heaven, light and beautiful
Irriz hegaldatu ***dun*** eta lehiarekin	Laughing as he flies
Handik, gutaz gaixoa oi! urrikal dadin	Thinking of us in glory
8.Ama, nahi nintzake apexa bezala	Mother, I would like to be like the bee
Agurka lorez-lore polliki dabila	Flitting from flower to flower
Zeruko lilietan ibiltzekotz hola	To be among heaven's flowers
Biak Battittarekin Jaunak deit gitzala	That God would call us to be with Battita

Here, at last, we see *noka* used in ways akin to other familiar forms: in an emotional moment, as a mother consoles her daughter about a baby's sudden death. As *noka* (and its male counterpart, *toka*) was once the only singular familiar pronoun in Basque—and the death of infants, unfortunately, quite common—one can imagine the ubiquity of this kind of usage; yet only this song uses *noka* in such a poignant scene. In the section below, we shall see that *noka* songs convey other heart-rending news as well.

My Country 'Tis of Thee

Love of the Basque Country and battles waged upon it comprise common themes in Basque song. Perhaps reflecting that battles and wars as well as the opportunities to leave the homeland for adventures elsewhere have historically been male perogatives, only four songs on these topics use *noka*.

Table 4.9: *Noka* Songs of Land and War (N = 4)

Song Title	**English Gloss**	**Provenance**	**Noka**
1. *Bereterretxen Khantoria*	The Song of Bereterretxe	Zuberoa, 1449	8
2. *Emazurtz*	Orphan	Gabriel Aresti (Bilbao, B)	20
3. *Errege Jan*	King John	IparANON	3
4. *Itziarren Semea*	Son of Itziar	Telesforo Mónzon (Bergara, G)	4
		TOTAL	**35**

The first two songs that use *noka* with regard to the land or country come from much earlier centuries from the northern side of Basque Country.[139] In "Errege Jan," King John returns home wounded from war, the day after his wife has borne him a son. He goes directly to his deathbed, asking his mother not to tell his wife of his imminent death. When the wife hears the servants weeping, the mother—using *noka*—lies that they mourn the death of a gray horse. When the wife hears singing for his funeral march outside, the mother lies that merely a procession passes by. The wife inevitably learns that her husband has died, and she asks to be buried with him in his grave.

The second of the *noka* songs in this category is also the oldest song in my corpus. Written in 1449 in the Zuberoan dialect, it recounts the assassination of a horseman named Bereterretxe:

Text 4.26: *Bereterretxen Khantoria*[140] (The Song of Bereterretxe)

1. Haltzak eztü bihotzik	The alder tree has no heart
Ez gaztanberak ezürrik	Fresh soft cheese, no bones
Enian uste erraiten ziela	I never used to believe
Aitunen semek gezürrik	That a nobleman would have lied
2. Andozeko ibarra	The valley of Andoz
Ala zer ibar lüzia!	What a long valley!
Hiruetan ebaki zaitan	My heart has been split in three
Armarik gabe bihotza	Without the use of my arms

3. Bereterretxek oheti
Neskatuari eztiki:
Abil, eta so egin ***ezan***
Gizonaik denez ageri?
4. Neskatuak berhala
Ikhusi zian bezala
Hiru dozena bazabiltzala
Bortha batetik bestila
5. Bereterretxek leihoti
Jaun Kuntiari goraintzi:
Ehun behi bazereitzola
Beren zezena ondoti
6. Jaun Kuntiak berhala
Traidore batek bezala:
Bereterretxe, aigü borthala:
Utzuliren hiz berhala
7. Ama, indazüt athorra
Mentüraz sekulakoa!
Bizi denak orhoit dü
Bazko-gaiherdi ondua!
8. Heltü nintzan Ligira
Buneta erori lürrera
Buneta erori lürrera eta
Eskurik ezin behera
9. Heltü nintzan Ezpeldoira
Han haritx bati esteki
Han haritx bati esteki
Eta bizia hesitan idoki
10. Mariasantzen lasterra
Bostmendietan behera!
Bi belhainez herrestan sartu da
Lakharri-Büstanobi
11. Büstonabi gasita
Ene anaie maitia
Hitzaz hunik ez baldinbada
Ene semia juan da
12. Arreba, *ago* ixilik!
Ez othoi egin nigarrik!
Hiri semia bizi bada,
Mauliala ***dun*** juanik
13. Marisantzen lasterra
Jaun Kuntiaren borthala!
Ai, ei, eta, jauna
Nun düzie ene seme galanta?
14. ***Hik*** *bahiena* semerik
Bereterretxez besterik?
Ezpeldoi-altian ***dün*** hilik
Abil, ***eraikan*** bizirik

From his bed, Bereterretxe
Says to the girl, sweetly:
Go and see
If any man has come for me
Right away, she looks
And sees
Three dozen men going
From door to door
From the window, Bereterretxe
Hails the Count, wishing him well
Offering a hundred cows
And their bull
Right away, the Count
Like a traitor:
Bereterretxe, go to the door
You'll return right away
Mother, let me have a shirt
Perhaps it will be my last!
All those living will remember
The morrow of Easter last
I was coming to Ligi
And my beret fell to the ground
Yes, my beret fell to the ground
I couldn't reach it
I was coming to Ezpeldo
Going along, nice and slow
Going along, nice and slow
And left my life behind
Mariasan ran downhill
Up and down five mountains!
Until she arrived, crawling
In Lakharri-Büstanobi
Young Büstonabi
My dear brother
There are no words for this
My son is gone
Sister, be quiet!
Please do not cry
If your son is alive
He has gone to Maule
Mariasan ran
To the Count's door
Ai, ai! My Lord
Where is my beautiful son?
Do you have a son
Other than Bereterretxe
He is dead on Ezpeldo's altar
Go, raise him up if you can

15. Ezpeldoiko jentiak	The people of Ezpeldo
Ala sendimentu-gabiak!	Have they no feelings?
Hila hain hüilan ükhen	A dead man in their midst
Eta deüsere etzakienak!	And they know nothing of it!
16. Ezpeldoiko alhaba	Daughter of Ezpeldo
Margarita deitzen da:	Margarita is her name:
Bereterretxen odoletik	Bereterretxe's blood
Ahurka biltzen ari da	She's trying to gather it with her hands
17. Ezpeldoiko bukhata	The end of Ezpeldoi
Ala bukhata ederra!	What a fine end!
Bereterretxen athorretarik	From Bereterretxe's shirt
Hirur dozena ümen da	Have sprung three dozen

Many Basque songbooks document this song, yet the use of *noka* to deliver the terrible news of a fatal blow to a woman's loved one has gone unremarked.

Indeed, it was an overtly political song that was my first introduction to *noka* in lyrics, though I was unaware of it at the time. *"Itziarren Semea"* is based on the arrest and torture of Andoni Arrizabalaga, a political activist against the Franco regime in the 1960s. Andoni's mother (Miren Basterretxea) told the story to Telesforo Monzón (1904-1981), a Basque minister-in-exile in *Iparralde* (northern Basque Country) at the time.

Text 4.27: *Itziarren Semeak* ("Son of Itziar")

1. Itziarren semeak	The son of Itziar
Ez du laguna salatzen . . .	Doesn't denounce his friends
Eta zakurren aurrean	And when confronting the dogs
Tinko ta ixilik egoiten.	Silently stands firm
2. Itziarren semea: hori **duk** mutila!	Son of Itziar—what a young man!
Nihor salatu baino nahiago du hila	He'd rather die than denounce anyone
Harro egon liteke Maji neskatila	Maji should be proud
Espetxetik jali ta joanen zaio bila!	She will go to him when he gets out of prison
Maji neskatila, hori ***dun*** mutila!	Maji, my girl, there you have your boy!
Nihor salatu baino nahiago du hila!	He'd rather die than denounce anyone
3. Haurra zer egin haute hola agertzeko?	Child, what did they do to you that you turn up like that?
Ama, jo egin naute mintza arazteko	Mother, they beat me to make me talk
Izenik eman al **duk**? Esan **zak** egia!	Did you give up any names? Tell the truth!
Ez ama, ez dut eman! Jali naiz garbia!	No, mother, I didn't! I left with a clean conscience
Jali *haiz* garbia?	You left with a clean conscience?
Bai ama, egia!	Yes, that's the truth!
Ta amak eskeini zion klabelin gorria[141]	And Mother asked him for a red carnation

4. Itziarren semea: hori **<u>duk</u>** mutila!
Nihor salatu baino nahiago du hila
Harro egon liteke Maji neskatila
Espetxetik jali ta joanen zaio bila!
Maji neskatila, hori ***dun*** mutila!
Nihor salatu baino nahiago du hila!
5. Zazpi gizon nituen joka inguruan
Makilaz hartu naute ostikoz lurrean

Bainan nik ez dut eman
Lagunen izenik!
Ta hantxe galditu dira
Fitsik jakin barik!
6. Lau aldiz sartu naute urean burua
Zangotik euki naute zintzilikatua
Bainan nik ez dut eman lagunen izenik
Ta hantxen gelditu dira filxik jakin barik!
Zangotik zintzilik, ni beti ixilik!
Ta hantxen gelditu dira fitxik jakin barik!
7. Itziarren semea: hori **<u>duk</u>** mutila!
Nihor salatu baino nahiago du hila
Harro egon liteke Maji neskatila
Espetxetik jali ta joanen zaio bila!
Maji neskatila, hori ***dun*** mutila!
Nihor salatu baino nahiago du hila!
8. Izerdia ta odola burutik behera
Ezpainak urratu ta azazkalak atera
Bainan nik ez dut eman lagunen izenik
Ta hantxen gelditu dira fitxik jakin barik!
Odolez beterik, ni beti ixilik!
Ta hantxen gelditu dira fitxik jakin barik!
9. Itziarren semea: hori **<u>duk</u>** mutila!
Nihor salatu baino nahiago du hila
Harro egon liteke Maji neskatila
Espetxetik jali ta joanen zaio bila!
Maji neskatila, hori ***dun*** mutila!
Nihor salatu baino nahiago du hila!
10. Itziarren semeak ez du laguna salatzen
Eta zakurren aurrean Tinko ta ixilik egoiten
Espetxerat igorri dute
Amak ez du ezagutu
Ta Majik, pulliki pulliki
Eman dioska bi musu.

Son of Itziar—what a young man!
He'd rather die than denounce anyone
Maji should be proud
She will go to him when he gets out of prison
Maji—there you have a boy!
He'd rather die than denounce anyone
Seven men surrounded me and beat me
They beat me with sticks and kicked me on the ground
But I didn't give up
My friends' names!
And they were left there
Learning nothing!
Four times they dunked my head in water
They strung me upside down
But I didn't give up my friends' names
And they were left there, learning nothing!
I hung there upside down, but I stayed silent!
And they were left there, learning nothing!
Son of Itziar—there you have a boy!
He'd rather die than denounce anyone
Maji should be proud
She will go to him when he gets out of prison
Maji—there you have a boy!
He'd rather die than denounce anyone
Sweat and blood dripped from my head
My lips torn and my nails ripped out
But I didn't give up my friends
And they learned nothing at all!
Dripping with blood, I stayed silent!
And they learned nothing at all!
Son of Itziar—what a young man!
He'd rather die than denounce anyone
Maji should be proud
She will go to him when he gets out of prison
Maji—there you have a boy!
He'd rather die than denounce anyone
Itziar's son doesn't denounce his friends
And confronted by the dogs, silently stays firm
They took him to jail
His mother didn't recognize him
And Maji, very gently
Gave him two kisses

Growing up, I was oblivious to the real significance of the lyrics and just sang happily along to the peppy version popularized by Pantxoa Carrere and Peio Ospital, whose soundtracks infused my childhood.

It is perhaps fitting that I close this chapter with a final political song that uses *noka* to address the Basque Country itself. Like the many examples discussed in chapter 2, this is an example of "prosopopeia" (or "apostrophe"), addressing an inanimate object as if it were a living being. Unlike the passage from Duvoisin's 1865 Old Testament that used *noka* to disparage the cities it referenced, however, Gabriel Aresti (1933-1975) uses *noka* to address the Basque Country in loving, even plaintive, terms:

Text 4.28: *Emazurtz* ("Orphan")

1. Emazurtz jaio *hintzen*	You were born an orphan
Lurraren erdira	In the middle of the land
Pobreen esperanztak	The hopes of the poor
Beneten zer dira?	What are they, really?
Ama urrikariak	Your poor mother
Hala ***zinan*** erran	Said it to you this way
Esperantza guztiak	That all our hopes
Hil zirela gerran	Died in the war
2. Baina inoren zorrik	But no one's debts
Ez ***dun*** ordainduko	Will you pay
Eure etorkizunak	Your future
Ditun apainduko	You will arrange
3. Sufritua ***giauden***	We suffered
Hamaika gosete	So many famines
Ez genien sabela	Our bellies
Alimentuz beta	Were not full
4. Beti gau eta egun	All day and night
Gogorrik lanean	We work hard
Jornal benetan pobre	In a struggle
Baten afanean	For truly miserly wages
5. Ezkondu *hintzenean*	When you got married
Bost gona *hituen*	You had five skirts
Bi *bahituan* jarri	You wore two
Bi saldu *hintuen*	You sold two
Soinean ***dunan*** hori	That skirt you have on
Diagon zaharra	Is old
Berriak erosteko	To buy new ones
Esperantza txarra	Your hopes are dim
6. Haurtxo bat sabelean	A child in your belly
Beste bat besoen	Another in your arms

Senarra erbestean
Artoa hauzoan
Hiru hilendi kentsu
Suaren ondoan
Beste argirik ez ***dun***
Hiretzat munduan
7. *Hi haiz* Euskal Herria
Herri nekatua
Inork ezagutzen du
Hire bekatua?
Baina inoren zorrik
Ez ***dun*** ordainduko
Heure etorkizunak
Ditun apainduko

A husband in exile
The neighborhood's corn
Three smoky embers
Beside the fire
There is no other light
For you in the world
You are the Basque Country
A weary country
Does anyone know
What your sin in?
But no one's debts
Will you pay
Your future
You will arrange

The band Oskorri familiarized fans in both *Euskal Herria* and the diaspora with Aresti's wistful words. To my knowledge, this is the first work to fully acknowledge its frequent and affirming uses of *noka* in doing so.

Conclusion

I began this chapter by outlining the social customs and legal dictates that have constrained girls and women from participating in—much less, producing—Basque song until the last few decades. Indeed, when women and girls do appear in song, they do so in songs produced almost entirely by men. And in those songs, women and girls engage primarily in passive or "traditional" roles. But if we take a look at the songs that use *noka*—whether proffered by women or men—we see not only more varied images of the female person but also more complex uses of the female pronoun, *noka*. A goodly number of the 125 *noka* songs discussed in this chapter echo the negative usages we saw in the Catholic texts discussed in chapter 2, that is, the use of *noka* to chastise or insult a female addressee.

The majority of these songs, however, use *noka* for a much wider range of purposes: to offer advice, to pine for a lover or loved one lost, to console the grieving, to condemn the living, to show solidarity, to exchange barbs, to comment on mundane activities. These songs feature females doing some surprising or "untraditional" things: cavorting with men other than their husbands, standing up to abusive or hard-drinking husbands, fending off unwanted advances, and vehemently negotiating potential mates. Girls and women resist the expectation that they be dutiful wives and daughters, finding ways to party or drink instead of working. Yet other songs sing the praises of women or girls who hold fast to "traditional" religious values, extolling them for their pious devotion—even to the point, in one case, of martyrdom. *Noka* songs do not always portray females in positive ways, yet they provide a more complete picture of Basque womanhood than the musical canon usually presents.

Further, like the folktales discussed in chapter 3, these songs provide evidence of the role women have played as creators of Basque culture. Of the 125 songs that use *noka*, 20 were told or written by women. While this only represents 16 percent of the total as compared to the 43 percent of songs (N = 52) attributed to men, it still compares favorably to the representation of women authors of the biblical materials discussed in chapter 2, all of whom were men. However, as indicated in tables 4.1–4.9, the provenance of many of these songs (N = 53, or 43 percent) was either "Anonymous" or had no attribution at all. As I gathered and researched these songs, I was often haunted by Virginia Woolf's famous line: "I would venture to guess that Anon, who wrote so many poems without signing them, was often a woman."[142] Given that female participation in singing Basque songs was proscribed by custom or overtly forbidden by law, would women (or girls) who wrote them be eager to claim their authorship? Would they fear censure for daring to write the verses they were not even supposed to sing? Songs have perhaps been (and continue to be) the most accessible venue for transmitting Basque language and culture. Even those who could not read or write could learn these songs by ear; Basque speakers who have not had the opportunity to become literate in *Euskera* can learn about their culture and history through singing or listening to these songs. To the extent that women have brought some of them into being, it is unfortunate that their roles in doing so have not been fully acknowledged.

We may never know the extent to which women and girls authored Basque songs. But we do have a record of songs directed to a female addressee, as they use *noka* in their lyrics. It may be that the 125 songs with *noka* comprise but a fraction of the total corpus of Basque song; yet they provide examples of female agency and female identity that we would not otherwise have. We cannot know whether these songs represent actual behaviors by women and girls and they can be interpreted in many ways, whether fact or fiction. The girls or women resisting "traditional" roles can be read (or heard) as role models—or as cautionary tales. Even so, the actions of the women and girls in these songs deserve to be deliberated upon if we are to more fully understand Basque culture and gender roles—and the role of songs in producing and contesting them.

Notes

1 Aulestia, *Improvisational Poetry.*

2 Ibid., 69.

3 Mikel Oteiza and Andréa Bidart-Oteiza assisted me in collecting some of these materials, for which I thank them.

4 Amuriza, *Bizkaiko Bertsogintza I-II;* Ansorena, *Cancionero Vasco and Euskal Kantak*; Arbelbide, *Piarres Topet Etxahun*; Azkue, *Cancionero Popular Vasca*; *The Alan Lomax Collection*; Manterola, *Cancionero Vasco*; Mujika, *Euskal Lirika Tradizionala I—IV*; Nehor and Dufau, "Aitak Erran Dio Alabari"; Ormaetxea, *Euskaldunak Poema*; Riezu, ed., *Cancionero Vasco P. Donostia*, vols. 6, 7, and 9; Urkizu, *Bertsolaritzaren Historia I-II*; Urkizu et al., *Historia de la Literatura Vasca*; Zavala, *Euskal Erromatzeak*; Zavala, *Ezkondu Bearreko Bertsoak*; Zavala, *Neska-Mutilen Arteko Bertsoek.*

5 When date of song's origin is unknown, dates of author's life are provided, when available.

6 Riezu, ed., *Cancionero Vasco P. Donostia*, vol. 7, 657.

7 Urkizu, *Bertso Zahar eta Berri Zenbaiten Bilduma*, 122–129.

8 Amuriza, *Bizkaiko Bertsogintza II*, 491–492.

9 Azkue, *Cancionero Popular Vasco III*, 43.

10 Riezu, ed., *Cancionero Vasco P. Donostia, Volumen VI*, 299–300. Gathered from the village of Hernani on September 15, 1912.

11 Azkue, *Cancionero Popular Vasca II*, 65–66.

12 Urkizu, *Bertsolaritzaren Historia . . . Kantak 2*, 757–758. 757–

13 Ibid., 758.
14 Azkue, *Cancionero Popular Vasca II*, 943–944.
15 Azkue, *Cancionero Popular Vasca I*, 154.
16 Urkizu, *Bertsolaritzaren Historia . . . Kantak 2*, 658.
17 Riezu, ed., *Cancionero Vasco P. Donostia*, vol. 9, 1928. Donostia collected this dance in August, 1918.
18 Arbelbide, *Piarres Topet Etxahun.*
19 Zavala, *Euskal Erromantzeak,* 326.
20 Riezu, ed., *Cancionero Vasco P. Donostia*, volumen VII, 605. Collected from the parish priest of Arrute on September 8, 1923.
21 Ibid.
22 Zavala, *Euskal Erromantzeak*, 380–381. However, Zavala notes that he found this song in "the late J.A. Donostia's papers."
23 Urkizu, *Bertsolaritzaren Historia: Lapurdi, Baxanabarre eta Zuberoako Bertso eta Kantak 2*, 621.
24 Zavala, *Euskal Erromantzeak,* 72–73. Zavala notes that Euloji Gorrotxatea learned this song from his mother.
25 Ibid., 35. A version of this song can be found on the CD (www.ilovenoka.com) *Bi Ahizpak.*
26 Nehor and Dufau, *Gure Herria*, 1.
27 Riezu, ed., *Cancionero Vasco P. Donostia*, vol. 7, 752. Donostia notes that he collected this "humorous" song from a sixty-six-year-old singer from Liginaga (Zuberoa) on September 19, 1927.
28 Amuriza, *Bizkaiko Bertsogintza I*, 186–187.
29 Urkizu, *Bertsolaritzaren Historia . . . Kantak 1*, 641.
30 Azkue, *Cancionero Popular Vasco VIII*, 736–737. Collected on January 15, 1913, from the village of Sara.
31 Riezu, ed., *Cancionero Vasco P. Donostia*, vol. 6, 157.
32 Urkizu, *Bertsolaritzaren Historia . . . Kantak 1*, 627.
33 Amuriza, *Bizkaiko Bertsogintza I*, 571; cf. Urkizu, *Bertsolaritzaren Historia . . . Kantak 1*, 539 for version without *noka.*
34 Zavala, *Ezkondu Bearreko Bertsoak*, 45–46.
35 Zavala, *Neska-Mutilen Arteko Bertsoek,* 81–83. Zavala notes he collected these verses from anonymous papers in a Zarautz farmhouse.
36 Zavala, *Ezkondu Bearreko Bertsoak,* 11–18.
37 Azkue, *Cancionero Popular Vasca II,* 58–59. A version of this song can be found on the CD, "NOKATU": www.ilovenoka.com.
38 Urkizu, *Bertsolaritzaren Historia . . . Kantak 1*, 376–378.
39 Amuriza, *Bizkaiko Bertsogintza I,* 555–557. Amuriza notes that this song was collected from "a young boy from Ermua" in 1908.
40 Urkizu, *Bertsolaritzaren Historia . . . Kantak 1*, 451–452.
41 Zavala, *Neska-Mutilen Arteko Bertsoek,* 97–99. A version of this song can be heard on the CD "Bi Ahizpak": www.ilovenoka.com.
42 Urkizu, *Bertsolaritzaren Historia . . . Kantak 1*, 460. Collected from Graziosa

Zabalo of Istiriz (Baxe Nafarroa).

43 Zavala, *Neska-Mutillen Arteko Bertsoak,* 131–133.

44 Riezu, ed., *Cancionero Vasco P. Donostia,* vol. 9, 31–32. According to Donostia, this song is a variant of "mutil dantza" (boys' dance) from 1943.

45 Azkue, *Cancionero Popular Vasco I,* 148–149.

46 Riezu, ed., *Cancionero Vasco P. Donostia,* vol. 6, 32–33. A version of this song can be heard on NOKA's CD, "NOKATU:" www.ilovenoka.com.

47 Arbelbide, *Piarres Topet Etxahun,* 36. A version of this song can be heard on the "Bi Ahizpak" CD: www.ilovenoka.com

48 Zavala, *Euskal Erromantzeak,* 50. According to Zavala, this song is also known as "Juan Almendu's Lamentation."

49 "Xarpa" refers to a "cloth that impedes procreation, used for animals" (Azkue, *Diccionario Vasco-Española-Frances,* 585).

50 Azkue, *Cancionero Popular Vasco II, 128–129.* His informant Leoncio Ituralde was from Elizondo in the Valley of Baztan, Nafarroa.

51 Azkue, *Cancionero Popular Vasco III,* 1088.

52 Bullen, "Gender and Identity in the Alarde," 64.

53 Urkizu, *Bertsolaritzaren Historia . . . Kantak 2,* 111–112. This song was translated by Alan R. King.

54 Ibid., 126–127. NOKA has recorded a version of this song: www.ilovenoka.com

55 Ibid.,122–123.

56 De Rijk, "Familiarity or Solidarity," 377.

57 Urkizu, *Bertsolaritzaren Historia . . . Kantak 1,* 27. Disturbingly, there is a category of "laughter and sexual touching" songs ("*Irri eta Zirri*") into which this song falls.

58 Riezu, ed., *Cancionero Vasco P. Donostia,* vol. 1, 256; and/or Urkizu, *Bertsolaritzaren Historia: Lapurdi, Baxanabarre eta Zuberoako Bertso eta Kantak 1,* 665–666.

59 Urkizu, *Bertsolaritzaren Historia . . . Kantak 1,* 439–440. A version of this song can be heard on the CD, "NOKA": www.ilovenoka.com.

60 Arbelbide, *Piarres Topet Etxahun,* 38.

61 Riezu, ed., *Cancionero Vasco P. Donostia,* vol. 6, 194–195.

62 Azkue, *Cancionero Popular Vasco II,* 995–996.

63 Ibid., 120–122.

64 Ibid., 127–128.

65 Riezu, ed., *Cancionero Vasco P. Donostia,* vol. 6, 189. Transcribed by P. Modesto Lecumberri.

66 Urkizu, *Bertsolaritzaren Historia . . . Kantak 1,* 173.

67 Azkue, *Cancionero Popular Vasco I,* 533–536.

68 This song uses the word "tuntun" which means "a foolish woman" (Aulestia, *Basque-English Dictionary,* 505). But as we saw above, the song "*Aita tun tun*" uses the insult for men as well as women.

69 Urkizu, *Bertsolaritzaren Historia . . . Kantak 2,* 302–305.

70 *The Alan Lomax Collection: The Spanish Recordings.* Basque Country: Navarre,

2004, liner notes.

71 Urkizu, *Bertsolaritzaren Historia . . . Kantak 2*, 300–301. A version of this song can be heard on the CD "NOKATU:" www.ilovenoka.com.

72 NOKA has recorded a version of this song: www.ilovenoka.com.

73 Riezu, ed., *Cancionero Vasco P. Donostia*, vol. 7, 683–684.

74 Zavala, *Euskal Erromantzeak*, 202–203. NOKA has recorded a version of this song with its alternative title, "Frantzesa dut Baino" ("She is French, but . . .). See www.ilovenoka.com.

75 Trask, *The History of the Basque Language*, 13.

76 Barandiaran, *El Mundo en la Mente Popular Vasca II*, 78.

77 Urkizu, *Historia de la Literatura Vasca*, 91.

78 Urkizu, *Bertsolaritzaren Historia . . .Kantak 1*, 96.

79 Azkue, *Cancionero Popular Vasco*, 1092–1093.

80 Ansorena, *Euskal Kantak*, 127–138. Historically, this song was sung during May Day festivals in the Valley of Baztan (Nafarroa). The Catholic Church forbade this festival in the seventeenth century, but towns like Arizkun and Arraiotz revived it in 1930. It was still celebrated at the time *Euskal Kantak* was published in 2000.

81 Urkizu, *Bertsolaritzaren Historia . . . Kantak 1*, 89–93.

82 Ibid.,121–122.

83 Ansorena, *Euskal Kantak, 203*

84 Urkizu, *Bertso Zahar eta Berri Zenbaiten Bilduma*, 130.

85 Urkizu, *Bertsolaritzaren Historia . . . Kantak 2*, 465–467.

86 Urkizu, *Bertsolaritzaren Historia . . . Kantak 1*, 281–286.

87 Ibid.

88 Ibid

89 Ibid

90 Ibid.

91 Urkizu, *Bertsolaritzaren Historia . . .Kantak 2*, 380–381.

92 Ibid.

93 Ibid.

94 Ibid.

95 Ibid.

96 Ibid.

97 Ibid.

98 Ormaetxea, *Euskaldunak Poema eta Olerki Guziak*, 333–336.

99 Alan R. King contributed to the translations of some of these verses. Belinda Thom wrote music for these lyrics, a recording of which is in progress: belindathom.com

100 Urkizu, *Bertsolaritzaren Historia . . . Kantak 2*, 426–428. A version of this song with its traditional tune can be heard on the CD, "NOKA": www.ilovenoka.com. A more contemporary version sung at The Library of Congress can be viewed at: www.loc.gov/concerts/folklife/noka.html.

101 See Henningsen, *The Witches' Advocate.*

102 McBrien, ed., *Encyclopedia of Catholicism,* 48.
103 Baroja, *The World of the Witches,* 236.
104 Henningsen, *The Witches' Advocate,* 57.
105 Ansorena, *Euskal Kantak,* 204. This is a dance mostly sung in the Valley of Baztan, Nafarroa. Belinda Thom wrote music for these lyrics, a recording of which can be found on belindathom.com.
106 Amuriza, *Bizkaiko Bertsogintza I,* 66.
107 Azkue, *Cancionero Popular Vasco I,* 351.
108 Amuriza, *Bizkaiko Bertsogintza I,* 153.
109 Gender of this narrator is unspecified.
110 Urkizu, *Bertsolaritzaren Historia . . . Kantak 1,* 186–187.
111 Ibid., 186.
112 Ibid., 248. Belinda Thom wrote music for these lyrics, a recording of which is in progress: belindathom.com.
113 Riezu, ed., *Cancionero Vasco P. Donostia,* vol. 6, 94–95.
114 Urkizu, *Bertsolaritzaren Historia . . . Kantak 1,* 665–666
115 Ibid.
116 Riezu, ed., *Cancionero Vasco P. Donostia,* vol. 6, 94–95. Donostia collected this song from Amantzi Urriolabeita of Lekeitio, Bizkaia, on April 9, 1941.
117 Ormaetxea, *Euskaldunak Poema eta Olerki Guziak,* 159–165.
118 Ibid., 365–365.
119 Ibid.
120 Azkue, *Cancionero Popular Vasco II,* 690–691.
121 Zavala, *Neska-Mutillen Arteko Bertsoek,* 106–108.
122 Urkizu, *Bertsolaritzaren Historia . . . Kantak 2,* 288–289. This song was written by M. Baluyan in 1858.
123 Ibid., 453–454. Leon Elizanburu (1816–1861) of Lapurdi authored this song.
124 Ibid., 442–444.
125 Urkizu, *Bertsolaritzaren Historia . . . Kantak 2,* 443–444.
126 Urkizu, *Bertso Zahar eta Berri,* 164–167.
127 Zavala, *Euskal Erromantzeak,* 74–77.
128 Azkue, *Cancionero Popular Vasco I,* 144.
129 Riezu, *Cancionero Vasco P. Donostia,* vol. 7, 658. This "humorous" song was collected from Azpilkueta in the Valley of Baztan (Nafarroa) on February 22, 1912.
130 Urkizu, *Bertsolaritzaren Historia . . . Kantak 1,* 167–168.
131 Azkue, *Cancionero Popular Vasco II,* 833–833.
132 Riezu, *Cancionero Vasco P. Donostia,* vol. 7, 532. Donostia collected this song from Mme. Harambure of Donibane-Garazi (Bizkaia) on July 2, 1937.
133 Ibid.
134 Riezu, ed., *Cancionero Vasco P. Donostia,* vol. 7, 658.
135 Azkue, *Cancionero Popular Vasco II,* 665.
136 Urkizu, *Bertsolaritzaren Historia . . . Kantak 1,* 718–719.
137 Azkue, *Cancionero Popular Vasco II,* 809.

138 Urkizu, *Bertsolaritzaren Historia . . . Kantak 1*, 74–75. A version of this song can be heard the CD, "NOKATU:" www.ilovenoka.com.

139 Urkizu, *Bertsolaritzaren Historia . . . Kantak 1*, 454–456.

140 Ibid., 438–439. Alan R. King contributed to the translation of this song. NOKA has recorded a version of this song: www.ilovenoka.com.

141 This could be a reference to socialism. I thank José Ignacio Hualde for his help in interpreting and translating the song. For more information on the historical context, see "El Correo," May 15, 2015.

142 Woolf, *A Room of One's Own*.

5

Counter *Noka* Narratives

Words Have Ancestors, Deeds Have Masters

—Lao Tzu

In the previous chapters, I have demonstrated that the loss of *noka* over time can be attributed to negative language ideologies ascribed it not only in biblical texts, but also to the not-necessarily-positive identities *noka* constructs in folktales and folksong. Perhaps more importantly, I have also shown that these negative meanings did not emerge on their own, nor are they immutable. To build upon the insight of ancient Chinese philosopher quoted above, I would argue that the negative associations attributed to *noka* can be attributed to particular deeds done to *noka* by particular Basque writers—most of whom were male, as they have held sway over the production and distribution of Basque texts: as translators, poets, versifiers, singers, folklorists, ethnologists, or priests.

I have also shown that positive or at least more nuanced uses of *noka* can be found by digging deeper into the archives, drawing on songs rarely sung around the table or folktales no longer told around the fire (or included in the canon). These uses of and meanings ascribed *noka* can be seen as ancestors—perhaps, better said, ancestresses—whose lessons have been overlooked or ignored when it comes to how *noka* can be used, and the identities it can construct. In this spirit, this chapter provides additional examples from each of the genres discussed—biblical materials, folktales, and song—of myriad uses of *noka*, in the hope that they may pass down to future generations of Basque speakers.

Counter *Noka* Narratives in Catholic Basque Bibles

Chapter 2 showed that Catholic texts—whether the Bible as a whole or individual scriptural passages—rarely use *hika*. To the extent they do, they use primarily *toka* (for a male addressee) asymmetrically. In these contexts, *toka* is employed overwhelmingly for negative interactional purposes—to cast out, to condemn, to curse, to castigate. The semiotic legacy of *noka*, however, is far worse. The Duvoisin Bible uses *noka* almost exclusively with inanimate addressees, metaphorically cast as female, using sexualized and violent imagery.

However, such did not need to be the case. An 1873 Catholic Bible, translated into the Zuberoan dialect by (surprisingly) a woman named Anna Uruthy, uses *noka* in John 11:28, when Jesus visits Martha and Mary soon after their brother Lazarus has died. Martha calls for her sister Mary: "Nausia heben ***dun***, eta *hire* galthoz ***dun***" (The Lord is here and is asking for thee).[1] This language parallels a similar scene in the Leizarraga text from three hundred years before: "Magistrua ***dun*** hemen, eta deitzen *au*." But Duvoisin renders this interaction in the formal *zu* instead: "Nausia hemen DA, eta ZURE galdea DU."

However, in 1858, José Antonio Uriarte (also sponsored by L. L. Bonaparte and presumably working with the same guidelines regarding translation as Duvoisin) did use the familiar *T* (*noka* and *toka*)—alongside *V* (*zu*) as well as Latin—in translating the Song of Solomon into the Gipuzkoan and Bizkaian dialects.[2] While I found no explanation of why Uriarte included both pronouns in this text, he nonetheless provides abundant and positive uses of *noka* in these eight chapters, unusual in a Catholic text.[3]

Table 5.1: *Noka* in the Song of Solomon

Chapter	*noka*	*toka*
1	13	24
2	18	2
3	15	2
4	45	3
5	16	4
6	19	0
7	25	12
8	29	25
	180	**72**

Alone among Catholic texts, then, the Song of Solomon uses more *noka* than *toka*, in part, because the verses more often address the female than the male lover. Further, these passages use *noka* for romantic, even erotic, purposes. In chapter 1, the male lover addresses his female beloved whose "cheeks are beautiful as the turtle-dove's: your neck, like necklaces/We will make you golden necklaces, inlaid with lines of silver" (Ederrak DIRA/***ditun*** ZURE/*ire* masallak ala nola usatortolarena: ZURE/*hire* lepoa lepandeak bezela, urrezko katechoak egingo DIZKIZUGU/***dizkiñagu***, zillarezko archoz margainduak).[4] Verse 14 provides yet more praise for the female lover: "Oh how beautiful you are, my lover, oh how beautiful you are! Your eyes are doves' [eyes]" ("Ai zeñ ederra ZERAN/*aizan*, nere adiskidea, ai zeñ ederra ZERAN/*aizan*! ZURE/*Ire* begiak usoenak DIRA/***ditun***"). These uses of *noka* to bestow compliments and jewels upon a female addressee contrast sharply from the Duvoisin text, discussed in chapter 2, which uses *noka* to malign the addressee's reputation or to strip "her" of adornments.

The second chapter of The Song of Solomon[5] continues this use of *noka* to praise the woman. In the thirteenth verse, the (male) lover calls to her: "Come, come quickly, my lover, my dove, my beauty: come" (Jaiki ZAITE/*adi*, neure adiskidea, neure ederra, eta ATOZ/*ator*). In the following verse, he pleads with her to "show me your face in the nooks of the rocks, the cranny of the wall, let your voice resound in my ears: for your voice is sweet, and your face beautiful" (Erakutsi ZADAZU/***zadan*** ZURE/*ire* arpegia, soñu egin beza ZURE/*ire* bozak nere belarrietan: zeren ZURE/ *ire* boza gozoa DA/***den***, eta ZURE/*ire* arpegia ederra).[6]

The first eight verses in chapter 4 compose a "description song" which details "the beloved part by part, usually in a loose hand-to-foot sequence and culminating in a summary declaration."[7] Verse 9 begins an "admiration song" that "describes the beloved's body as a whole rather than part by part ... [It] is concerned mainly with the beloved's impact on the speaker:"[8]

Text 5.1 *Salomenen Kanten Kanta*, Chapter 4[9]

1. Zen ederra ZERAN/*aizan*, nere idiskidea, zen ederra ZERAN/ ***aizan***! ZURE/*Ire* begiak usonak DIRA/***ditun***, barrenen ezkutaturik DAGOENA/***zeagona*** gabe. ZURE/*Ire* illeak Galaad-ko mentikan igo ZIRAN/***itunan*** auntzen taldeak bezelakoak

HOW beautiful you are my lover, how beautiful you are! Your eyes are doves' [eyes], without that which is hidden inside. Your hair, like the herds of goats that went up Mount Gilead

2. ZURE/*Ire* ortzak garbitokitik igo ZIRAN/***itunan*** artalde moztuak bezalakoak, guztiak ume bizkiakin, eta umegaberik ez DA/***den*** beren artean

Your teeth, like the shorn flocks of sheep that went up from the washing place, all with twin lambs, and there is none childless among them

3. ZURE/*Ire* ezpañak, granazko lokarria bezelakoak: eta ZURE/*ire* izkuntza, gozoa. Granadaren akatsa bezela, ala DIRA/***ditun*** ZURE/*ire* masallak, barrenen ezkutaturik DAGOENA/***zeagona*** gabe

Your lips, like scarlet string: and your speech, sweet. As fragments of pomegranate, such are your cheeks, without that which is hidden inside

4. Dabiden torrea bezela ZURE/*ire* lepoa, egina DAGOENA/ ***zeagona*** baluarteakin: milla ezkutua DAUDE/***zeauden*** zinzillika beratatikan, errusten armapilla guztia

Like David's tower your neck, which is built with a bulwark: there are a thousand shields hanging from it, all the armament of the warriors

5. ZURE/*ire* bular biak, lirio artean bazkatzen DIRAN/***ditun*** basaunzkume bizki biak bezelakoak

Your two breasts, like two twin wild fawns that graze among the lilies

6. Eguna argitu, eta itzalak alde DITEZEN/***diteznan*** bitartean, joango NAIZ/***naun*** mirrako mendira, eta intzentzoaren munora

At the break of dawn, while the shadows vanish, I will go to the mountain of myrrh, to the hilltop of incense

7. Guziori ZERA/*aiz* ederra, nere adiskidea, eta mancharik ez DA/***den*** igan

You are altogether beautiful, my lover, and there is no flaw in you

8. ATOZ/*Ator* Libanotik, nere ezkongaya ATOZ/*ator* Libanotik, ATOZ/*ator*: izango ZERA/*aiz* koronatua Amanako buruarekin, Sanir eta Hermon-go tontorrarekin, leoen saizuloakin, eta leoenabarren mendiakin

Come from Lebanon, my betrothed, come from Lebanon, come: you will be crowned with the summit of Amana, with the mountain top of Senir and Hermon, with the lions' den, and with the leopards' mountains

9. Zauritu DEZU/***den*** nere biotza, nere arreba ezkongaya, azurite DEZU/***den*** nere biotza ZURE/*ire* begietatik batekin, eta ZURE/*ire* lepoko ille batekin

You have wounded my heart, my betrothed sister, you have wounded my heart with one of your eyes, and with a hair of your neck.

10. Zen ederrak DIRAN/***ditun*** ZURE/*ire* bularrak, nere arreba ezkongaya! Ederragoak DIRA/***ditun*** ZURE/*ire* titiak ardo bano, eta ZURE/*ire* okenduen usaya aroma guzien ganetikoa

You have wounded my heart, my betrothed sister, you have wounded my heart with one of your eyes, and with a hair of your neck. How beautiful are your breasts, my betrothed sister! Your nipples are more beautiful than wine, and the scent of your lotions is superior to all the spices

11. ZURE/*Ire* ezpañak, ezkongaya, abaraska jarioa DUTENAK/***ditenak***, eztia ta esnea ZURE/*ire* miñganaren azpian: eta ZURE/*ire* soñekoen usaiña intzentzoren usaiña bezelakoa

Your lips, betrothed, [are like] a honeycomb dripping honey and milk under your tongue: and the smell of your clothes, like the smell of incense

12. Baratz ichia ZERA/*aiz*, nere arreba ezkongaya, bartz ichia, iturri sillutua

You are a closed garden, my betrothed sister, a closed garden, a sealed fountain

13. ZURE/*Ire* moteak granadazko berjela sagarren frutuakin. Ziproak nardoarekin

Your buds, a pomegranate orchard with fruit of the apple tree. Cyprus with nard

14. Nardoa ta azafraya, kanabera usaitsua, eta kanela Libanoko zur guzitakin, mirra ta zabila okendurik onen guztiakin

Nard and saffron, fragrant grass, and cinnamon with all the woods of Lebanon, myrrh and aloe with all the finest ointments

15. Baratzetako iturria: Libanotikan bultzadaka DIJOAZEN/***zijoazen*** ur bizien putzua

Garden fountain; well of living waters that flow rushing from Lebanon

16. Jaiki ZAITE/*adi*, Ifarra, eta ATOZ/*ator*, Egoa, ZABILTZA/*abill* nere baratzetik, eta jario bitez beraren aromak

Rise, north wind, and come, south wind, blow through my garden, and let their fragrances flow

While the amorous intent of this passage might be obvious, it perhaps bears mentioning that the dove "is known for its delicacy and softness,"[10] and the flock of shorn sheep can be likened to "white, matched teeth;"[11] the pomegranate evokes red cheeks, and the twin fawns can be read as a simile for graceful breasts.[12] All of these features would be particularly praiseworthy—and difficult to attain—in a young woman who has toiled her whole life in the fields. Nonetheless, the male lover's effusiveness about her continues unabated: "Just one glance of her eyes, indeed, just one strand of her necklace, is enough to capture his heart."[13] Like Egyptian love poetry, the man calls his beloved "sister" as an expression of affection rather than of biological relationship as well as the "bride" he hopes she will one day be for him. His praise reaps rewards by the end of the chapter: the woman "invites him into her locked garden, opening it to him alone."[14]

These metaphors of love and sexual longing continue in chapter 5. Upon entering his beloved's "garden," the man declares (in verse 1): "I have come to my garden, my betrothed sister, I have reaped my myrrh with my spices: I have eaten honeycomb with my honey, I have drunk my wine with my milk: eat, lovers, and drink, and be drunk, beloved ones" (Etorri NAIZ/***naun*** nere baratzera, nere arreba ezkongaya, igitaitu DET/***diñat*** nere mirra nere aromakin: jan DET/***diñat*** abaraska nere eztiarekin, edan DET/***diñat*** nere ardoa nere esnearekin: jan ezazute, adiskideak, eta edan ezazute, eta orditu zaitezte, chit maiteak). In the following verse, he begs his beloved to "Open for me, my sister, my lover, my dove, my unblemished one: for my head is full of dew, and my locks with night-drops" (Idiki ZADAZU/***zadan***, nere arreba, nere adiskidea, nere usoa, nere manchagabea: zeren nere burua intzez beterik DAGO/***zeagon***, eta nere kartzetak gauetako tantoz).

Chapter 6, verse 3, continues this litany of praise: "You are beautiful, my lover, sweet and gentle like Jerusalem" (Ederra ZERA/*aiz*, nere adiskidea, eztia, eta emaguritsua Jerusalen bezela). In verse 5, he repeats the metaphors extolling the woman's beauty: "Your teeth, like the flock of sheep that went up from the washing place, all with twin lambs, and there is none childless among them" (ZURE/*Ire* ortzak garbitokitik igo ZIRAN/***itunan*** ardien taldea bezala, guztiak ume bizkiakin, eta umegaberik ez DA/***den*** beren artean). In the twelfth and final verse, he pleads with her again, asking her to come to him "so that we may look at you" (Itzuli ZAITE/*adi*, itzuli ZAITE/*adi*, begiratu DIZUGUN/***azanagun***).

The two remaining chapters use *noka* profusely. In the opening verse of chapter 7, the male besotted declares: "How beautiful are your steps in shoes, prince's daughter! Your thigh joints [are] like bracelets that have been made by the hands of an artisan" (Zeñ ederrak DIRAN/***ditun*** ZURE/*ire* pausoak oñetakoetan, prinzipearen alaba! ZURE/*Ire* isterren giltzak, langillearen eskuz egiñak izan DIRAN/***ditun*** eskumuturrekoak bezela). In verse 5, he goes on to praise her navel, belly, breasts, neck, eyes. "How beautiful you are, and how gentle, most beloved, in pleasures!" (Zeñ ederra ZERAN/*aizan,* eta zeñ emaguritsua, chit maitea, atsegiñetan!). The power of love seems all-consuming in chapter 8, verse 7: "Many waters cannot quench affection, and nor can rivers drown it: even if a man were to give everything in his house for love, it will disdain him as nothing" (Ur askok ezin ZUTEN/***ziñaten*** itzali karidadea, eta ibayak ere ez DUTE/***diten*** urpetuko: emango BALU/***baliñ*** ere gizonak bere echeko izate guztia amorioa gatik, deus bezela mespreziatuko DU/***diñ***).

Thus, while often interpreted as a metaphor for God's relationship to his people during the latter's exodus from Egypt[15]—in line with the marriage metaphors we saw in the books of the Latter Prophets in chapter 2—the Song of Solomon contains sexually explicit dialogue between unmarried adolescents. In fact, the "couple's relationship is strikingly egalitarian, as if bracketed out for the moment from the assumptions of patriarchal society . . . their possession is mutual (2:16), their desires indistinguishable."[16]

Here, then, pronominal parity prevails: *hika* is shown alongside *zuka,* and *noka* equals *toka* in sociolinguistic terms: a female and male use the familiar pronoun symmetrically to construct each other as social equals, as mutual objects of romantic desire. If these 180 uses of *noka* had been included by Duvoisin, it could have gone a long way in mitigating the violent imagery associated with *noka* use in the Latter Prophets. Alas, Duvoisin did not do so. His Song of Solomon uses mutual *zu*, the "pragmatically unmarked"[17] mode of address.

Counter *Noka* Narratives in Basque Folklore

Alternative uses and meanings of *noka*, including the power of sexual desire, can also be found in Basque myths and legends featuring figures other than Mari, witches, and the sirens. The folktale "*Pagomari*" ("Beech Mari") features the pretty, young Mari who, despite being a "hardened shepherd girl," grows weary of the solitude of tending sheep: "sometimes, although she felt a twinge of sinfulness and guilt, she would lie on her back on the grass and start to stroke and caress her body. She would visualize a gentleman riding a white horse who came over to her, got off his horse in front of her, and sat down next to her."[18] This fantasy becomes all too real one day; a "slender young man"[19] appears by her side and touches her:

Text 5.2: *Pagomari* (excerpt 1)[20]

Neskak kilika gozo bat sentitu zuen bere gorputzaren barnean, eta mutil hura nor zen jakiteko irrikaz bazegoen ere, ez zuen galderarik egin; erabat haren mende utzi zuen bere burua. Gero mutilaren ezpainek neskarenak ukitu zituzten leunki, samur, busti; besoez neskaren gorputz bildu zuen hurrena, eta besarkada gozo estu batean elkartu ziren azkenean.

Gau iluna zen elkar agurtu zutenean. Mari txora-txora eginda zegoen, eta nekatu itxura zuen, arropak nahasiak eta izerditan blai. Mutilarengandik banandu beharrak, horrek biziki ez zion begitartea iluntzen; gainerakoan, poz-pozik zegoen. Mutila bertan gera zedin saiatu zen hitzik esan gabe . . . Hain zegoen gustura harekin! Zergatik joan nahi ote zuen horren agudo? Maitasun benetakoa, dagoeniko munduko plazerrik handiena bezala zeukana harengandik ikaski berri . . . eta orain bazihoakiola ondotik!

Mariren aurpegian tristura azaleratzen ari zela ikusirik, mutilak hitz batzuk xuxurlatu zizkion belarrira: "Datorren Gabon gauen hemen bertan elkartuko ***gaitun***!"

Eta Mariri musu eman ondoren, handik abiatu eta berehala desagertu zen. Emakumea estasian geratu zen, mutilaren ezpainek ukitu zuten azal zati batoiza behatzez ferekatuz.

Handik aurrera Mari emakume desberdina izan zen. Mendian bere ardiekin eta bakarrik segitzen bazuen ere, herrira jaisten zenean pozik eta alai agertzen zen denen aurrean. Herriko emakume batzuk, hala ere, aldaketaz harriturik, berehala hasi ziren haren lepotik gaizki esaka. Mariri ordea bost axola zitzaikion atso zahar haien txutxumutxu eta berritsukeriak!

Beech Mari (excerpt 1)

As soon as she felt his gentle touch, a new world of pleasures unfolded inside her heart, and she was filled with a delicious sensation. Since she didn't resist (quite the contrary!), he carried on caressing her body: her shoulder, her neck . . . Mari lay down on the ground with her eyes closed while he slowly stroked her eyes, nose, mouth and cheeks. She sensed a tickling feeling all through her body, and although she wondered who he could possibly be, she didn't ask; she surrendered herself to him completely. Then his lips touched hers softly, tender and moist; next he enfolded her body in his arms, and finally they came together in a sweet, tight, calm embrace.

It was late at night when they said goodbye. Mari was enraptured. She looked tired, her clothes were rumpled and she was covered with perspiration. The only thing that brought furrow to her brow was having to separate from him, but apart from that she was filled with joy. Without saying a word she did what she could do to get him to stay. She was so happy with him, why did he have to go so soon? She had only just learned from him the world's greatest pleasure, true love, yet now he would leave her!

When he saw Mari's sadness written on her face, he whispered in her ears: "We will meet in this spot next Christmas Eve!"

After kissing Mari he started off and quickly disappeared. In ecstasy, the woman stroked with her fingers each part of her skin that his lips had touched.

From then on, Mari was a different woman. Although she was still alone with her sheep on the mountain, whenever she went down to the village she was always happy and cheerful in front of everybody. However, some of the village women who noticed the change with surprise soon started spreading rumors behind her back. But Mari couldn't care less about the whispering and chattering of those old hags!

Alas, the chatterers knew whereof they spoke. Mari agonizes as she waits for her next rendezvous with the gentleman:

she wonders where he has gone and whether he is married. Christmas Eve finally arrives and she returns to the beech tree where they had agreed to meet; but the young man does not appear:

Text 5.3: *Pagomari* (excerpt 2)
Horrela pasa zituen egun batzuk, pagoaren ondotik mugitu gabe. Elurra egiten hasi zuen, mara-mara, eta dena zuritu zuen. Orduan ere ez zen mugitu. Goseak, hotzak eta tristurak ahiturik, hantxe bertan hil zen Mari gajoa.

Egun batzuk geroago aurkitu zuten haren gorputza, izoztua, pagoaren ondoan. Harrezkero Pagomari esaten zaio pagoari eta inguruari.

Beech Mari (excerpt 2)
[Mari] continued so for several days, not moving from the side of the tree. It started to snow and everything became white. She still didn't move. Overcome by hunger, cold and grief, the unfortunate Mari died there.

Her frozen body was discovered a few days later next to the beech, which was ever since known, as is the surrounding area, as *Pagomari* (Beech Mari).

Thus, "Beech Mari" conveys both the power and the danger of sexual desire, and it uses *noka* to do so. The mysterious young gentleman uses *noka* in wooing the lonely shepherdess and in making false promises to her. Other Basque folktales feature male mythological figures also causing harm to innocent young girls, and using *noka* when doing so. One such figure is the "*basajaun*" or "man-of-the-forest" who takes the shape of a large man, covered in hair; the hair on his head reaches below his knees. Sometimes the *basajaun* is represented as a benevolent power, as the first agriculturalist or first miller.[21] Other times, the *basajaun* exerts malevolent powers, as in the story below:

Text 5.4: Basajaun Bahitzaile[22]

Behin batez, basajaun batek harrapatu zizun Behorlegi Etxepareko alaba bat Elhorrietan, Behorlegimendin, eta ereman zizun berekin leizerat. Zenbait egunen buruian handik jalgi Behorlegiko bistara, eta han jarri zitzun ekhitala. Neskatoren altzoan basajaunak phausatzen dizu buruia eta lokhartzen duzu. Neskatoak emekiño azturrez tabliera mozturik, emekiño phausatzen dizu buria buria tablieraren barnean. Bainan basajaunak, okharturik, burhau egin ziakozun, eta erran ziakozun:

"Balinba leher eginen ***dun*** extean sartzearekin."

Eta neskatoak etxean sartzean, zango bat alhartzearen barnean eta bertze bat kanpoan, leher egin zizun.

The Kidnapping Man-of-the-Forest

Once upon a time, a *basajaun* [Man-of-the-Forest] kidnapped a daughter from the Behorlegi Etxepare farm in Elhorrieta, on Mount Behorlegi, and took her to his cave. After a few days, they emerged from the cave in sight of Behorlegi and sat in the sun. The *basajaun* lays his head on the girl's lap and falls asleep. The girl, carefully cutting her apron with a pair of scissors, places his head inside her apron. But the *basajaun* realized and cursed her, saying:

"May you burst the moment you get home!"

And as the girl was entering her house, with one foot on the threshold and the other outside, she burst.

While such is not made explicit, we can easily surmise what transpired between the *basajaun* and girl during her internment in his cave. Why the girl is punished by death when she escaped from her captor—one might hope the girl's bravery and resourcefulness might have been rewarded instead—the sociolinguistic point here is that the *basajaun* uses *noka* in cursing her. *Noka* is very powerful pronoun indeed.

In other stories, it is more amorphous forces that wield *noka* so effectively as a curse. Barandiaran collected "Katherine's

Punishment"[23] in 1926 from his hometown (Ataun, Gipuzkoa): a spinner named Katherine bets that she can defy local lore that "you must not turn around a house three times at night, unless you hold a laurel branch in your hand." She goes around a house twice, but disappears on her third attempt. Afterwards, these words are heard on a bridge nearby: "Kataliñ deabruk eaman ***diñ***" (Katherine has been taken by the devil). Katherine was never heard from again.

A similar fate befalls other daring girls in stories from across the Basque Country. In a story told by his mother to Barandiaran himself, a girl takes a dare to bring water from a certain spring, by moonlight. Her fellow spinners call out to her now and again (in *noka*) asking where she is, and she responds several times, but her voice becomes ever fainter. Eventually, the girl's voice falls silent to this one: "The night is for the night creatures and the day is for the day creatures!" And the girl disappears forever.

In a story collected by Cerquand from a sixty-eight-year-old woman named Catherine Osinaga, a girl servant dares to carry out a task a boy servant will not:

Text 5.5: Arrasteluko Neska[24]

Bithirinan, oraino ikhusten den Inhurri deithu etxean, bi muthil neska sehi zauden. Arrats batez, etxe hartako jendeak artho xuritzen ari ziren, bethi bezala, ezkaratzean. Muthila ohartzen da, langiletarat arthoaren hurbiltzeko zerbitzatzen zen hirur hortzetako arrastelua, landetan urrunxko zen etxola batean ahantzirik utzi zutela. Gaua beltza zelakotz, tresnaren bilha joaiteko lotsa zen. Neskatoak, ongi trufatu ondoan, erraiten dio:

"Jokhatzen daizkiat bortz sos nihaur bilha joaiten naizela."

Parioa onhartua da, eta neska gaztea partitu zen ilhunperen erdian. Hainitz denbora gabe aditzen dituzte horren gibelerat ethortzeko urhatsak. Bainan ez zen etxean sarthu. Bortha gaina idekia bait zen, handik arthikitzen du arrastelua erranez: "Hor duzue falta zinutena. Ni, ene diru gosearen gaztigutan, ezin ikhusizko esku batek eramaten nau."

Gisa hortan airez aire zaramatelarik, Mendibeko 'capilla'-ren gainerat heldu, eta oihu egiten du: "Salbatore, laguntzerat ethor zaizkit!"

Orduan boz batek ihardesten dio: "Barur itxiki ***duna***?"

"Nik ez, bainan ene amak urthe guziez begiratzen du."

"Horrek salbaturen hau," dio bozak.

Ordu berean hil hotza phausatua da "capilla'-ren athean. Ez da gauaz pariorik behar.

The Rake Girl

In Bithirina, in a house named Inhurri which still stands, there were two servants, one male and one female. One evening, the people in the house were on the porch shelling maize as usual. The servant boy realizes that the three-pronged rake used to shift the maize to where the workers were had been forgotten in a distant shed. As it was a dark night, he was scared to go and fetch it. The girl, after scoffing at him, says:

"I bet you five *sous* that I'll go and get it myself."

He accepted the bet and the young girl set out into the pitch-dark night.

Not long afterwards, they hear her steps returning. But she did not enter the house. As the upper half of the door was open, she throws the rake inside saying: "There you have what you needed. As for me, in punishment for my greed, an invisible hand is carrying me away."

Carried in this fashion through the air, she reaches the chapel of Mendibe where she shouts: "Savior, come and help me!"

Then a voice answers: "Did you fast?"

"I didn't; but my mother fasts every year."

"That will help you," the voice replies.

At that very moment she dropped dead at the chapel door. One should not bet at night!

As the girls above meet unfortunate ends, one could argue that these stories should be suppressed rather than disseminated:

why perpetuate stories of female victimization? However, such tales—like all stories—can be interpreted many ways and one could also argue that these ill-fated girls also exhibit bravery, cunning, and daring in their final moments: not unlike male characters who engage in "heroes' journeys" which do not always turn out so well. In this sense, stories like the *basajaun*-escaping girl, the spinner, and the rake girl illustrate Basque Communist Dolores Ibarruri's famous slogan: "Better die on your feet than live on your knees."

Even so, Basque folklore also contains some stories where female cunning and bravery best the devil himself:

Text 5.6: San Martinen Errota[25]

San Martin'ek errota berria in omentzuen; baino ezin ibilazi. Aldiz debruak ere errota bai omentzuen eta ai omentzen lanean. Emazteki bat gan omentzen San Martin'en errotara, eta galdetu zertako etzuen ibilartzen errota.

San Martin'ek erran omentzion, bere errotak utsen bat bazuela, baino zer zen etzekiela. Emazteki hura gan omentzen debruain errotara, eta erran debruai: "Hay *aiz*, hay *aiz*."

"Ba hai ***naun***."

"Hai **duk** ba San Martin e, hai **duk**, dabla, dabla."

"Haltzeko kokoxa eman ***zion*** beaz"?

"**Etziok** eman, baino emain **ziok**." Emaztekiak San Martin'i erran omentzion, debruak zer errantzuen.

Ala San Martin'ek ikasi omentzuen nola errota ibilazi.

Saint Martin's Mill

The story goes that Saint Martin built a new mill, but couldn't get it to work. Meanwhile the devil also had a mill, which was working. A woman went to Saint Martin's mill and asked why he didn't get the mill up and running. Saint Martin told her that his mill had something wrong with it but he didn't know what it was.

The woman went to the devil's mill, and said to the devil: "You're at it, you're at it."

"Yup, I'm at it."

"Well, Saint Martin is at it too, he's at it dabla dabla."

"So, he has installed a bed of alder-wood for the millstones, then?

"He hasn't, but he will!"

The woman told Saint Martin what the devil had said. And that's how Saint Martin learnt how to get the mill to work.

Thus, the heroine of this story not only tricks the devil into revealing his secret—which ultimately benefits the (male) miller, quite a selfless act—she exhibits fearlessness when faced with the devil as well as the quick-thinking and equanimity necessary to trick him: qualities admirable in any person, male or female.

Even in this brief foray into Basque folktales "starring" figures other than Mari, witches, or sirens, we see *noka* used to construct images of human females not usually captured in texts representing Basque culture. Like human males, these females exhibit sexual desire, bravery, cunning, and agency. And like boys and men, these girls and women sometimes are rewarded for their attributes and actions; other times, they are punished. Either way, such stories round out the kinds of identities and activities women and girls can inhabit. To the extent that gender equity is about showing the whole range of human experience for both sexes—for men and women—we are all enriched when the restricted view, or allowable portrayals of one sex (in this case, the female), is expanded to encompass more of the human experience.

Counter *Noka* Narratives in Basque Song

As we saw in chapter 4, Basques have a long history of singing about all aspects of the human experience: life and death, history and war, daily life and work, religion, friendship, family and love.[26] We have also seen that few women have had the privilege to use song to express themselves on these topics. As a long overdue corrective to this androcentric tradition, over twenty years ago two Basque-American women (Andréa Bidart and Catherine Petrissans) and I formed the trio NOKA, which focuses on songs about women or those that use *noka* (www.ilovenoka.com). NOKA has produced four CDs with a fifth in progress.[27] In addition to the 125 songs in *noka* I have uncovered through my research, discussed in chapter 4, I have written or cowritten over 40 songs, many of which use *noka*. I conclude this chapter, then, with a sampling of these songs.

Daily Life and Work

The first song I wrote using *noka* was autobiographical. My parents were immigrants from Orabidea, a mountain community in the Valley of Baztan (from whence, perhaps coincidentally, many of the "witches" burned at the 1610 Logroño trials came). Each was one of seven surviving siblings living on the traditional "*baserri*" (farmhouse), in which the oldest child (regardless of gender) inherited the farm, with the understanding that s/he would (usually with his or her spouse) care for the heir's parents in old age. But my parents grew up during the dictatorship of Francisco Franco (1939-75) and his autarkic economic policies that impoverished much of the country, especially the rural areas that fought against him during the Spanish Civil War such as the Basque-speaking areas. During the 1950s, my father (and his brothers) availed themselves of a program that allowed Basque men to come to the United States to work as shepherds. My father worked for seven years to save enough money to marry my mother, and they eventually settled in Chino, California, near other siblings who had also immigrated to the United States. My first language, and that of my siblings and first cousins, was Basque; I spoke *Euskera* with my parents at home, with my aunts and uncles during our weekly visits with each other, and with other immigrants who had settled in southern California.

However, like other children of immigrants, I had no institutional support for my native language outside the home. English became the language I used with my siblings, cousins, and my peers, even if they spoke Basque. This concerned my mother, who was determined that her children would remain Basque speakers. "*Kafesneari Esker*" ("Thanks to Coffee-Milk") explains how she ensured that my siblings and I did so:

Text 5.7: *Kafesneari Esker* ("Thanks to Coffee-Milk")[28]

1. Euskal alaba naiz ni, sortzez Chino-koa	I am a Basque daughter from Chino
Aita Ansonekoa, Ama Arnoskoa	My dad's home is Ansonea; my mom's, Arnos
Aspaldi ganak dira, Ameriketara	They went to America long ago
Nola hazi ninduten, eskualdun alaba?	How did they teach me Basque?
2. Beren etxe berrietan, Chinon izan arren	Even in their Chino home
Baztanen bezalaxe, eskuaraz mintzatzen	They spoke Basque, like in Baztan
Haurrak eskolatu 'ta, Ingelesa sartu zen	But we children learned English in school
Eskuara atxitzeko, ba al zen itxaropen?	Was there any hope for Basque?
3. Echeverria denekin, ardura, bai, biltzen	We often gathered with all the Echeverrias
Helduak eleketan, gazteak jolasten	The adults talked and the children played
Etxeratzekoan nik amari galde egiten:	On the way home, I asked my mother:
Kafesnea, faborez, afaldu ondoren?	After dinner, can I have coffee-milk?
4.Amari ideia gogoratu orduan	Then it occurred to my mother
Ama hizkuntza nola ongi gorde dezan	How to keep the mother tongue alive
Bere boz eztiekin, hauxe erran zautan:	In her sweet voice she said:
Kafesnea nahi ***badun***, eskuaraz mintza ***zan***	If you want coffee-milk, speak Basque
5. Egunero eskatzen nion kafesnea	Every day I asked for coffee-milk
Amak neri: Orduan, mintza ***zan*** eskuaraz	My mother said: Then speak Basque
Ongi haunditzekotan, haurra, *hi* bezala	For it to grow up well, like you,
Eskuara berdin zaindu, eman maitasuna	You must care for it, give it love
6. Gorputzeri kafesneak dio, bai, indarra	Coffee-milk gives the body strength
Eta eskuarak, aldiz, arimari goza	And Basque lifts up the soul
Ene azken hitz hauek, nere Amari poza?	Do these last words make my mother happy?
Kafesnea bezala, maite dut eskuara!	Like coffee-milk, I love Basque!

While my ability to speak (and affection for) *Euskera* is a tribute primarily to my mother's determination, my love for Basque singing is due primarily to my father, who knew perhaps hundreds of songs by heart. Our birthdays were two days apart, and his mother—who he said knew even more songs by heart despite being illiterate—died on the day between our birthdays, long before I was born. Even when my father wasn't singing, every now and again he would tell a story which was fodder for song. The following is a composite of stories he told me over the years, about himself and others:

Text 5.8: *Gizon Gazte Nintzala* (I Was A Young Man)[29]

1. Gizon gazte nintzala
Bizarra kentzen
Alde bat zen egina
Lagun bat etortzen:
Falange heldu zela!
Leiotik ateratzen
Bestealderat pasatu 'ta
Bestealdea finitzen
2. Mendian bide ***badun***
Bestekin gurutzatzen
Hemendik mezarat
Handik kontrabanden
Debekatua izan 'ta
Pekatu ez ***zunen***
Frankoren pobrezian
Jan behar genuen
3. Oihanean, Frantzian
Lanean nintzen
Ijitoa nerekin
Euskaraz mintzatzen
Gabezian bizi zela
Ez nuen laguntzen?
Bere haurrak neri
Saltzeko prest ***zunen***
4. Kantu hau aditzeagatik
Ditut eskerrrak ematen
Explikatu nahi du
Miseriak zer egiten duen
Bakoitzeak berea
Nola zaintzen duen
Jainkoa, barkatu
Ez ***dinat*** iñor juzkatzen

I was a young man
Shaving my beard
I had one side done
When a friend came to me:
The Spanish Fascists are coming!
I escaped through a window
Passed to the other side of the border
And finished shaving the other side
In the mountains
There is a crossroad
I took one road to go to Mass
And the other to smuggle goods
That was forbidden
But not a sin
In Franco's poverty
We had to eat
In the forests of France
Where I was working
A gypsy came up to me
Speaking Basque
He was living in poverty
Couldn't I help him?
He was ready
To sell me his own children
For listening to this song
I thank you
It explains
What misery can do
And how everyone
Looks out for themselves
God forgive us
I judge no one

History and War

On April 26, 1937, the town of Gernika[30] (Bizkaia) was bombed by Hitler's Condor legion, with Francisco Franco's blessing. Hitler wanted to try out his new "Luftwaffe's terror bombing strategy" and Franco offered him this town, for since the Middle Ages the Basques had assembled under an oak tree in Gernika to make their laws. To Franco, this town was the symbol of democracy and of resistance to his Nationalist forces during the Spanish Civil War. It was the first civilian target in history to be completely decimated by aerial bombing. Terrified that more bombings were to come, many Basques and Spaniards sent their children to countries friendly with the Republican cause for protection, such as France, the USSR, Mexico, or Great Britain: twenty thousand children in all, called "The Gernika Generation."[31]

I knew little of this exodus of refugee children until I met a British woman of Basque descent whose father had been evacuated to England, along with his brother. But when England entered World War II in 1939, politicians and the public called for the Basque children to be returned home; they had their own children to worry about. In the case of my British friend's father, things did not turn out so well: his mother asked for his brother back, but not for him. He died many decades later, never knowing why his mother had left him behind.

Based loosely on this story, my play *Picasso Presents Gernika* tells the story of a mother who makes a similar choice: sending both her daughter and son to England after the bombing; she only asks for her son back. It is only at the end of the play that the daughter (by then, in her eighties) learns why:

Text 5.9: *Bonbarazi du Gernika* (He Had Gernika Bombed)[32]

1. Bonbarazi du Gernika	He had Gernika bombed
Bonbak hil du ene senarra	A bomb killed my husband
Bi haurrekin gelditu ni	Alone with two children
Alarguna eta pobrea	I was left a poor widow
2. Inglaterrak bidali du untzia	England sent a boat
Salbatzeko Gernikako haurrak	To save Gernika's children
Semea, alaba, nigarrez	My son and daughter cried
Sarrarazi ditut barkoan	As I put them on that boat
3. O Ama Birjina	O, Virgin Mary
Uzten ditut ene haurrak	I leave my children
Zure beso artean	In your arms
O Ama Birjina	O, Virgin Mary
Zaindu zaindu ene haurrak	Please protect my children
Etxeratu arte	Until they come home
4. Frankok hil du demokrazia	Franco killed our democracy
Munduko bigarren gerra hasi da	World War II began
Inglaterrak bere umeak	England wanted to help
Lagundu nahi 'ta itzuli gureak	Its own children and send ours home
5. Frankok kendu ditu eskubideak	Franco took away our rights
Bereziki emazte eta neskenak	Especially from girls and women
Semea 'karrazi, alaba han utzi	I asked for my boy back, left my girl there
Izanen ***dun*** bizi hobea?	Will you have a better life?

A less known facet of the Spanish Civil War and Franco's dictatorship thereafter was revealed only in the last few years. A reporter from the Spanish newspaper, *El País*, visited the grave of his baby sister, who (he had been told) had died shortly after birth decades before. But he found the grave empty, and uncovered a scheme carried out during the Franco regime whereby the babies of women whose politics opposed Franco were given away to his supporters to raise as their own. This tragic story inspired the lyrics below:

Text 5.10: *Alargun Gaztea Nintzen*[33] (I Was a Young Widow)

1. Alargun gaztea nintzen haurdun gelditua	I was a pregnant young widow
Eusko-gudaria zen nere gizon hila	My dead husband, a Basque soldier
Goizegi etorri zen gure haur gaixoa	Our poor child came too early
Serorak erran zaten: Galdu ***dun*** alaba	The nun told me: You lost your daughter
2. Astero hilarrian uzten ditut loreak	Every week I left flowers at the tomb
Bataio egin partez eman ditut nigarrak	I baptized her with my tears
Denok ***dinagu*** gurutze, erran du apezak	We all have a cross to bear, the priest said
Ezin du konprenitu haurgaltzearen pena	Not understanding the loss of a child
3. Handik hogeibat urte serora etorri	Twenty years later the nun came
Konfesio egitera: utsa zen hilobi	To confess: the tomb was empty
Nere alaba gaixoa "xuriekin" bizi	My poor daughter was living with "Whites"
Ez zutelako gehiago nahi "gorriak" hazi	To prevent the raising of more"Reds"

The Immigrant Experience

While my parents were from the Baztan Valley in Nafarroa, Spain, the farmhouses where they grew up are only about five miles from the northern Basque Country (*Iparralde*). A road called Izpegi traverses the two sides of the border through rugged mountain terrain; it can be difficult to travel not only because of potholes but also because sheep, goats, or *pottokak* (a breed of horse native to the Basque Country) sometimes block the way. It occurred to me that Izpegi was an apt metaphor for the Basque language itself: that sometimes its dissemination is blocked by the obstacles speakers (or would-be speakers) put in its way:

Text 5.11: *Izpegi* ("Izpegi Road")[34]

1. Izpegiko bidean	On Izpegi road
Nengokinan beldur	I was afraid
Ibiltzen mantso mantso	I drove very slowly
Batzuk enekin samur	Some got angry with me

Bainan egun Izpegi
Harrapatzen ***dinat*** labur
Fite fite 'ta zuzen
Nahiz izan oso kizkur
2. Poxelamenduz bete
Zitzainan lehenago
Ez ***nindunan*** hain trebe
Izpegin ibiltzeko
Oztopo izan 'ta ere
Berdin zait oraingo
Beldurrez ibiltzea
Ez ***dinagu*** balio
3. Izpegia omen ***din***
Muga eta zubi
Gauza bera gertatzen
Euskaldun guztieri
Ipar- 'ta Hegoalde
Zenbat hitz-gidari?
Elkarrekin mintzatuz
Ulerbide garbi
4. Euskalerritik kanpo
Izpegi ailegatu
Guretako nola
Hizkuntza mantendu?
Diasporen akatsak
Hobe ***ditun*** barkatu
Eskualbide estua
Dezagun zabaldu

But now Izpegi
I find to be very short
Fast and straight
Even though it's a winding road
I used to find Izpegi
Full of potholes
And I wasn't very skilled
At driving on Izpegi
By now I don't mind
If there are obstacles
There's no point
In being afraid
Izpegi is both
A border and a bridge
The same is true
Of all Basques
From north to the south side
How many wordsmiths are there?
By speaking with each other
We can create understanding
Outside the Basque Country
Izpegi has arrived
How do we maintain
This language for us?
By forgiving the mistakes
Made in the diaspora
We widen the narrow road
Of the Basque language

The image of the lone Basque shepherd has become an important symbol of the American West: the rugged immigrant male toughing it out in a new land with an unfamiliar language, until finding success beyond his dreams by working hard. While many Basque immigrant men—and women—have indeed lived the American Dream, others struggled with loneliness and despair, spending months on end with no human company as they tended to thousands of sheep on their own, with little to no training. The aspen trees across the American West testify to the alienation so many of them faced.[35] The lyrics below convey what the tragic consequence of such isolation and disappointment could be:

Text 5.12: *Sos Bat Gehiago* (One More Dollar)

1. Baserritarra nauzu
Mendia dut laketu
Bainan ez nintzen premu

I am a farm boy
I love the mountain
But I was not the heir

Orduan gan nintzen	So I went
Diruen bila	To make my fortune
Segiduan lan aurkitu	And found a job right away
2. Sos bat gehiago	Just a little more money
'ta etxera	Then I'll go home
Sos bat	A little more money
'ta nahikoa	That will be enough
Sorlekutik, beharra	I left my homeland poor
Etxeratu, sosduna	And will go home rich
3. Neska bat ezagutu	I met a girl
Eni begi bota du	She gave me this look
Harekin nahi nuen ezkondu	I wanted to marry her
Aski diru bildu arte, Nerea	Until I earn enough money
Eginen ***dun*** esperatu?	Will you wait for me?
4. Zazpi urte pasatu	Seven years passed
Etxea ez ***diñat*** lortu	And I still have no house
Neska beste batekin ezkondu	My girl married someone else
Esku baten ***diñat*** arrosarioa	I have a rosary in one hand
Bestean eskopeta	And a shotgun in the other

Friendship

Given that *noka* ostensibly marks familiarity and solidarity, I found it surprising that few songs use *noka* in dialogue addressing a female friend. The song below aspires to use *noka* in keeping with its sociolinguistic function as a pronoun of solidarity:

Text 5.13: *Oroit Hadi* ("Remember Me")

1. Ele eztiena laztanari erraten da	The sweetest word, you say to your beloved
Zakarrena, banatzen denean	The harshest one, when you separate
Nahigabetsu sentitzen *haizenean*	When you feel heart-broken
Oroit *hadi*, ***naun*** *hirekin* beti	Remember, I am with you always
2. Oroit *hadi*	Remember me
Nitaz, une tristeetan	In your sad moments
Heldu dela soilik zori txarra	When only bad luck comes
Oroit *hadi*	Remember me
Nitaz, ordu beltzeetan	In your darkest hours
Nitan ***badun***	You will always
Laguntasun beti	Have a friend in me
3. Bizi hoberena ametsetan da	The best life is in your dreams
Txarrena, bete ez direnean	The worst, when they don't come true
Porrotaldi egiten ***badun*** ere	Even if you fail
Oroit *hadi*, berdin ***zaidan*** neri	Remember, it doesn't matter to me
4. Lagun leialenak hitz betetzen du	The best friend keeps her word
Falsuenak, isilpeak saldu	The worst one tells your secrets
Konfiantza galdu ***badun*** ezaguneekin	If you've lost faith in those you know
Oroit *hadi*, adiskide ***naun*** ni	Remember, I am your friend

The song below, however, shows that even mutual use of *noka* does not guarantee that the friendship itself is one based on mutual respect and solidarity:

Text 5.14: *Osane eta Nerea* (Mine and Remedy)

1. Itsaso aldean bi lagun badira	Near the sea are two friends
Ahizpak bezain estuak, Osane eta Nerea	As close as sisters, Osana and Nerea[36]
Batek betzeari ematen belarri	One always lends an ear
Edozein arazoaz, konpontzerat ari	To listen to any problem
Bertzeak, aldiz, bakarrik ageri	But the other only shows up
Zerbait behar duelarik:	When she needs something:
Nolako zigorraldi?	How will she be punished?
2. Goazen laguna, behar ***dinat*** laguntza	Let's go, friend, I need help
Nere katukumea nonbait ***din*** galdua	To find my lost kitten
Zeregin utzi 'ta, Osane etorri da	Osane dropped everything:
Hire katua harrapatzea, hori ***din*** importa	The most important thing is to find it
Handik bi astera, harena galdua	Two weeks later, hers goes missing
Nereak ez lagundu	But Nerea did not help
Zagon hondarretan	She had gone to the beach
3. Eskolako-lanak, ***ditun*** oso zailak	This homework is so hard
Eneganat etorriko *haiz*, laguntza ematera?	Will you come help me?
Jakina, Nerea, ez dago problema	No problem, Nerea,
Etxekolanak egin 'ta, jinen segiduan	I'll come as soon as I finish my chores
Handik bi astera, Osana beharrean	Two weeks later, Osane needed something
Nerea gana ***zunan*** igerri egitera	But Nerea had gone swimming
4. Begira, Osane, mutil eder hori	Look, Osana, at that cute boy
Mintzatzera hari ez ***dinat*** ausarpenik	I'm not brave enough to talk to him
Lasai, ene laguna, ez izan kezka	Calm down, my friend, don't worry
Badakinat dela *hitaz* agradatua	I know he likes you
Mutil horrek begi botatzen ***din*** eni?	Do you think that other boy likes me?
Gizongaiarekin ***dun*** Nerea	But Nerea had left with her boyfriend
Ez ***din*** ihardestsi	And did not answer
5. Osane, eri nago 'ta ene gizonak	Osane, I am ill
Laguntzarik emaiteko ez ***din*** ahalmena	And my husband cannot help me
Aut hi lagundako, heldu ***naun*** berehala	I will come right away
Beharrik bereburua ***dun*** ene senarra	Thank goodness, my husband is independent
Handik bi astera, Osana hil dela	Two weeks later, Osane died
Nerearen gaitz hartu 'ta	Having caught Nerea's illness
Osane: Hosanna!	Glory be to Osana!

Family and Love

As discussed in chapter 1, one of the manifestations of the androcentricism of Basque culture has been the social exclusion of girls and women from public participation in activities such as sports. Females who engaged in sports or other domains deemed "masculine" were called "*Mari Mutikoa*" or "*Mutil Gizonak*"[37] an epithet which loosely translates as "Tomboy," though it has more negative connotations than the English term. Some Basque women who immigrated to America found the proscriptions on their behavior loosened in the diaspora:

Text 5.15: *Mari Mutikoa* ("Tomboy")[38]

1. Galdegin zautan ene aitak	My father asked me:
Zer egin nahi ***dun***, ene alaba?	What do you want to do, my daughter?
Anaiekilan igo arbola	Climb a tree with my brothers
Ezin ***dun*** edo mari mutikoa	You can't or they'll call you 'tomboy'
2. Galdegin zautan ene aitak	My father asked me:
Zer egin nahi ***dun***, ene alaba?	What do you want to do, my daughter?
Anaiekilan joka pilota	Play ball with my brothers
Ezin ***dun*** edo mari mutikoa	You can't or they'll call you 'tomboy'
3. Galdegin zautan ene aitak	My father asked me:
Zer lan nahi egin ***dun***, ene alaba?	What work would you like to do, my daughter?
Zu bezala, izan zurgintza	I want to be a carpenter like you
Ezin ***dun*** edo mari mutikoa	You can't or they'll call you 'tomboy'
4. Galdegin zautan ene aitak	My father asked me:
Ameriketan zer *haiz*, ene alaba?	What are you doing in America, daughter?
Zu eta anaiak bezala	Like you and my brothers
Pilotan eta mus-ean joka	I'm playing handball and mus[39]
5. Galdegin zautan ene aitak	My father asked me:
Zer lan egiten ***dun***, ene alaba?	What work do you do, my daughter?
Ostatuko jabea naiz, Aita	I own a restaurant, Father
Gizonarekilan batera	With my husband
6.Galdegin zautan ene aitak	My father asked me:
Haurrik ***badun***, ene alaba?	Do you have children, my daughter?
Alaba politta, Aita	A lovely daughter, Father
Ni bezala Mari Mutikoa	A tomboy like me

Perhaps the fictional protagonist of "*Mari Mutikoa*" met her husband at a dance; many a couple (in the Basque Country and the diaspora) met this way. But the song below imagines a not-so-happy ending to a romance begun at such a dance:

Text 5.16: *Baztango Itzulia* (The Dance in Baztan)

1. Ni dantzen ari nintzen nere maiteñorekin	I was dancing with my sweetheart
Lagun bat etorri zitzaidan neri	A friend came up to me
Elgarrekin hasi ziren bi jira egiten	They took a turn on the dance floor
Oraindik dire dantzatzen	And they are dancing still

2. Oroitzen naiz ongi, Baztango itzuli	I remember well the dance in Baztan
Amodioa galdu nuelarik	When I lost my beloved
Ene maiteño betiko ene lagunandako	And my love to my friend forever
Eta ni gelditu bakarrik	And I was left alone
3. *Hi* dantzatzen ari *hintzen* ene lagunarekin	You were dancing with my friend
Hi galtzea ez ***ninan*** beldurrik	I was not worried about losing you
Diñat ene bizi guzia dantzatzeko *hirekin*	I have my whole life to dance with you
Bi jira ***ditun*** berdin harekin	I don't mind one dance with my friend
4. Oroitzen ***naun*** ongi, Baztango itzuli	I remember well the dance in Baztan
Amodiogabe utzirik	I was left without love
Dantzatuko *haiz* betiko ene lagunarekin	You will dance with my friend forever
Ez al ***dun*** lotsa baterik?	Have you no shame?
5. Ni dantzatzen ari nintzen hire lagunarekin	I was dancing with your friend
Bat-batean ni xoraturik	Suddenly, I was enchanted
Diat nere bizi guzia dantzetzeko harekin	I have my whole life to dance with him
'ta barka lortzeko higanik	And to earn your forgiveness
6. Oroitzen nauk ongi, Baztango itzuli	I remember well the dance in Baztan
Amodio ezagutu nuelarik	When I knew love
Dantzatuko nauk betiko hire lagunarekin	I will always dance with your friend
Hire barka estatzen **diat** nik	I ask your forgiveness

Religion

Another key domain from which Basque women have been excluded is religion. As we saw in chapter 4, laws passed in the fifteenth century prohibited women from leading the funeral dirges that had been their purview. The Roman Catholic faith, hegemonic in the Basque Country since the tenth century, excludes women from the priesthood even today. And this marginalization of female identity extends to *noka* as well. While the seventeenth century priest and writer Pedro Axular used *noka* to address the human soul,[40] contemporary texts no longer do so. But women in the Basque Country and immigrant communities continue to play key roles behind the scenes as sacristans (*serorak*), catechism teachers, Eucharistic ministers, as well as singers during mass. Indeed, my fellow NOKA members and I are among the many women[41] who have unwittingly reclaimed Basque women's historic roles in funerals, as cantors. As a reflection of this, the following song uses *noka* to address the soul of a departing loved one:

Text 5.17: *Gogoan Haugu* (We Keep You In Mind)

1. Gure laguna ospatzera	To celebrate our friend
Bilduak ***gaitun*** kantuz	We gather, singing
Adiskide hunen arima	We lift this spirit
Airatzen ***dinagu*** kantuz	Through our song
Gogoan *haugu*	We remember you
Beti Gure Bihotzetan	Always in our hearts
2. Hil hunen ondare ***din*** gure artean	The legacy of the departed is among us
Onartzen ***dinagu*** kantuz	We honor it
Gure laguna bakean dela	That our friend is in peace
Ospatzen ***dinagu*** kantuz	We celebrate in song
3. Adiskideri amodioa	Love, to our friend
Bidaltzen diogu kantuz	We send, through song
Gure laguna ospatzera	To celebrate our friend
Bilduak ***gaitun*** kantuz	We gather, singing

Life and Death or Carpe Diem

Indeed, one of the ways Basques have kept the memory of loved ones alive is by commemorating them through song. While most such songs that survive in written documents concern historical personages like Napoleon and Saint Ignatius Loyola (founder of the Jesuits), some "ordinary" people undoubtedly have been remembered by their family and friends via songs transmitted orally. I wrote the following song in honor of my mother after she passed away suddenly, eleven years ago:

Text 5.18: *Gerokoa Maitea* (The Future, My Dear)[42]

1. Gerokoa maitea	The future, my dear,
Ez ***dinagu*** gurea	Is not ours
Ez ***dun*** inoir sortuko	No one is born
Baizik ez hiltzeko	Who will not die
2. Emandako abrigua	The coat given me
Eskolako, gorria	For school, the red one
Urteak pasatu dira	The years passed
Han dago, dilindan	And it still hangs there
3. Mundua ikusi nahirik	I wanted to see the world
Maleta prestatu, nik	And prepared my suitcase
Baina memoriarik	But instead of memories
Ez du, errautsa baizik	It just gathered dust
4. Egindako eskulanak	My handiwork
Kutxa hartan paratuak	I put away in that trunk
Ongi konserbatzeko	There to be preserved
Han ni hil arteo	Until I died

Finally, many Basque songs attempt to communicate the writer's perspectives or philosophies of life. I found no songs in *noka* that did so from a woman's point of view. I would like to conclude this section then with a song using *noka* expressing mine:

Text 5.19: *Utzi Zan* (Let Go)

1. Utzi ***zan*** airoski	Let go, with grace
Bizia ez ***zainana***[43] komeni	The life not meant for you
Ospatu *hire* zori	Celebrate your destiny
Hire baitana, eman ***zan*** argi	Give light to what's within you
2. Haien ideiak ez ***diten*** *hireak*	Their ideas are not yours
Bertzeen iritziak ez izan behar *hireak*	Their opinions need not be
Ospatu *hire* zori	Celebrate your destiny
Hirea ez ***badun*** erraiten, nork erranen ***din***?	If you don't say it, who will?
Hirea ez ***badun*** egiten, nork eginen ***din?***	If you don't do it, who will?
Hirea ez ***badun*** bizitzen, nork biziko ***din***?	If you don't live your life, who will?

Conclusion

In this chapter, I have attempted to show that to the extent that the loss of *noka* is due to its stigmatization by particular deeds done to it—rather than some problem inherent to the pronoun itself—that countering these "misdeeds" with alternative *noka* texts might undo some of the semiotic damage that has been done to *noka*. It is my hope that in so doing, such examples might become the "ancestresses" to *noka*, taken up by current and future speakers of *Euskera*. Toward those ends, I proffer some final lyrics I wrote that summarize the social history of *noka*:

Text 5.20: *NOKAnta* (The NOKA Song)[44]

1. Gure eskuara sortu zelarik	When our Basque language was born
Batekin mintzatzekoan	In order to speak to one person
Izenordea, bakar-bakarra	There was only one pronoun
Ez zen zuka baizik hika	Called *zu*, not *hi*
Lehenbizian zuka zen plural	*Zu* used to be a plural pronoun
Denborakin bihurtu da	But over time things changed
Orain zuka da guztiz formala	Now *zu* is formal
Eta hika informala	And *hi* is informal
2. Hitanoa moldatzekotan	To use *hitanoa*
Grammatika jakin behar da	One must know the grammar
Gizonkiekin forma **duk** toka	The male form is *toka*
Emazteekin ***dun*** noka	And the female form is *noka*

Hikari berdin ***zaion*** mintzaile
Bereixten duena, entzulea
Eta “zu”, aldiz,
Da berdin berdin
Edozeineikin da untsa
3. Hika ongi erabiltzekotan
Ez omen ***dun*** hain errexa
Alokutiboa erabil behar da
Batzutan, beti ez, oha
Zuka ondoan delako zaila
Omen ***dun*** *hi* baztertua
Halere toka
Eta ez noka
Entzun ***dinagu*** tarteka
4. Etxepareren liburuetan[45]
Zuka ***dun*** nahiago duena
Batzutan toka agertzen bainan
Behin ere ikusten ***dun*** noka
Garai horetan baita ***ditinagu***
Noka erabiltzen testuak
Leizarragena eta “promesa”
Nafarroan lehen errana
5. Chinoko euskaldunen artean
Baditun nokalariak
Konfiantzekoa
Lagun artekoa
Atxeman ***diten*** noka
Bertzeak nahi ***zitenan*** mintzatu
Bainan *hunan* debekatua
Nokalariak die eroxkak,
Buhameak eta sorginak
6. Chinoko alabak ***gaitun*** gu
Hemen euskera aditua
Gure xedea
Dun famatzea
Eskual kultura mundura
Nokaren aberastasuna
Kantuetan gorestea
Erabilera onartzea ‘ta
Ahalbada zabaltzea

Hi doesn’t care about the speaker
Only about the addressee
But *zu*
Is always the same
It’s appropriate for everybody.
To use *hika* well
Is not easy
The “allocutive” is used
But only sometimes
Because it’s more difficult than *zuka*
Hi has been left behind
Even so, *toka*
But not *noka*
Is heard now and then
In Etxepare’s books
He prefers *zuka*
Sometimes *toka* is used
But never *noka*
In that time period
Other texts use *noka*
Like Leizarraga’s
And marriage vows from Nafarroa[46]
Among Chino Basques
We have some *noka* speakers
To express trust
And show friendship
Is what they use it for
Others wanted to speak it
But it was forbidden them:
Noka spakers are crazy,
Gypsies, or witches
We daughters of Chino
Heard Basque here
Our wish
Is to celebrate
The Basque culture
As well as the richness of *noka*
Through song
To make it acceptable to speak
And, hopefully, to spread its use

Notes

1 Uruthy, *Ebanjelio Santia*, 73. My translation.

2 Uriarte, *Canticum Canticorum Salomonis,* 1858.

3 However, Satrustegui found another romantic context in which only *hika* was used, among a couple taking wedding vows in 1547. Here are the *noka* verses: “Nic Martin, *y* Joanna, ***arçenaut*** neure alaroçacat eta ***hic arnaçan*** *yre* sposaçat,

eta prometacen ***dinat*** ez verçe emazteric eguiteko *y* vaycen vici nayçen artean eta guardaçeco lealtadea" ("I, Martin, take thee Joanna as my wife and you take me as your spouse, and I promise to take no other wife as long as thou shalt live and to be loyal as long as I shall live.") My translation. *See* Satrustegui, "Promesa matrimonial."

4 Alan R. King translated these passages in The Song of Solomon (also known as "The Song of Songs").

5 Uriarte, *Canticum Canticoum Salomonis,* 191–225.

6 The third chapter contains no *noka* (or *toka*), perhaps because it is the only chapter which contains no dialogue between the lovers.

7 Fox, "Song of Songs," 474.

8 Ibid.

9 Uriarte, *Canticum Canticorum Salomis,* 207–210.

10 May, "Song of Songs," 474.

11 Ibid.

12 Ibid.

13 Ibid.

14 Ibid.

15 Sweeney, *Tanak,* 426

16 Fox, "The Song of Songs," 473.

17 Errington, "On the Nature of the Sociolinguistic Sign."

18 Dueso, *Lamiak eta Sorginak,* 41.

19 Ibid., 43.

20 Ibid.

21 Barandiaran, *Diccionario,* 39.

22 Cerquand, *Ipar Euskal Herriko Legenda eta Ipuinak II,* 21.

23 Barandiaran, *El Mundo en la Mente Popular Vasca, II,* 92-93.

24 Cerquand, *Ipar Euskal Herriko Legenda eta Ipuinak II,* 10–11.

25 Barandiaran, *De Etnografía de Navarra,* 34.

26 See also Aulestia, *Improvisational Poetry,* 35-36.

27 A performance of many of these original songs with *noka* lyrics can be viewed at: www.loc.gov/concerts/folklife/noka.html.

28 This appeared in the *Diasporako Bertsoak,* an anthology of verses from the diaspora. A version of this song can be found on the CD, "NOKATU": (www.ilovenoka.com).

29 A version of this song is in progress: belindathom.com

30 Spanish spelling, "Guernica."

31 See Legarreta, *The Guernica Generation.*

32 Belinda Thom has written music for these lyrics. A recording of the song is in progress: belindathom.com.

33 Babcock, "Trial Could Shed Light," *Los Angeles Times,* A1, A4. Belinda Thom has written music for these lyrics, a recording of which is in progress: belindathom.com.

34 This appeared in the *Diasporako Bertsoak,* an anthology of verses from the diaspora. A performance of this song can be viewed on: www.loc.gov/concerts/folklife/noka.html. It is also available on the CD, *"NOKA Lau":* www.ilovenoka.com.

35 See Mallea-Olaetxe, *Speaking Through the Aspens*, 2000. A recording of this song is in progress: www.ilovenoka.com.

36 Osane and Nerea are female names for "Remedy" and "Mine", respectively.

37 Ugalde, "Apuntes Sobre el Género," 290.

38 A recording of this song is in progress: belindathom.com

39 *Pilota* is Basque handball; *mus* is a card game.

40 Axular, *Gero*, 1643. While this is a negative use of *noka*, to curse the soul of a sinner (see chapter 2), it begs the question of whether the soul was once conceptualized as female, as in other languages (e.g., "*la arima*" in Castilian and "*l'ame*" in French).

41 Germaine Lanathoua, originally from Ezterenzubi (Baxe Nafarroa) is the most prominent of these in the Chino immigrant community. American-born Maite Maisterrena, whose father hailed from the Baztan Valley (Nafarroa), also helps lead Basque song at funerals.

42 A version of this can be found on the CD, "*Bi Ahizpak*": www.ilovenoka.com.

43 I take this allocutive form from Leizarraga (see Text 2.10, line 28), though I have modernized its spelling. A recording of this song is in progress: www.ilovenoka.com.

44 A version of this song can be found on the CD, "*NOKATU*": www.ilovenoka.com

45 Etxepare, *Linguae Vasconum Primitiae*, 1545.

46 Satrustegui, "Promesa Matrimonial del Año 1547," 1977.

6

Noka as Synecdoche: Conclusions and Implications

Synecdoche: A figure of speech by which a part is put for the whole.

—Merriam-Webster's Dictionary

This book began as an archival journey to answer questions that arose from my experience as a speaker of *Euskera* and ethnographic work I have conducted in the Basque Country and the diaspora over thirty years. It is perhaps a testament to the privileges I have enjoyed growing up outside the Basque Country that I was unaware for so long how much my heritage favored its male members. I participated in Basque dance groups from the age of seven until I left home for college, oblivious that many of the dances exported from the Basque Country—such as the tell-tale "*Mutikoak*" (Boys' Dance)—were historically performed only by male dancers. My sister, Candida, and other American-born women played sports such as *pala* (not to mention, many American sports) without the sting of the "*Mari Mutikoa*" (Tom Boy) epithet suffered by our mothers' generation who pursued athletic pursuits. Without realizing it, my fellow NOKA members and I have bucked the centuries-old proscriptions against females singing in public for two decades. Perhaps most importantly as *Euskera* is an endangered language, we daughters of Basque immigrants have kept apace with the sons when it comes to speaking the language of our parents, as many of the moorings undergirding androcentric language ideologies did not survive the trip across the Atlantic.

However, this journey has demonstrated that without a fuller understanding of how the language we use and the cultural information it transmits, even native and heritage speakers can inadvertently promote inequitable images of the language communities in which they (we) participate. I have focused here on the inequities that lie along gender lines, but scholars of other endangered languages could identify the inequalities along other social categories that language ideologies in those communities perpetuate. I have shown that despite their linguistic equivalence as second person singular pronouns, *noka* (for a female addressee) and *toka* (for a male addressee), *noka* suffers more negative meanings, and greater attrition, than *toka*. This has not only restricted the linguistic resources that can be used to address a girl or a woman (by male and female speakers) as compared to those that can be used to address a boy or man—an inequity in and of itself—but also limited the kinds of identities that can be forged with *noka*.

Noka as Synecdoche

One might wonder why anyone should care about any of this: Why should it matter if such a small part of the Basque language dies? Why should it matter what it used to mean, how it was used in the past and the consequences of these for contemporary usage? Especially given that Basque is a small language when it comes to the global stage, why should we bother to educate its speakers and potential speakers about such a small part of the language? Isn't saving this endangered language in and of itself enough to do?

I would argue that it is precisely because Basque is an endangered language that we should care about even such a small aspect of it as *noka*. For even the infrequent uses of *noka* in the archives provides us with much information about Basque cultural values, relationships between speakers, and conversational norms that would otherwise be lost without *noka*. In this sense, *noka* can be seen as a synecdoche: the vitality (or lack thereof) of this part of speech stands in for the Basque language and culture as a whole. The marginalization of *noka* is not just about the pronoun itself; it reflects the gender inequities suffered by actual girls and women *noka* is (linguistically speaking) intended to address. Until recently, social convention proscribed women from attending or participating the *bertsolaritza* contests; laws prohibited women from singing in public; insults like "*Mari Mutikoa*" discouraged women and girls from engaging in sports; prestige adhered to male-dominated activities like the Basque Language Academy, while the names of the women who quietly taught their children Basque at home (or clandestinely in *ikastolas* during the Franco dictatorship) remain unacknowledged; male folklorists and ethnographers are celebrated but their many female informants are smuggled into footnotes (anthologies often omit their names altogether). Images in the public domain and in curricular materials celebrate the "Man of the Plaza" (*Plazako Gizona*) who "stands out and knows how to act in public"[1] through self-possession and feats of strength. But images usually portray women not as active agents in their own right but playing supportive roles to others in the private realm despite the inroads women have made in the educational and occupational spheres in the last fifty years.

As goes *noka* as a part of speech, I would argue, so go the social conditions of the actual girls and women *noka* is meant to address.

Implications for Endangered Languages

The loss of *noka* has implications beyond the Basque-speaking community. *Noka*—especially when used in the allocutive—is perhaps the most imperilled aspect of the endangered Basque language. Everyone, not just Basque speakers, loses an important window into the human experience whenever such an unusual aspect of a language disappears. That is, we lose not only access to insights into the particular culture's knowledge, insights, and values. We also lose models for how we might use language—in this case, "merely" a pronoun—to interact in nuanced ways with others; to signal friendship, animosity, and everything in between; and to construct various kinds of identity. Much crucial information about Basque culture and history—especially regarding gender roles, language ideologies, and identity—have been (perhaps irrevocably) lost because canonical literary genres and pedagogical materials have not attended to *noka* already. As with whole languages, so with its parts: To the extent that *noka* provides unique perspectives on the world, these are likely to be lost even if the language itself survives. As a language isolate, *Euskera* has no linguistic relatives to which it could bequeath *noka*'s unique sociolinguistic legacies.

I hope that this work also shows the value of using a historical sociolinguistic approach to understand how language ideologies affect language use and effect language change. Especially when contemporary models of particular speech forms are not widely available—as with *noka*, which has practically disappeared from speech—it is crucial that such models be made available through archival materials. We have seen that biblical materials, songs, and folklore provide rich sources for a robust sociolinguistic understanding of *noka*, yet educational efforts to teach *Euskera* (in the Basque Country or in the diaspora) do not mine these materials nearly to the extent they could to teach either the language itself or the culture in which it is embedded. Indeed, *noka* rarely makes an appearance in school curricula or other pedagogical materials. To the extent that it does, it is used in ways that present a very restricted view of its meanings (mostly negative) and its users.[2] If it is to be used for daily interaction, *noka* must become a more palatable pronoun and the models for such uses lie in the archives.

I argue for the imperative of utilizing, and mining, as wide a swath as possible of a given language's cultural artifacts in teaching that language. It is perhaps understandable that efforts to revitalize threatened languages mimic the literary genres of the cultures who have dominated them in attempting to take their place alongside them on the global linguistic stage. It is perhaps good strategy that such efforts focus on making dictionaries and textbooks in teaching the language. But my work shows the peril of focusing on such "learned" materials and "literary" genres to the exclusion of "vernacular" texts often more familiar to "ordinary" native speakers, such as folktales and songs. Such sources have been overlooked, in part, not only because they remain in the purview of the "uneducated masses" but because they are often the domain of women. Basque women have transmitted these folklores from hearth to hearth over the centuries. As Bourdieu might say, perhaps it was to "distinguish"[3] themselves from such "old wives' tales" that the men who have made themselves the primary agents in efforts to revitalize *Euskera* have pushed folktales outside the bounds of the literary canon.

Scholars of many languages have shown that revitalization efforts often (unwittingly) redraw boundaries between speakers (those who are "authentic" versus those who are not) and language varieties ("standard" versus "dialect"), as well as reinscribe language ideologies that privilege certain kinds of identities and values over others.[4] Scholars have also shown that literature, especially officially sanctioned genres, can go a long way in imposing standards.[5] If an endangered language is to be a living language, it must become a language for living—for every interactional purpose, the mundane as well as the profound, by individuals of every social group, status, and situation.

While educational movements understandably often focus their efforts on increasing the prestige of their language vis-à-vis the language that has dominated them (often, using the "master's tools to undo the master's house"), a language that lives also is used to express friendship, to build bonds of solidarity. Obviously, friendship and solidarity cannot be forced upon speakers. However, I would argue that it would behoove efforts to revitalize endangered languages if they were to provide as wide a use of the target language for solidarity purposes as possible, that speakers and learners could draw on, on their own, for such purposes—and such can often be found in vernacular genres rather than the dictionary, textbook, or the literary canon.

The Basque case also suggests that efforts to save endangered languages should focus not just on teaching students and speakers, "How do I say that?", but also "What kind of person do I seem to be when I say that?" A language cannot be saved if it is not savored, as a way to express the range of identities and emotions that its (potential) speakers feel or aspire to become. A language will not survive if it is seen as something that is just for school, for passing exams, for getting into college, or obtaining a job that requires it. It cannot remain or become a language ascribed only instrumental values; it must also be associated with affective values that encompass the entire human experience—the good, the bad, and the indifferent—and compatible with many kinds of identities. I hope I have shown how a historical sociolinguistic approach can provide the means by which such uses can be recovered for contemporary purposes.

Finally, the Basque case shows the difference gender makes when it comes to the state, fate, or status of endangered languages. Language, gender, and religion are all used to create social boundaries, construct personal identities, and carry out interactional functions. Yet few scholars have examined how ideologies of language and gender interact with theologies or belief systems and how these interactions affect linguistic practices or effect language change. I hope I have shown that value of examining all these constructs simultaneously.

Conclusion

In this book, I have drawn on archival materials since the fifteenth century to document how *noka*—linguistically, "just" a familiar second person singular pronoun for a female addressee in the Basque language—attained such negative language ideologies that it is disappearing from contemporary speech. I have also uncovered from the archives more complex, nuanced, and positive uses of *noka* (and created some of my own through song) in the hopes that these will counter *noka*'s "semantic derogation"[6]—and perhaps, restore its use. But the more likely scenario is that

I will have to settle for achieving only the first goal. Actually saving *noka* from extinction seems very unlikely, given the small number of Basque speakers who use or even know about *noka*. But there is a Basque saying: Whatever has a name, exists ("*Izan duan guztia omen da*").[7] To the extent that this book rounds out all the things *noka* has been and could be for Basque speakers and Basque culture, perhaps the more positive of these will restore *noka*'s good name—they too will become part of *noka*'s sociolinguistic legacy.

And there is something to be said for that. To paraphrase the old Basque saying: "As *noka* lived well, may she die well."

Notes

1 Fernandez, *Mujer, Ritual y Fiesta*, 83.
2 Echeverria, "Language Ideologies and Practices."
3 Bourdieu, *Distinction*.
4 Dorian, "The Value of Language Movements"; Eckert, "Diglossia."
5 Inoue, "Gender, Language and Modernity."
6 Schultz, "Semantic Derogation."
7 Barandaiaran, *Diccionario de Mitologia Vasca*, 112.

Bibliography

Achtemeier, Paul J., ed. *The HarperCollins Bible Dictionary*. San Francisco: HarperCollins, 1989.

Addiss, Stephen, and S. Lombardo. *Lao-Tzu: Tao Te Ching*. Indianapolis: Hackett Publishing Company, 1993.

The Alan Lomax Collection: The Spanish Recordings. Basque Country: Navarre, 2004.

Alberdi, Xabier. "Euskarazko Tratamenduen Ikuspegia: I. Historia Apur Bat." *AJSU* 20 (1986): 149-202.

———. *Hika Tratamenduari Buruzko Ihardunaldiak*. Arrasate: San Frantzisko Ikastola, 1992.

———. "The Development of the Basque System of Terms of Address and the Allocutive Conjugation." In *Towards a History of the Basque Language*, edited by José Ignacio Hualde, Joseba Lakarra, and R. L. Trask, 275–293. *Current Issues in Linguistic Theory*, 131. Amsterdam: John Benjamins, 1995.

———. *Euskararen Tratamenduak: Erabilera*. Bilbo: Euzkaltzaindia, 1996.

Amuriza, Xabier. *Bizkaiko Bertsogintza I: Izengabeak*. Bilbo: Bizkaiko Foru Aldundia, 1995.

———. *Bizkaiko Bertsogintza II: Izendunak*. Bilbo: Bizkaiko Foru Aldundia, 1998.

———. *Bizkaiko Bertsogintza III: Gerraurreko Emoitza*. Bilbo: Bizkaiko Foru Aldundia, 2006.

Anderson, Benedict. *Imagined Communities: Reflections on the Origin and Spread of Nationalism*. London and New York: Verso, 1991.

Ansorena, José Ignacio. *Cancionero Popular Vasco*. Donostia: Erein, 2008.

———. *Euskal Kantak*. Donostia: Erein, 2000.

Antonov, Anton. "Verbal Allocutivity in a Crosslinguistic Perspective." *Linguistic Typology* 19, no. 1 (2019): 55–85.

Arbelbide, Xipri, *Piarres Topet Etxahun: Bertso Bilduma (Zuberoera-Batua)*. Donostia: Elkar, 1987.

Aretxaga. Begoña. *Los Funerales en el Nacionalismo Radical Vasco*. San Sebastian: La Primitiva Casa Baroja, 1988.

Arriaga, José Luis. *Euskal Mitologia*. Bilbo: Gero, 2000.

Auer, Anita and Anja Voeste. "Grammatical Variables." In *The Handbook of Historical Sociolinguistics*, edited by Juan M. Hernández-Campoy and J. Camino Conde-Silvestre, 254–270. Oxford: Wiley-Blackwell.

Aulestia, Gorka. *Basque-English Dictionary*. Reno: University of Nevada Press, 1989.

———. *Improvisational Poetry from the Basque Country*. Reno: University of Nevada Press, 1995.

Axular, Pedro. *Gero*. Bordeaux, 1643.

Azkue, Resurreccion Maria. *Cancionero Popular Vasco I*. Acedo: Wilsen Editorial, 1968.

———. *Cancionero Popular Vasco II*. Acedo: Wilsen Editorial, 1968.

———. *Diccionario Vasco-Española-Frances, II*. Bilbao: La Gran Enciclopedia Vasca, 1969.

———. *Euskaleriaren Yakintza: Literatura Popular del Pais Vasco I—Costumbres y Supersticiones*. Bilbao & Madrid: Euskaltzaindia & Espasa Calpe, 1989.

———. *Lamiak Euskalerrian*. Bilbo: Eusko Argitaldaria, 1927.

Azkue, Resurreccion María, J. M. Barandiaran, J. Barbier, J. F. Cerquand, and J. Garmendia Larrañaga. *Euskal Herriko Leienda Hautatuak*. Donostia: Hiria, 2002.

Azkue, Resurreccion María, J. M. Barandiaran, J. Barbier, J. F. Cerquand, J. Garmendia Larrañaga, J. Gereño, J., and W. Webster. *Euskal Herriko Mito Hautatuak*. Donostia: Hiria, 2002.

Babcock, James. "Trial Could Shed Light on Spain's Stolen Babies Saga." *Los Angeles Times*, June 25, 2018.

Bahktin, Mikhail. "Discourse in the Novel." In *The Dialogic Imagination*. Austin: University of Texas Press, 1981.

Barandiaran, Asier. *Diasporako Bertsoak: Euskal Kultura Bilduma*, vol. 79. Buenos Aires: EKIN, 2016.

Barandiaran, José Miguel. *Brujería y Brujas en los Relatos Populares Vascos*. Donostia: Txertoa, 2002.

———. *De Etnografía de Navarra*. Donostia: Txertoa, 1987.

———. *Diccionario de Mitología Vasca*. San Sebastian: Txertoa, 2003.

———. *Diccionario de Mitología Vasca: Creencias y Leyendas Tradicionales*. Donostia: Txertoa, 2003.

———. *El Mundo en la Mente Popular Vasca I*. San Sebastian: Colección Auñamendi, 1960.

———. *El Mundo en la Mente Popular Vasca III*. San Sebastian: Colección Auñamendi, 1962.

———. "Folklore en le Montaña Alavesa." *Eusko-Folklore*. 1921.

———. *Tradiciones y Leyendas. Eusko-Folklore. Obras Completas*. Bilbo: Editorial La Gran Enciclopedia Vasca, 1973.

———. *The Selected Writings of José Miguel de Barandiaran: Basque Prehistory and Ethnography*, edited by J. Altuna. Reno: University of Nevada Press, 2008.

———. *A View from the Witch's Cave: Folktales of the Pyrenees*, edited by Luis de Barandiaran Irizar; translated by Linda White. Reno: University of Nevada Press, 1991.

Barbier, Jean. *Ixtorio-Mixtorio: Bernardo Garro 'Otxolua.'* Bilbao: Labayru Ikastegia & Bizkaiko Aurrezki Kutxa, 1999.

———. *Légendes du Pays Basque: d'aprés la Tradition*. Paris: Libraire Delagrave, 1931.

Blenkinsopp, Joseph. "Introduction to the Prophetic Books." In *Bible Commentary*, edited by James L. Mays, 480–488. New York: Harper One, 1988.

Bonaparte, Lucien Luis. *Formulaire de Prone Conserve dans 'Eglise d'Arbonnne (Pregariac Bayonaco Diocezacotz)*. London: Strangeways & Walden, 1866 [1651].

Bourdieu, Pierre. *Distinction: A Social Critique of the Judgement of Taste*. Cambridge: Harvard University Press. 1984.

———. "The Economics of Linguistic Exchanges." *Social Science Information* 16 (1977): 645–668.

Brown, Roger, and Albert Gilman. "The Pronouns of Power and Solidarity." In *Style in Language*, edited by Thomas Sebeok, 253–276. Cambridge: Technical Press of the Massachusetts Institute of Technology, 1960.

Bullen, Margaret. "Gender and Identity in the Alardes of Two Basque Towns." *Basque Studies Program Occasional Paper Series* 5 (1999): 149–177.

Caro Baroja, Julio. *The Basques*. Reno: The Center for Basque Studies, 2009 [1949].

———. *The World of the Witches*. Chicago: The University of Chicago Press, 1968.

Carthaigh, Criostoir Mac. "Midwife to the Fairies (ML 5070): The Irish Variants in Their Scottish and Scandinavian Perspective." *Bealoideas: The Journal of the Folklore of Ireland Society* 59 (1991): 133–144.

Cerquand, Jean-François. *Ipar Euskal Herriko Legenda eta Ipuinak*. Donostia: Txertoa, 1986 [1875–1876].

———. *Légendes et Récits du Pays Basque I*. Paris: Leon Ribaut, 1875.

———. *Légendes et Récits du Pays Basque II*. Paris, Leon Ribaut, 1876.

Chamberlayne, Joanes, ed. *Oratio Dominica*. Amsterdam: Guilielmi & Davidis Goerei, 1715.

Clark, Robert. "Euzkadi: Basque Nationalism in Spain since the Civil War." In *Nations Without a State: Ethnic Minorities in Western Europe*, edited by Charles R. Foster, 75–100. New York: Prager Publishers.

Conde-Silvestre, J. Camilo, and Juan M. Hernández-Campoy. "Introduction." In *The Handbook of Historical Sociolinguistics*, edited by Juan M. Hernández-Campoy and J. Camilo Conde-Silvestre, 1–8. Oxford: Wiley-Blackwell, 2012.

Cosem, Michel. *Euskal Herriko Kondairak*. Euba-Amorebieta: Ibaizabal, 2000.

Craddock, Fred D. "Luke." In *Bible Commentary*, edited by James L. Mays, 925–955. New York: Harper One, 1988.

De Lancre, Pierre. *Tableau de L'Inconstance des Mauvais Anges et Demons ou il est Amplement Traite des Sorciers et de la Sorcellerie*. Paris, 1612.

Del Valle, Teresa. *Mujer Vasca: Imagen y Realidad*. Barcelona: Anthropos, 1985.

De Rijk, R.P.G., "Familiarity or Solidarity: The Pronoun Hi in Basque." *Revista Internacional de Estudios Vascos* 36 (1991): 373–378.

———. "El Género en la Construccion de la Identidad Nacionalista." *Forum Hispanica de los Paises Bajos* 16 (2000): 37–44.

Diccionario Enciclopedico Vasco. San Sebastian: Editorial Auñamendi, 1988.

Dodgson, E.S. "Appendix B. List of Translations of the Bible or Parts of it into Basque)." In *The Earliest Translation of the Old Testament into the Basque Language (A Fragment)*, D'Urte, Pierre edited by Llewelyn Thomas, 158-163. Clarendon Press: Oxford, 1894.

Dorian, Nancy. "The Value of Language Movements That Are Unlikely to Succeed." *International Journal of the Sociology of Language* 68 (1981): 57–67.

Dueso, José. *Lamiak eta Sorginak*. Donostia: Honena, 1998.

———. *Nosotros Los Vascos: Mitos, Leyendas y Costumbres, I Mitología*. Grafman: Lur, 1987.

D'Urte, Pierre. *Grammaire Cantabrique Basque*. Bagneres-de-Bigorre: Imrimerie D. Berot, 1900 [1712].

———. *The Earliest Translation of the Old Testament into the Basque Language (A Fragment),* edited by Llewelyn Thomas. Clarendon Press: Oxford, 1894.

Duvoisin, Jean Baptiste. *Bible Saindua, La Santa Biblia: Version Euskerica de la Vulgata Realizada por El Capitan Duvoisin.* Bilbao: La Gran Enciclopedia Vasca, 1972 [1865].

Echeverria, Begoña. "Capturing Basque Witches, Releasing Lyrical Resources: From Historical Cases to Folk Song." *Preternature* 3, no 1 (2014): 110–146.

———. "(En)gendering Basque culture: Musical Notes from the Archives." BOGA: Basque Studies Consortium Journal, 2004.

———. "Indexing Religious Identity in the French Basque Country: Toward a Theory of Pronominal Shift." In *Studies in Basque and Historical Linguistics in Memory of R. L. Trask*, edited by Joseba Lakarra and Jose Ignacio Hualde, 273–291. Donostia; Bilbo: Gipuzkoako Foru Aldundia and Euskal Herriko Unibersitatea, 2006.

———. "Language Ideologies in (En)gendering the Basque Nation." *Language in Society* 32, no. 3 (2003): 383–414.

———. "Language Lessons, Gender Lessons: Androcentric Inscription in a Basque-English Dictionary." Hizkunea, 2007

———. "Of Harlots, Whores but Not Lovers: Dressing Down the Pronoun for a Female Addressee in a Basque Old Testament." In *Gender in the Periphery: Grammatical and Social Gender from the Margins*, edited by Julie Abbou and Fabienne H. Baider, 353–379. Amsterdam/Philadelphia: John Benjamins, 2016.

———. "What of the Siren That Has No Song? Lessons from The Basque Lamina." *Western Folklore* 75, no. 2 (2016): 165–190.

Eckert, Penelope. "The Paradox of Minority Language Movements." *Journal of Multilingual and Multicultural Development* 4 (1980): 289–300.

Errington, Joseph. "On the Nature of the Sociolinguistic Sign: Describing the Javanese Speech Levels." In *Semiotic Mediation*, edited by Elizabeth Mertz and Richard J. Parmentier, 287–310. Orlando: Academic Press, 1985.

Esteban, M.L., and Amurrio, M., Eds. *Feminist Challenges in the Social Sciences: Gender Studies in the Basque Country.* Reno: University of Nevada Press, 2010.

Estornes Lasa, Bernardo. "Erronkari'ko Uskaraz Elestak (Fraseologia Roncalesa)." *Fontes Linguae Vasconum: Studia et Documenta* 40 (1982): 461–484.

Etcheberri, Joanes. *Manuel Devotionezcoa, edo Ezperen, Oren Oro Escuetan Errabilltceco Liburuchoa: Escarazco Versutan Eguina eta Guztia Bi Partetan Berecia (Bi-garren Liburuar. Guiristinoac Erran Behar Lituvquen Othoitzcez).* Bordeaux: Mongiron & Millagnes, 1669.

Etxebarria Ayesta, Juan Manuel. *Bizkaialdeko Ipuin-Esaundak.* Euba-Amorebieta: Ibaizabal, 2002.

Etxepare, Beñaut. *Linguae Vacsconum Primitiae.* Bordeaux, Morpain. 1545.

Fernandez de Larrinoa, Kepa. *Mujer, Ritual y Fiesta: Género, Antropología y Teatro de Carnival en el Valle de Soule.* Iruñea: Pamiela, 1997.

Fox, Michael V. "The Song of Songs." In *Bible Commentary*, edited by James L. Mays, 472– 477. New York: Harper One, 1988.

Gal, Susan, and Judith Irvine. "The Boundaries of Languages and Disciplines: How Ideologies Construct Difference." *Social Research* 62 (1995): 967–1001.

Gallop, Rodney. *A Book of the Basques*. Reno: University of Nevada Press, 1970 [1930].

Garmendia Larrañaga, J. *Jentilak, Sorginak eta Beste: Euskal Pentsamendu Magikoa II.* Donostia: Elkar, 1994.

Goffman, Erving. *Frame Analysis: An Essay on the Organization of Experience.* Cambridge: Harvard University Press, 1974.

Gumperz, John. "Linguistic and Social Interaction in Two Communities." *American Anthropologist* 66, no. 6, part 2 (1964): 137–152.

Haramburu, Jean. *Debocino Ezcuarra, Mirailla eta Oracinoteguia: Virginaren Debocinoa, Marinelena, eta San Francesen Heren Ordena.* Bordeaux, 1635.

Haraneder, Joannes. *Jesu Christoren Evangelio Saindua*. Bilbo: Euskaltzaindia, 1990.

Haritschelhar, Jean. "Ideologiak Lore Jokoetako Kantuetan (Ideology in the Songs of the Floral Games)." In *Antoine d'Abbadie 1897–1997: Congres International* (Hendaya, 1997), 621–653. Donostia & Bilbao: Eusko Ikaskuntza, 1998.

Harizmendi, C. *L'Office de la Vierge Marie, en Basque Labourdin.* Chalon-sur-Saone, 1901 [1658].

Haskins, Susan. *Mary Magdalen: The Essential History.* London: Harper-Collins, 1993.

Heiberg, Marianne. *The Making of the Basque Nation.* Cambridge: Cambridge University Press, 1989.

Henningsen, Gustav. *The Witches' Advocate: Basque Witchcraft and the Spanish Inquisition (1604–1614).* Reno: University of Nevada Press, 1980.

———. "Basque Country." In *Encyclopedia of Witchcraft: The Western Tradition, Volume I, A–D*, edited by Richard Golden. Santa Barbara: ABC-CLIO, 2006.

———, ed. *The Salazar Documents: Inquisitor Alonso de Salazar Frías and Others on the Basque Witch Persecution.* Leiden & Boston: Brill, 2004.

Hooper, John. *The Spaniards: A Portrait of the New Spain.* Middlesex: Viking, 1986.

Idoate, Florencio. *La Brujería en Navarra y Sus Documentos. Diputacion Foral de Navarra: Pamplona*, 1978.

Inoue, Miyako. "Gender, Language and Modernity: Toward an Effective History of 'Japanese Women's Language.'" *American Ethnologist* no. 29 (2002): 392–422.

Kalmanofsky, Amy. "The Dangerous Sisters of Jeremiah and Ezekiel." *Journal of Biblical Studies* 130, no. 2 (2011): 299–312.

Kalzakorta, Jabier. *Lamia, Sorgin eta Tartaroen: Erresuma Ezkutua.* Bilbao: Labayru Ikastegia & Bilbao Bizkaia Kutxa, 1997.

Kselman, John S. "Genesis." In *HarperCollins Bible Commentary*, edited by James L. Mays, 83–118. New York: Harper One, 1988.

Kuipers, Joel C. *Language, Identity and Marginality in Indonesia.* Cambridge: Cambridge University Press, 1998.

Lea, Henry Charles. *A History of the Inquisition of Spain*, volume 4. New York: AMS Press, Inc., 1966.

Legarreta, Dorothy. *The Guernica Generation: Basque Refugee Children of the Spanish Civil War.* Reno: University of Nevada Press, 1984.

Leizarraga, Joanes. *Jesus Christ Gure Jaunaren Testamentu Berria Othoitza Ecclesiasticoen Forma Catechismea.* Bilbao: Euskaltzaindia, 1990 [1571].

Llande, Pierre. *Dictionnaire Basque-Français.* Paris: Gabriel Beauchesne, 2001 [1926].

McBrien, Richard, ed. *Encyclopedia of Catholicism: A Comprehensive, Illustrated Reference on the People, Places, History, Theology, Art, Sacraments, and Spirituality of the World's Largest Religious Tradition.* San Francisco: Harper, 1989.

McCarter, P. Kyle. "Exodus." In *HarperCollins Bible Commentary*, edited by James L. Mays, 119–144. New York: Harper One, 1988.

Mallea-Olaetxe, Joxe. *Speaking through the Aspens: Basque Tree Carvings in California and Nevada.* Reno: University of Nevada Press, 2000.

Manterola, José. *Cancionero Vasco.* Donostia: Sendoa, 1981.

March, W. Eugene. "Micah." In *Bible Commentary*, edited by James L. Mays, 660–664. New York: Harper One, 1988.

Materre, Estebe. *Dotrina Christiana.* Bordeaux, 1623.

Matthews, Victor. *The Hebrew Prophets and Their Social World: An Introduction.* Grand Rapids, MI: Baker Academic, 2012.

Michelena, Luis. *Textos Arcaicos Vascos.* Madrid: Minotaurio, 1964.

Mujika, Luis M. *Euskal Lirika Tradizionala I.* San Sebastian: Haranburu, 1985.

———. *Euskal Lirika Tradizionala II.* San Sebastian: Haranburu, 1985.

———. *Euskal Lirika Tradizionala III.* San Sebastian: Haranburu, 1985.

———. *Euskal Lirika Tradizionala IV.* San Sebastian: Haranburu, 1985.

Nehor and Dufau, C. "Aitak Erran Dio Alabari." In *Bertsolaritzaren Historia: Lapurdi, Baxanabarre eta Zuberoako Bertso eta Kantak I: Anonimoak*, by Patri Urkizu, 621. Donostia: Etor, 2003.

Nettle, Daniel, and Suzanne Romaine. *Vanishing Voices: The Extinction of the World's Languages.* New York: Oxford University Press, 2000.

Nuñez, Luis. *Clases Sociales en Euskadi.* San Sebastian: Editorial Txertoa, 1977.

Ochs, Elinor. "Indexing Gender." In *Rethinking Context*, edited by Alessandro Duranti and Charles Goodwin, 335–358. Cambridge: Cambridge University Press, 1992.

Onaindia, Santiago. *Lamiñak Orrazi-Eskean.* Amorebieta: 1978.

Ormaetxea, Nicolas. *Euskaldunak Poema eta Olerki Guziak: Poema los Lascos y Poesias Completas.* San Sebastian: Editorial Auñamendi, 1972.

Ott, Sandra. *The Circle of Mountains: A Basque Shepherding Community.* Oxford: Oxford University Press, 1981.

———. "Indarra: Some Reflections on a Basque Concept." In *Honour and Grace*, edited by J. Peristany and J. Pitt Rivers, 193-214, 1990.

Overholt, Thomas W. "Jeremiah." In *Bible Commentary*, edited by James L. Mays, 538–576. New York: Harper One, 1988.

Oyharçabal, Bernard. "Verb Agreement with Non Arguments: On Allocutive

Agreement." In *Generative Studies in Basque Linguistics*, edited by José I. Hualde, and Jon Ortiz de Urbina, 189–220. *Current Issues in Linguistic Theory 105*. Amsterdam: John Benjamins, 1993.

Payne, Stanley. *Basque Nationalism*. Reno: University of Nevada Press, 1987.

Richelieu, Cardinala. *Guiristinoaren Dotrina*. Bilbo: Labayru Ikastegia, 2006 [1618].

Riezu, Jorge, ed. *Cancionero Vasco P. Donostia*, vol. 6, *I Canciones*. Donostia: Eusko Ikaskuntza, 1994.

———. *Cancionero Vasco P. Donostia*, vol. 7, *II Canciones*. Donostia: Eusko Ikaskuntza, 1994.

———. *Cancionero Vasco P. Donostia*, vol. 9, *IV Danzas*. Donostia: Eusko Ikaskuntza, 1994.

Romaine, Suzanne. "English: A Man-Made Language?" In *Communicating Gender*, 91–117. Mahwah, New Jersey: Lawrence Erlbaum Associates. 1999.

Ruiz Arzalluz, I. "Notas Sobre Algunas Traducciones Vascas del Nuevo Testamento." *ASJU* 22, no. 3, 1987: 709-725.

Satrustegui, Jose Mari. 1977. "Promesa Matrimonial del Año 1547 en Euskera de Uterga." *Fontes Linguae Vasconum: Studia et Documenta* 25 (1977): 109–114.

Scholz Williams, Gerhild, trans. *On the Inconstancy of Witches: Pierre de Lancre's Tableau de L'Inconstance des Mauvais Anges et Demons (1612)*. Tempe: Arizona State University Press, 2005.

Schulz, Muriel. "The Semantic Derogation of Woman." In *Language and Sex: Difference and Dominance*, edited by Barrie Thorne, and Nancy Henley, 64–75. Rowley, MA: Newbury House, 1975.

Sheppard, Gerald T. "Isaiah." In *Bible Commentary*, edited by James L. Mays, 489– 532. New York: Harper One, 1988.

Silverstein, Michael. "Language and the Culture of Gender: At the Intersection of Structure, Usage and Ideology." In *Semiotic Mediation*, edited by Elizabeth Mertz and R. J. Parmentiers, 209–259. Orlando: Academic Press, 1985.

Smith, D. Moody. "John." In *HarperCollins Bible Commentary*, edited by James L. Mays, 956–986. New York: Harper One, 1988.

Soziolinguistika Klusterra, "Measurement of the Street Use of Language." Andoain, 2017.

Stuhlmueller, Carroll. "Psalms." In *Bible Commentary*, edited by James L. Mays, 394–446. New York: Harper One, 1988.

Sweeney, Matthew. *Tanak: A Theological and Critical Introduction to the Jewish Bible*. Minneapolis: Fortress, 2012.

Tartas, Juan. *Onsa Hilceco Bidia*. Arantzazu: Jakin, 1975 [1666].

Trask, Robert L. *The History of Basque*. London and New York: Routledge, 1997.

Ugalde, Mercedes. "Apuntes Sobre el Género Como Categoría y De Análysis Para La Historia Del Nacionalismo. El Caso Vasco Del Primer Tercio De Siglo." In *Nationalism in Europe Past and Present*, volume 1, edited by Justo G. Beramendi, 353–380. Santiago de Compostela: Universidad de Santiago de Compostela, 1994.

UNESCO. *Atlas of the World's Languages in Danger.* First edition, 1996, Wurm, Stephen. (ed.); Second edition, 2001, Wurm, Stephen. (ed.); Third edition, 2010, Moseley, Christopher. (ed.). Paris: UNESCO Publications Office.

Uriarte, Jose Antonio. *Canticum Canticorum Salomonis; Tribus Vasconice Linguae Dialectis in Hispania Vigentibus Versum.* London: Impensis Ludovici Luciani Bonaparte, 1858.

Urkizu, Patri. *Bertsolaritzaren Historia: Lapurdi, Baxanabarre eta Zuberoako Bertso eta Kantak I: Anonimoak.* Donostia: Etor, 2003.

———. *Bertsolaritzaren Historia: Lapurdi, Baxanabarre eta Zuberoako Bertso eta Kantak II.* Donostia: Etor, 2003.

———. *Bertso Zahar eta Berri Zenbaiten Bilduma.* Durango: Durangoko Udala, 1987.

Urkizu, Patri, María Jose Olaciregui Alustiza, et al. *Historia de la Literatura Vasca.* Madrid: Universidad Nacional de Educación a Distancia, 2000.

Urla, Jacqueline. "Outlaw Language: Creating Alternative Public Spheres in Basque Free Radio" (reprint). In *The Politics of Culture in the Shadow of Capital,* edited by Lisa Lowe and David Lloyd, 280–300. Durham: Duke University Press, 1997.

———. *Reclaiming Basque: Language, Nation, and Cultural Activism.* Reno: University of Nevada Press, 2012.

Uruthy, Anna. *Ebanjelio Santia Jesus-Kristena Johaneren Arabera.* Bayonne, 1873.

Veyrin, Philippe. *The Basques of Lapurdi, Zuberoa, and Lower Navarre: Their History and Their Traditions.* Reno: The Center for Basque Studies, 2011 [1949].

Videgain, Xarles. *Laminosine: 80 Ipuin Labur.* Donostia: Elkar, 2009.

Vinson, Julien. *Literatura Popular del Pais Vasco.* Donostia: Txertoa, 1988.

Webster, Wentworth. *Basque Legends: Collected, Chiefly in the Labourd.* London: Walbrook & Company, 1879.

———. *Ipuinak I.* Donostia: Klasikoak, 1993.

———. *Ipuinak II.* Donostia: Klasikoak, 1993.

White, Linda. 1999. "Mission for the Millenium: Gendering and Engendering Basque Literature for the Next Thousand Years." In *Basque Studies Program Occasional Paper Series* 5 (1999): 134–148.

Wilson, Robert R. "Ezekiel." In *Bible Commentary,* edited by James L. Mays, 583–622. New York: Harper One, 1988.

Woolard, Kathyrn. *Double Talk: Bilingualism and the Politics of Ethnicity in Catalonia.* Stanford: Stanford University Press, 1989.

———. "Language Variation and Cultural Hegemony: Towards an Integration of Sociolinguistic and Social Theory." *American Ethnologist* 12 (1985): 738–748.

Woolard, Kathryn, and Bambi Schieffelin. "Language Ideology." *Annual Review of Anthropology* 23 (1994): 55–82.

Woolf, Virginia. *A Room of One's Own.* Harcourt, Brace & World: New York, 1929.

Zavala, Antonio. *Ezkondu Bearreko Bertsoak.* Zarautz: Auspoa Liburutegia, 1985.

———. *Neska-Mutilen Arteko Bertsoek.* Zarautz: Auspoa Liburutegia, 1985.

———. *Euskal Erromantzeak (Romancero Vasco).* Zarautz: Auspoa Liburutegia, 1998.

Ziarnko, Jan. *Description et Figure Du Sabbat Des Sorcieres.* 1613.

Zulaika, Joseba. "The Tragedy of Carlos." In *Basque Politics: A Case Study in Ethnic Nationalism,* edited by William A. Douglass, 309–331. Reno: University of Nevada Press, 1985.

Index

Note: Page numbers followed by "t" indicate tables.

Acknowledgments

This book has been a long time coming, and many people have helped me get it across the finish line. In addition to those acknowledged in the endnotes, I would like to thank the following individuals for their support along the way:

Jeanette Bidart, Mike Bidart, Jane Collier, William Durham, Roslyn Frank, Marjorie Goodwin, Shirley Brice Heath, José Ignacio Hualde, Lea Hubbard, Ezaiku Komeni, N.A.M., Margaret Nash, Sandra Ott, Pello Salaburu, Steve Smith, Jacqueline Urla, and Kathryn Woolard. Portions of some chapters have appeared in an earlier form in various publications as indicated in the bibliography. Many thanks to the editors and anonymous reviewers of those journals, as well as to those at the Center for Basque Studies who provided such thorough and thoughtful feedback on this manuscript.

I also thank the following repositories for the many hours I spent gloriously basque-ing in their collections as I researched this book: Archivo Biblioteka Euskaltzaindia (Vitoria-Gazteiz); Koldo Mitxelena Liburutegia, HABE Liburutegia, UPV/EHE Biblioteka Carlos Santamaria, Udal Liburutegia Nagusia, Bilbioteka Playa La Concha, ERESBIL: Musikaren Euskal Artxibioa (Donostia/San Sebastian); Archivo Real y General de Navarra and Archivo Diocesano del Pamplona (Iruña/Pamplona); Madrid's Archivo Histórico Nacional and Biblioteca Nacional de España; Rome's Archivum Romanum Societatus Jesu, Archivio Segreto Vaticano, Biblioteca Apostolica Vaticana, Biblioteca Casanatense; Oxford's Bodleian Library; London's British Library; Paris' Bibliothèque Nationale de France; and the Jon Bilbao Basque Library at the University of Nevada, Reno. This research was made possible by various grants from the University of California, Riverside, as well as the National Academy of Education/Spencer Foundation.

Mila esker deneri, bihotz-bihotzez!

About the Author

BEGOÑA ECHEVERRIA, daughter of Basque immigrants to California, is a native Basque speaker and a Professor at UC Riverside. Her research on Basque schooling, language, and identity has appeared in academic journals in education, sociolinguistics, early modern history, anthropology, and folklore. *The Hammer of Witches,* her novel based on the 1610 burning of Basque "witches," was the Historical Novel Society's Editor's Choice for May, 2015. Her docudrama *Picasso Presents Gernika* considers the fate of refugees of the 1937 bombing of Gernika, as well as the artistic journey of Picasso's anti-war masterpiece, *Guernica.* She is also a singer-songwriter with the musical trio, NOKA (www.ilovenoka.com) whose 60+ domestic and international appearances include performances at The Kennedy Center, the Library of Congress, and the Smithsonian Folklife Festival. She is writing a second novel, *Apparitions,* which explores the supposed appearances of the Virgin Mary to Basque children amid the tumult preceding the Spanish Civil War.

www.ingramcontent.com/pod-product-compliance
Lightning Source LLC
Chambersburg PA
CBHW070614310726
48982CB00001B/77

* 9 7 8 1 9 4 9 8 0 5 4 0 6 *